Stock Investing For Dummies, 2nd Edition

Checking Out the Ten Most Important Points about Stock Investing

1. You're not buying a stock; you're buying a company.

2. The only reason you buy a stock is because the company is making a profit.

3. If you buy a stock when the company isn't making a profit, then you're not investing; you're speculating.

4. A stock (or stocks in general) should never be 100 percent of your assets.

5. In some cases (such as a severe bear market), stocks aren't a good investment at all.

6. A stock's price is dependent on the company, which in turn is dependent on its environment, which includes its customer base, its industry, the general economy, and politics.

7. Your common sense and logic can be just as important in choosing a good stock as the advice of any investment expert.

8. Always have well-reasoned answers to questions such as "Why are you investing in stocks?" and "Why are you investing in a particular stock?"

9. If you have no idea about the prospects of a company (and sometimes even if you think you do), always use stop-loss orders.

10. Even if your philosophy is "buy and hold for the long term," continue to monitor your stocks and consider selling them if they're not appreciating or if general economic conditions have changed.

Flipping through a Mandatory Reading List for Investors

- The company's annual report
- The 10K and 10Q reports that the company files with the SEC
- *Standard & Poor's Stock Guide*
- *The Wall Street Journal* and/or *Investor's Business Daily*
- The stock investing Web sites listed in Appendix A

For Dummies: Bestselling Book Series for Beginners

Stock Investing For Dummies, 2nd Edition

Cheat Sheet

Looking at Four Important Parts of a Company's Fundamentals

- **Earnings:** This number should be at least 10 percent higher than the year before.
- **Sales:** This number should be higher than the year before.
- **Debt:** This number should be lower than or about the same as the year before. It should also be lower than the company's assets.
- **Equity:** This number should be higher than the year before.

Knowing the Best Financial Measures

- **Price-to-Earnings ratio (PE):** For large cap stocks, the ratio should be under 20. For all stocks (including growth, small cap, and speculative issues), it shouldn't exceed 40.
- **Price to sales ratio (PSR):** The PSR should be as close to 1 as possible.
- **Return on equity (ROE):** ROE should be going up by at least 10 percent per year.
- **Earnings growth:** Earnings should be at least 10 percent higher than the year before. This rate should be maintained over several years.
- **Debt-to-asset ratio:** Debt should be half or less compared to assets.

Remembering Nine Events That Could Spell Trouble for Your Stock

- A bear market
- Heavy insider selling
- A lawsuit/investigation by the government
- Excessive government taxation
- Excessive government regulation
- Pending government intervention (nationalizing an industry)
- An economic slowdown or decline in the industry or sector
- National or international conflict (such as war or acts of terrorism)
- Acts of nature (such as a hurricane or tsunami)

Copyright © 2006 Wiley Publishing, Inc. All rights reserved.

Item 9903-8.

For more information about Wiley Publishing, call 1-800-762-2974.

For Dummies: Bestselling Book Series for Beginners

Stock Investing

FOR

DUMMIES®

2ND EDITION

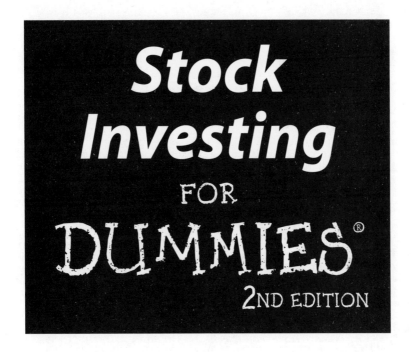

Stock Investing FOR DUMMIES® 2ND EDITION

by Paul Mladjenovic

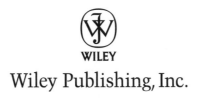

Wiley Publishing, Inc.

Stock Investing For Dummies®, 2nd Edition

Published by
Wiley Publishing, Inc.
111 River St.
Hoboken, NJ 07030-5774
www.wiley.com

Copyright © 2006 by Wiley Publishing, Inc., Indianapolis, Indiana

Published simultaneously in Canada

For general information on our other products and services, please contact our Customer Care Department within the U.S. at 800-762-2974, outside the U.S. at 317-572-3993, or fax 317-572-4002.

For technical support, please visit www.wiley.com/techsupport.

Wiley also publishes its books in a variety of electronic formats. Some content that appears in print may not be available in electronic books.

Library of Congress Control Number: 2005935151

ISBN-13: 978-0-7645-9903-3

ISBN-10: 0-7645-9903-8

Manufactured in the United States of America

10 9 8 7 6 5 4 3

2O/QZ/RS/QV/IN

WILEY

About the Author

Paul Mladjenovic is a certified financial planner practitioner, writer, and public speaker who has a Web site at www.mladjenovic.com. His business, PM Financial Services, has helped people with financial and business concerns since 1981. In 1985 he achieved his CFP designation. Since 1983, Paul has taught thousands of budding investors through popular national seminars such as "The $50 Wealthbuilder" and "Stock Investing Like a Pro." Paul has been quoted or referenced by many media outlets such as Bloomberg, MarketWatch, CNBC, and many financial and business publications and Web sites. As an author, he has written the books *The Unofficial Guide to Picking Stocks* (Wiley, 2000) and *Zero-Cost Marketing* (Todd Publications, 1995). In 2002, the first edition of *Stock Investing For Dummies* was ranked in the top 10 out of 300 books reviewed by *Barron's*. In recent years, Paul accurately forecasted many economic events, such as the rise of gold and the decline of the U.S. dollar. At press time he has been warning his students and clients about the coming decline in housing. He maintains a financial database for his readers and students at www.supermoneylinks.com

Dedication

For my beloved Fran, Adam, Joshua, and a loving, supportive family, I thank God for you.

I also dedicate this book to the millions of investors who deserve more knowledge and information to achieve lasting prosperity.

Author's Acknowledgments

First and foremost, I offer my appreciation and gratitude to the wonderful people at Wiley. It has been a pleasure to work with such a top-notch organization that works so hard to create products that offer readers tremendous value and information. I wish all of you continued success! There are some notables there whom I want to single out.

The first person is Jennifer Connolly (my project editor). She is a true publishing and writing professional who has been extremely helpful, understanding, and patient. Those words are not enough to express my thanks for her fantastic guidance. May God bless her growing family! (Jennifer took over in mid-stream for the wonderful Sherri Pfouts.)

Sarah Faulkner (my copy editor) has made sure my mish-mash of content is readable and professional (no small feat). I thank her sincerely and I am grateful she worked on this book with her impressive editing skills.

The technical editor Steven Dolvin is a superb financial pro. His expertise and insights have helped me improve the content for you and have helped me learn as well. I wish him continued success.

My gratitude goes out to the acquisitions editor Stacy Kennedy for making this *For Dummies* book happen. *For Dummies* books don't magically appear at the bookstore, they happen due to the foresight and efforts of people like Stacy. Wiley is fortunate to have her (and the others also mentioned)!

Fran, Lipa Zyenska, you helped make those late nights at the computer more tolerable, and you helped me focus on the important things. Te amo and I thank God that you are by my side. With you and the rest of my loving family, I know that the future will be bright.

Lastly, I want to acknowledge you, the reader. Over the years, you have made the *For Dummies* books what they are today. Your devotion to these wonderful books created a foundation that played a big part in the creation of this book and many more yet to come. Thank you!

Publisher's Acknowledgments

We're proud of this book; please send us your comments through our Dummies online registration form located at www.dummies.com/register.

Some of the people who helped bring this book to market include the following:

Acquisitions, Editorial, and Media Development

Project Editor: Jennifer Connolly

Acquisitions Editor: Stacy Kennedy

Copy Editor: Sarah Faulkner

Technical Editor: Steven Dolvin, PhD, CFA

Editorial Managers: Christine Meloy Beck, Michelle Hacker

Editorial Supervisor: Carmen Krikorian

Editorial Assistants: Hanna K. Scott, Nadine Bell

Cartoons: Rich Tennant (www.the5thwave.com)

Composition Services

Project Coordinator: Adrienne Martinez

Layout and Graphics: Carl Byers, Andrea Dahl, Stephanie D. Jumper, Heather Ryan

Proofreaders: Carl Pierce, TECHBOOKS Production Services

Indexer: TECHBOOKS Production Services

Publishing and Editorial for Consumer Dummies

> **Diane Graves Steele,** Vice President and Publisher, Consumer Dummies
>
> **Joyce Pepple,** Acquisitions Director, Consumer Dummies
>
> **Kristin A. Cocks,** Product Development Director, Consumer Dummies
>
> **Michael Spring,** Vice President and Publisher, Travel
>
> **Kelly Regan,** Editorial Director, Travel

Publishing for Technology Dummies

> **Andy Cummings,** Vice President and Publisher, Dummies Technology/General User

Composition Services

> **Gerry Fahey,** Vice President of Production Services
>
> **Debbie Stailey,** Director of Composition Services

Contents at a Glance

Table of Contents

Introduction

●●

*S*tock Investing For Dummies, 2nd Edition, has been an honor for me to write. I'm grateful that I can share my thoughts, information, and experience with such a large and devoted group of readers.

Although the stock market has served millions of investors for nearly a century, recent years have shown me that a great investing vehicle such as stocks can be easily misunderstood, misused, and even abused. The great bull market of 1982–1999 came to a screeching halt in 2000. During 2000–2002, millions of investors lost a total of over 5 trillion dollars. What bothers me is that much of that loss was easily avoidable. Investors at the tail end of a bull market often think that stock investing is an easy, carefree, certain way to make a quick fortune. How wrong they are! The countless stories of investors who lost tremendous amounts of money speculating in tech stocks, dot-coms, and other flashy stocks are lessons for all of us. Successful stock investing takes diligent work and knowledge like any other meaningful pursuit. This book can definitely help you avoid the mistakes others have made and can point you in the right direction.

Explore the pages of this book and find the topics that most interest you regarding the world of stock investing. Let me assure you that I have squeezed over two decades of experience, education, and expertise between these covers. My track record is as good (or better) as the track records of the experts who trumpet their successes. More importantly, I share information to avoid common mistakes (some of which I made myself!). Understanding what not to do can be just as important as figuring out what to do. In all the years that I have counseled and educated investors, the single difference between success and failure, between gain and loss, boils down to one word: knowledge. Take this book as your first step in a lifelong learning adventure.

About This Book

The stock market has been a cornerstone of the investor's passive wealth-building program for over a century and continues in this role. The period of 1995–2005 was one huge roller coaster ride for stock investors. If it was a stock chart, the graph would look like Mt. Everest. Fortunes were made and lost. With just a little more knowledge and a few wealth-preserving techniques, more investors could have held onto their hard-earned stock market fortunes. With all the media attention, all the talking heads on radio and TV, and the books with titles like *Dow at 36,000,* the investing public still didn't avoid losing trillions in a historic stock market debacle. Sadly, even the so-called experts who understood stocks didn't see the economic and geopolitical forces that acted like a tsunami on the market. This book also gives you a "heads up" on those megatrends and events that will affect your stock portfolio. While other books may tell you about stocks, this book tells you about stocks and what affects them.

This book is designed to give you a realistic approach to making money in stocks. It provides the essence of sound, practical stock investing strategies and insights that have been market tested and proven from nearly a hundred years of stock market history. I don't expect you to read it cover to cover, although I'd be delighted if you read every word! Instead, this book is designed as a reference tool. Feel free to read the chapters in whatever order you choose. You can flip to the sections and chapters that interest you or those that include topics that you need to know more about.

Stock Investing For Dummies, 2nd Edition, is also a book that is quite different from the "get rich with stocks" titles that have crammed the bookshelves in recent years. It doesn't take a standard approach to the topic; it doesn't assume that stocks are a sure thing and the be-all and end-all of wealth building. At times in this book, I tell you *not* to invest in stocks. This book can help you succeed not only in up markets but also in down markets. Bull markets and bear markets come and go, but the informed investor can keep making money no matter what. To give you an extra edge, I have tried to include information about the investing environment for stocks. Whether it is politics or hurricanes (or both), you need to know how "the big picture" affects your stock investment decisions.

Conventions Used in This Book

To make navigating through this book easier, I've established the following conventions:

- ✔ *Italic* highlights new terms that are defined.
- ✔ Monofont is used for Web addresses.
- ✔ Sidebars, shaded gray boxes of text, are filled with interesting information that isn't pertinent to your understanding of the topic, but is interesting nonetheless.

What You're Not to Read

Sidebars (gray boxes of text) in this book give you a more in-depth look at a certain topic. While they further illuminate a particular point, these sidebars aren't crucial to your understanding of the rest of the book. Feel free to read them or skip them. Of course, I'd love for you to read them all, but my feelings won't be hurt if you decide to skip them over.

The text that accompanies the Technical Stuff icon can be passed over as well. The text associated with this icon gives some technical details about stock investing that are certainly interesting and informative, but you can still come away with the information you need with or without reading this text.

Foolish Assumptions

I figure you've picked up this book for one or more of the following reasons:

- ✔ You're a beginner and want a crash course on stock investing that's an easy read.
- ✔ You're already a stock investor, and you need a book that allows you to read only those chapters that cover specific stock investing topics of interest to you.
- ✔ You need to review your own situation with the information in the book to see if you missed anything when you invested in that hot stock that your brother-in-law recommended.
- ✔ You need a great gift! When Uncle Mo is upset over his poor stock picks, you can give him this book so he can get back on his financial feet. Be sure to get a copy for his broker, too. (Odds are that the broker was the one who made those picks to begin with.)

How This Book Is Organized

The information is laid out in a straightforward format. The parts progress in a logical approach that any investor interested in stocks can follow very easily.

Part 1: The Essentials of Stock Investing

This section is for everyone. Understanding the essentials of stock investing and investing in general will only help you, especially in uncertain economic times. Stocks may even touch your finances in ways not readily apparent. For example, stocks are not only in individual accounts; they're also in mutual funds and pension plans.

An important point is that stocks are really financial tools that are a means to an end. Investors should be able to answer the question "Why am I considering stocks at all?" Stocks are a great vehicle for wealth building, but only if investors realize what they can accomplish and how to use them.

One of the essentials of stock investing is understanding risk. Most people are clueless about risk. Chapter 4, on risk, is one of the most important chapters that serious stock investors should read. You can't avoid every type of risk out there. (Life itself embodies risk.) However, this chapter can help you recognize it and find ways to minimize it in your stock investing program.

Part II: Before You Start Buying

Once you're ready to embark on your career as a stock investor, you'll need to use some resources to gather information about the stocks you're interested in. Fortunately, you live in the information age. I pity the investors from the 1920s, who didn't have access to so many resources, but today's investors are in an enviable position. This part tells you where to find information and how to use it to be a more knowledgeable investor (a rarity in recent years!). For example, I explain that stocks can be used for both growth and income purposes, and I discuss the characteristics of each. See Chapters 8 and 9 for more information.

When you're ready to invest, you'll invariably have to turn to a broker. There are several types, so you should know which is which. The wrong broker could make you . . . uh . . . broker. Chapter 7 helps you choose.

Part III: Picking Winners

Part III is about picking good stocks by using microeconomics, meaning that you look at the stocks of individual companies. I explain how to evaluate a company's products, services, and other factors so that you can determine whether a company is strong and healthy.

One of the major differences with this edition versus the first edition is the emphasis on emerging sector opportunities. If I can steer you toward those segments of the stock market that show solid promise for the coming years, then that alone would make your stock portfolio thrive. Putting your money into solid companies that are in thriving industries has been the hallmark of superior stock investing throughout history. It's no different now. Check out Chapter 13 if you want to know more about emerging sector opportunities.

Where do you turn to find out about a company's financial health? In Chapter 11, I show you the documents you should review to make a more informed decision. Once you find the information, you'll discover how to make sense of that data as well. While you're at it, check out Chapter 12 (on analyzing industries).

I compare buying stock to picking goldfish. If you look at a bunch of goldfish to choose which ones to buy, you want to make sure that you pick the healthiest ones. With stocks, you also need to pick companies that are healthy. Part III can help you do that.

Part IV: Investment Strategies and Tactics

Even the stocks of great companies can fall in a bad investing environment. This is where you should be aware of the "macro." If stocks were goldfish, the macro would be the pond or goldfish bowl. In that case, even healthy goldfish can die if the water is toxic. Therefore, you should monitor the investing environment for stocks. Part IV reveals tips, strategies, and resources that you shouldn't ignore.

Once you understand stocks and the economic environment in which they operate, choose the strategy and the tactics to help steer you to your wealth-building objectives. Chapter 17 reveals some of my all-time favorite techniques for building wealth and holding on to your stock investment gains. (Definitely check it out.)

You may be an investor, but that doesn't mean that you have deep pockets. Chapter 18 tells you how to buy stocks with lower (or no) transaction costs. If you're going to buy the stock anyway, why not save on commissions and other costs?

As an investor, you must keep an eye on what the company insiders are doing. In Chapter 19, I explain what it may mean if the company's management is buying or selling the same stock that you're considering.

After you spend all your time, money, and effort to grow your money in the world of stocks, you have yet another concern: holding on to your hard-earned gains. This challenge is summarized in one word: taxes. Sound tax planning is crucial for everyone who works hard. After all, taxes are the biggest expense in your lifetime (right after children!). See Chapter 20 for more information.

Part V: The Part of Tens

I wrap up the book with a hallmark of *For Dummies* books — the Part of Tens. These chapters give you a mini crash course in stock investing, including ten ways to protect yourself from fraud.

In this part, I offer some clues that signal a stock price increase and how to recognize the warning signs of a stock poised to fall. Also review the list of ten challenges and opportunities that face stock investors (Chapter 24). This is a new chapter that I feel is critical for your investing strategy.

Part VI: Appendixes

Don't overlook the appendixes. I pride myself on the resources I can provide my students and readers so that they can make informed investment decisions. Whether the topic is stock investing terminology, economics, or avoiding capital gains taxes, I include a treasure trove of resources to help you. Whether you go to a bookstore, the library, or the Internet, Appendix A gives you some great places to turn to for help. In Appendix B, I explain financial ratios. These important numbers help you better determine whether to invest in a particular company's stock.

Icons Used in This Book

This icon flags a particular bit of advice that just may give you an edge over other investors.

When you see this icon, I'm reminding you about some information that you should always keep stashed in your memory, whether you're new to investing or an old pro.

Pay special attention to this icon because the advice can prevent headaches, heartaches, and financial aches.

The text attached to this icon may not be crucial to your success as an investor, but it may enable you to talk shop with investing gurus and better understand the financial pages of your favorite business publication or Web site.

Where to Go from Here

You may not need to read every chapter to make you more confident as a stock investor, so feel free to jump around to suit your personal needs. Since every chapter is designed to be as self-contained as possible, it won't do you any harm to "cherry-pick" what you really want to read. But if you're like me, you still may want to check out every chapter because you never know when you can come across a new tip or resource that will make a profitable difference in your stock portfolio. I want you to be successful so that I can brag about you in the next edition!

Part I

The Essentials of Stock Investing

In this part . . .

*M*any investors do things in reverse; they buy stock first and learn "some lessons" afterward. Your success is dependent on doing your homework before you invest your first dollar in stocks. Most investors don't realize that they should be scrutinizing their own situations and financial goals at least as much as they scrutinize stocks. But how else can you know which stocks are right for you? Too many people risk too much simply because they don't take stock of their current needs, goals, and risk tolerance before they invest. The chapters in this part tell you what you need to know to choose the stocks that best suit you.

Chapter 1

Exploring the Basics

• •

In This Chapter

▶ Knowing the essentials

▶ Doing your own research

▶ Recognizing winners

▶ Exploring investment strategies

• •

Stock investing became all the rage during the late 1990s. Even tennis stars and punk rockers got into the act. Investors watched their stock portfolios and stock mutual funds skyrocket as the stock market was reaching the mania stage at the tail-end of an 18-year upswing (or bull market) in stocks. (See Chapter 15 for more information on bull markets.) Investment activity in the United States is a great example of the popularity that stocks experienced during that time period. By 1999, over half of U.S. households became participants in the stock market. Yet millions lost money when the stock market fell big time (the bear market — see Chapter 15) during 2000–2002. People invested. Yet they really didn't know exactly what they were investing in. If they had a rudimentary understanding of what stock really is, perhaps they could have avoided some expensive mistakes. The purpose of this book is not only to tell you about the basics of stock investing but also to let you in on some solid strategies that can help you profit from the stock market. Before you invest your first dollar, you need to understand the basics of stock investing.

Understanding the Basics

The basics are so basic that few people are doing them. Perhaps the most basic (and therefore most important) thing to grasp is the risk you face whenever you do anything (like putting your hard-earned money in an investment like a stock). When you lose track of the basics, you lose track of why you invested to begin with. Find out more about risk (and the different kinds of risk) in Chapter 4.

When the late comedian Henny Youngman was asked "How is your wife?" he responded "Compared to what?" This applies to stocks. When you are asked "how is your stock?" you can very well respond that it's doing well especially when compared to an acceptable "yardstick" such as a stock index (such as the S&P 500). Find out more about indexes in Chapter 5.

The bottom line is that the first thing you do in stock investing is not send your money to a brokerage account or go to a Web site to click "buy stock." The first thing you do is find out as much as you can about what stocks are and how to use them to achieve your wealth-building goals.

Getting Prepared before You Get Started

Gathering information is critical in your stock-investing pursuits. There are two times to gather information on your stock picks: before you invest . . . and after. You obviously should become more informed before you invest your first dollar. But you also need to stay informed about what's happening to the company whose stock you are buying and also about the industry and the general economy. To find the best information sources, check out Chapter 6.

When you are ready to invest, you will need a brokerage account. How do you know which broker to use? Chapter 7 provides some answers and resources to help you choose a broker.

Knowing How to Pick Winners

Once you get past the basics, you can get to the "meat" of stock picking. Successful stock picking is not mysterious, but it does take some time, effort, and analysis. It's worth it since stocks are a convenient and important part of most investors' portfolios. Read the following section and be sure to "leap frog" to the relevant chapters to get the inside scoop on "hot stocks."

Recognizing stock value

Imagine that you like eggs and you're willing to buy them at the grocery store. In this example, the eggs are like companies, and the prices represent the prices that you would pay for the companies' stock. The grocery store is the stock market. What if two brands of eggs are very similar, but one costs

50 cents while the other costs 75 cents? Which would you choose? Odds are that you would look at both brands, judge their quality, and, if they were indeed similar, take the cheaper eggs. The eggs at 75 cents are overpriced. The same is true of stocks. What if you compare two companies that are similar in every respect but have different share prices? All things being equal, the cheaper price has greater value for the investor. But the egg example has another side.

What if the quality of the two brands of eggs is significantly different but their prices are the same? If one brand of eggs is stale, of poor quality, and priced at 50 cents and the other brand is fresh, of superior quality, and also priced at 50 cents, which would you get? I'd take the good brand because they're better eggs. Perhaps the lesser eggs are an acceptable purchase at 10 cents, but they're definitely overpriced at 50 cents. The same example works with stocks. A badly run company isn't a good choice if you can buy a better company in the marketplace at the same — or a better — price.

Comparing the value of eggs may seem overly simplistic, but doing so does cut to the heart of stock investing. Eggs and egg prices can be as varied as companies and stock prices. As an investor, you must make it your job to find the best value for your investment dollars. (Otherwise you get egg on your face. You saw that one coming, right?)

Understanding how market capitalization affects stock value

You can determine the value of a company (and thus the value of its stock) in many ways. The most basic way to measure this value is to look at a company's market value, also known as market capitalization (or market cap). *Market capitalization* is simply the value you get when you multiply all the outstanding shares of a stock by the price of a single share.

Calculating the market cap is easy. It's the number of shares outstanding multiplied by the current share price. If the company has 1 million shares outstanding and its share price is $10, the market cap is $10 million.

Small cap, mid cap, and large cap aren't references to headgear; they're references to how large the company is as measured by its market value. Here are the five basic stock categories of market capitalization:

- ✔ **Micro cap (under $250 million):** These stocks are the smallest and hence the riskiest available.

- ✔ **Small cap ($250 million to $1 billion):** These stocks fare better than the microcaps and still have plenty of growth potential. The key word here is "potential."

✔ **Mid cap ($1 billion to $5 billion):** For many investors, this category offers a good compromise between small caps and large caps. These stocks have some of the safety of large caps while retaining some of the growth potential of small caps.

✔ **Large cap ($5 billion to $25 billion):** This category is usually best reserved for conservative stock investors who want steady appreciation with greater safety. Stocks in this category are frequently referred to as "blue chips."

✔ **Ultra cap (over $25 billion):** These stocks are also called "mega caps" and obviously refer to companies that are the biggest of the big. Stocks such as General Electric and Exxon Mobil are examples.

From a safety point of view, the company's size and market value do matter. All things being equal, large cap stocks are considered safer than small cap stocks. However, small cap stocks have greater potential for growth. Compare these stocks to trees: Which tree is sturdier — a giant California redwood or a small oak tree that's just a year old? In a great storm, the redwood holds up well, while the smaller tree has a rough time. But you also have to ask yourself which tree has more opportunity for growth. The redwood may not have much growth left, but the small oak tree has plenty of growth to look forward to.

For beginning investors, comparing market cap to trees isn't so far-fetched. You want your money to branch out without becoming a sap.

Although market capitalization is important to consider, don't invest (or not invest) just based on it. It's just one measure of value. As a serious investor, you need to look at numerous factors that can help you determine whether any given stock is a good investment. Keep reading — this book is full of information to help you decide.

Sharpening your investment skills

Investors who analyze the company can better judge the value of the stock and profit from buying and selling it. Your greatest asset in stock investing is knowledge (and a little common sense). To succeed in the world of stock investing, keep in mind these key success factors:

✔ Analyze yourself. What do you want to accomplish with your stock investing? What are your investment goals? Chapter 2 can help you figure it out.

✔ Know where to get information. The decisions you make about your money and what stocks to invest in require quality information. If you want help with information sources, turn to Chapter 3.

✔ Understand why you want to invest in stocks. Are you seeking appreciation (capital gains) or income (dividends)? Look at Chapters 8 and 9 for information on these topics.

✔ Do some research. Look at the company whose stock you're considering to see whether it's a profitable company worthy of your investment dollars. Chapters 10 and 11 help you scrutinize the company.

✔ Choosing a winning stock also means that you choose a winning industry. You'll frequently see stock prices of mediocre companies in "hot" industries rise higher and faster than solid companies in floundering industries. Therefore, choosing the industry is very important. Find out more about analyzing industries in Chapter 12.

✔ Understand how the world affects your stock. Stocks succeed or fail in large part due to the environment in which they operate. Economics and politics make up that world, so you should know something about them. Chapter 14 covers these topics, but also take a look at Chapter 2.

✔ Understand and identify megatrends. Doing so makes it easier for you to make money. This edition spends more time and provides more resources helping you see the opportunities in emerging sectors and even avoid the problem areas (see Chapter 13 for details).

✔ Use investing strategies like the pros do. In other words, how you go about investing can be just as important as what you invest in. Chapter 16 highlights techniques for investing to help you make more money from your stocks.

✔ Keep more of the money you earn. After all your great work in getting the right stocks and making the big bucks, you should know about keeping more of the fruits of your investing. I cover taxes in stock investing in Chapter 20.

✔ Sometimes, what people tell you to do with stocks is not as revealing as what people are actually doing. This is why I like to look at company insiders before I buy or sell that particular stock. To find out more about "insider buying and selling," read Chapter 19.

Actually, every chapter in the book offers you valuable guidance on some essential aspect of the fantastic world of stocks. The knowledge you pick up and apply from these pages has been tested over nearly a century of stock picking. The investment experience of the past — the good, the bad, and some of the ugly — is here for your benefit. Use this information to make a lot of money (and make me proud!). And don't forget to check out the Appendixes!

Stock market schizophrenia

Have you ever noticed a stock going up even though the company is reporting terrible results? How about seeing a stock nosedive despite the fact that the company is doing well? What gives? Well, judging the direction of a stock in a short-term period — over the next few days or weeks — is almost impossible.

Yes, in the short term, stock investing is irrational. The price of a stock and the value of its company seem disconnected and almost schizophrenic. The key phrase to remember is "short term." A stock's price and the company's value become more logical over an extended period

of time. The longer a stock is in the public's view, the more rational the performance of the stock's price. In other words, a good company continues to draw attention to itself; hence, more people want its stock, and the share price rises to better match the value of the company. Conversely, a bad company doesn't hold up to continued scrutiny over time. As more and more people see that the company isn't doing well, the share price declines. Over the long run, a stock's share price and the value of the company eventually become equal for the most part.

Boning Up on Strategies and Tactics

Successful investing isn't just what you invest in, it's also the way you invest. I am very big on strategies such as trailing stops and limit orders. You can find out more in Chapter 17.

Buying stocks doesn't always mean that you must buy through a broker and that it must be 100 shares. You can buy stock for as little as $25 using programs such as dividend reinvestment plans. Chapter 18 tells you more.

Getting Some Good Tips

Protecting yourself from downside exposure is what separates investors from speculators, and Chapter 21 gives you ten warning signs regarding a stock's decline. I know that when I see some of these signs that (at the very least) I'll put on a stop loss order (Chapter 17) so that I can sleep at night. Sometimes the return *on* your money is not as good as the return *of* your money.

If stocks give off "negative signals," then there must also be "positive" ones as well. Chapter 22 gives you ten of the best signs that are commonly seen before a stock is ready to rise. What better time to jump in?

You should be aware about the risks that fraud presents you. It's tough enough to make money with stocks in an honest market. Yet we must always be aware of those that would take our hard-earned money from us without our consent. That's why I include Chapter 24 — since you and I will always deal with a part of the universe that will always give us problems . . . humanity.

Chapter 24 is (I believe) one of the best chapters in the book. It is very important to understand if the environment for a particular stock is good or bad. The best stocks in the world sink in a tough market while the worst stocks can go up in a jubilant and rising market. Ideally, you avoid those stocks that are in the tough market and find good stocks in a good market. This chapter will clue you in regarding those markets.

Chapter 2

Taking Stock of Your Current Financial Situation and Goals

· ·

In This Chapter

▶ Preparing your personal balance sheet

▶ Looking at your cash flow statement

▶ Determining your financial goals

· ·

*Y*es, you want to make the big bucks. Or maybe you just want to get back the big bucks you lost in the stock market debacle of 2000–2003. (Investors who followed the guidelines from the first edition of this book did much better than the crowd!) Either way, you want your money to grow so that you can have a better life. But before you make reservations for that Caribbean cruise you're dreaming about, you have to map out your action plan for getting there. Stocks can be a great component of most wealth-building programs, but you must first do some homework on a topic that you should be very familiar with — yourself. That's right. Understanding your current financial situation and clearly defining your financial goals are the first steps in successful investing.

This chapter is undoubtedly one of the most important chapters in this book. At first, you may think it's a chapter more suitable for some general book on personal finance. Wrong! Unsuccessful investors' greatest weakness is not understanding their financial situation and how stocks fit in. Often, I counsel people to stay out of the stock market because they aren't prepared for the responsibilities of stock investing — they haven't been regularly reviewing the company's financial statements or tracking the company's progress. Very often, investors aren't aware of the pitfalls of stock investing during bear markets.

Investing in stocks requires balance. Investors sometimes tie up too much money in stocks, putting themselves at risk of losing a significant portion of their wealth if the market plunges. Then again, other investors place little or no money in stocks, and therefore miss out on excellent opportunities to grow their wealth. Investors should make stocks a part of their portfolios, but the operative word is *part.* You should only let stocks take up a *portion* of your money. A disciplined investor also has money in bank accounts, bonds, and other assets that offer growth or income opportunities. Diversification is key to minimizing risk. (For more on risk, see Chapter 4.)

Establishing a Starting Point

Whether you're already in stocks or you're looking to get into stocks, you need to find out about how much money you can afford to invest in stocks. No matter what you hope to accomplish with your stock investing plan, the first step a budding investor should take is figuring out how much you own and how much you owe. To do this, prepare and review your personal balance sheet. A *balance sheet* is simply a list of your assets, your liabilities, and what each item is currently worth so you can arrive at your net worth. Your net worth is total assets minus total liabilities. I know that these terms sound like accounting mumbo jumbo, but knowing your net worth is important to your future financial success, so just do it.

Composing your balance sheet is simple. Pull out a pencil and a piece of paper. For the computer savvy, a spreadsheet software program accomplishes the same task. Gather all your financial documents, such as bank and brokerage statements and other such paperwork — you need figures from these documents. Then follow the steps that I outline in the following sections. Update your balance sheet at least once a year to monitor your financial progress (Is your net worth going up or not?).

A second document to prepare is an income statement. An income statement lists your total income and your total expenses to find out how well you are doing. If your total income is greater than your total expenses, then you have net income (Great!). If your total expenses meet or exceed your total income, then that's not good. You better look into increasing your income or decreasing your expenses. You want to get to the point that you have net income so that you can use that money to fund your stock purchases.

Your personal balance sheet is really no different from balance sheets that giant companies prepare. (The main difference is a few zeros, but you can use my advice in this book to work on changing that.) In fact, the more you find out about your own balance sheet, the easier it is to understand the balance sheet of companies in which you're seeking to invest.

Step 1: Making sure you have an emergency fund

First, list cash on your balance sheet (see the next step for more on listing your assets). Your goal is to have, in reserve, at least three to six months' worth of your gross living expenses in cash. The cash is important because it gives you a cushion. Three to six months is usually enough to get you through the most common forms of financial disruption, such as losing your job. Finding a new job can take anywhere from three to six months.

If your monthly expenses (or *outgo*) are $2,000, you should have at least $6,000, and probably closer to $12,000, in a secure, FDIC-insured, interest-bearing bank account (or other relatively safe interest-bearing vehicle such as a money market fund). Consider this account an emergency fund and not an investment. Don't use this money to buy stocks.

Too many Americans don't have an emergency fund, meaning that they put themselves at risk. Walking across a busy street while wearing a blindfold is a great example of putting yourself at risk, and in recent years, investors have done the financial equivalent. Investors piled on tremendous debt, put too much into investments (such as stocks) that they didn't understand, and had little or no savings. One of the biggest problems during 2000–2003 was that savings were sinking to record lows while debt levels were reaching new heights. People then sold many stocks because they needed funds for — you guessed it — paying bills and debt.

Resist the urge to start thinking of your investment in stocks as a savings account generating over 20 percent per year. This is dangerous thinking! If your investments tank, or if you lose your job, you will have financial difficulty and that will affect your stock portfolio (you might have to sell some stocks in your account just to get money to pay the bills). An emergency fund helps you through a temporary cash crunch.

Step 2: Listing your assets in decreasing order of liquidity

Liquid assets aren't references to beer or cola (unless you're Anheuser-Busch). Instead, *liquidity* refers to how quickly you can convert a particular *asset* (something you own that has value) into cash. If you know the liquidity of your assets, including investments, you have some options when you need cash to buy some stock (or pay some bill). All too often, people are short on cash and have too much wealth tied up in *illiquid investments* such as real estate. *Illiquid* is just a fancy way of saying that you don't have the immediate cash to meet a pressing need. (Hey, we've all had those moments!) Review your assets and take measures to ensure that you have enough liquid assets (along with your illiquid assets).

Listing your assets in order of liquidity on your balance sheet gives you an immediate picture of which assets you can quickly convert to cash and which ones you can't. If you need money *now,* you can see that cash in hand, your checking account, and your savings account are at the top of the list. The items last in order of liquidity become obvious; they're things like real estate and other assets that can take a long time to convert to cash.

Selling real estate, even in a seller's market, can take months. Investors who don't have adequate liquid assets run the danger of selling assets quickly and possibly at a loss because they scramble to accumulate the cash for their short-term financial obligations. For stock investors, this scramble may include prematurely selling stocks that they originally intended to use as long-term investments.

Table 2-1 shows a typical list of assets in order of liquidity. Use it as a guide for making your own asset list.

Table 2-1	John Q. Investor: Personal Assets as of December 31, 2006	
Asset Item	*Market Value*	*Annual Growth Rate %*
Current Assets		
Cash on hand and in checking	$150	0
Bank savings accounts and certificates of deposit	$500	2%
Stocks	$2,000	11%
Mutual funds	$2,400	9%
Other assets		
(Collectibles, etc.)	$240	
Total current assets	**$5,290**	
Long-term assets		
Auto	$1,800	−10%
Residence	150,000	5%
Real estate investment	$125,000	6%

Asset Item	Market Value	Annual Growth Rate %
Personal stuff (such as jewelry)	$4,000	
Total long-term assets	$280,800	
Total assets	$286,090	

The first column of Table 2-1 describes the asset. You can quickly convert *current assets* to cash — they're more liquid; *long-term assets* have value, but you can't necessarily convert them to cash quickly — they aren't very liquid.

Please take note. I have stocks listed as short-term in the table. The reason is that this balance sheet is meant to list items in order of liquidity. Liquidity is best embodied in the question "How quickly can I turn this asset into cash?" Because a stock can be sold and converted to cash very quickly, it is a good example of a liquid asset. (However, that is not the main purpose for buying stocks.)

The second column gives the current market value for that item. Keep in mind that this value is not the purchase price or original value; it's the amount you would realistically get if you sold the asset in the current market at that moment.

The third column tells you how well that investment is doing, compared to one year ago. If the percentage rate is 5 percent, that item increased in value by 5 percent from a year ago. You need to know how well all your assets are doing. Why? To adjust your assets for maximum growth or to get rid of assets that are losing money. Assets that are doing well are kept (increase your holdings?), and assets that are down in value are candidates for removal. Perhaps you can sell them and reinvest the money elsewhere. In addition, the realized loss has tax benefits (see Chapter 20).

Figuring the annual growth rate (in the third column) as a percentage isn't difficult. Say that you buy 100 shares of the stock Gro-A-Lot Corp. (GAL), and its market value on December 31, 2003, is $50 per share for a total market value of $5,000 (100 shares × $50 per share). When you check its value on December 31, 2004, you find out the stock is at $60 per share (100 shares times $60 equals a total market value of $6,000). The annual growth rate is 20 percent. You calculate this by taking the amount of the gain ($60 per share less $50 per share = $10 gain per share), which is $1,000 (100 shares times the $10 gain), and dividing it by the value at the beginning of the time period ($5,000). In this case, you get 20 percent ($1,000 divided by $5,000). What if GAL also generates a dividend of $2 per share during that period; now what?

In that case, GAL generates a total return of 24 percent. To calculate the total return, add the appreciation ($10 per share times 100 shares equals $1,000) and the dividend income ($2 per share times 100 shares equals $200) and divide that sum ($1,000 + $200, or $1,200) by the value at the beginning of the year ($50 per share times 100 shares or $5,000). The total is $1,200 ($1,000 of appreciation and $200 total dividends), or 24 percent ($1,200 ÷ $5,000).

The last line lists the total for all the assets and their current market value. The third column answers the question "How well did this particular asset grow from a year ago?"

Step 3: Listing your liabilities

Liabilities are simply the bills that you're obligated to pay. Whether it's a credit card bill or a mortgage payment, a liability is an amount of money you have to pay back eventually (with interest). If you don't keep track of your liabilities, you may end up thinking that you have more money than you really do.

Table 2-2 lists some common liabilities. Use it as a model when you list your own. You should list the liabilities according to how soon you need to pay them. Credit card balances tend to be short-term obligations, while mortgages are long-term.

Table 2-2	Listing Personal Liabilities	
Liabilities	*Amount*	*Paying Rate %*
Credit cards	$4,000	15%
Personal loans	$13,000	10%
Mortgage	$100,000	8%
Total liabilities	$117,000	

The first column in Table 2-2 names the type of debt. Don't forget to include student loans and auto loans if you have any of these. Never avoid listing a liability because you're embarrassed to see how much you really owe. Be honest with yourself — doing so helps you improve your financial health.

The second column shows the current value (or current balance) of your liabilities. List the most current balance to see where you stand with your creditors.

The third column reflects how much interest you're paying for carrying that debt. This information is an important reminder about how debt can be a wealth zapper. Credit card debt can have an interest rate of 18 percent or more, and to add insult to injury, it isn't even tax deductible. Using a credit card to make even a small purchase costs you if you maintain a balance. Within a year, a $50 sweater at 18 percent costs $59 when you add in the potential interest you pay.

If you compare your liabilities in Table 2-2 and your personal assets in Table 2-1, you may find opportunities to reduce the amount you pay for interest. Say, for example, that you pay 15 percent on a credit card balance of $4,000 but also have a personal asset of $5,000 in a bank savings account that's earning 2 percent in interest. In that case, you may want to consider taking $4,000 out of the savings account to pay off the credit card balance. Doing so saves you $520; the $4,000 in the bank was earning only $80 (2 percent of $4,000), while you were paying $600 on the credit card balance (15 percent of $4,000).

If you can't pay off high-interest debt, at least look for ways to minimize the cost of carrying the debt. The most obvious ways include the following:

- ✔ Replacing high-interest cards with low-interest cards. Many companies offer incentives to consumers, including signing up for cards with favorable rates that can be used to pay off high-interest cards.

- ✔ Replacing unsecured debt with secured debt. Credit cards and personal loans are *unsecured* (you haven't put up any collateral or other asset to secure the debt); therefore, they have higher interest rates because this type of debt is considered riskier for the creditor. Sources of secured debt (such as home equity line accounts and brokerage accounts) provide you with a means to replace your high-interest debt with lower-interest debt. You get lower interest rates with *secured debt* because it's less risky for the creditor — the debt is backed up by collateral (your home or your stocks).

The year 2004 was the eighth consecutive year that personal bankruptcies surpassed the million mark in the United States. Corporate bankruptcies were also at record levels. Make a diligent effort to control and reduce your debt, or the debt can become too burdensome. If you don't, you may have to sell your stocks just to stay liquid. Remember, Murphy's Law states that you *will* sell your stock at the worst possible moment! Don't go there.

Step 4: Calculating your net worth

Your *net worth* is an indication of your total wealth. You can calculate your net worth with this basic equation: total assets (Table 2-1) less total liabilities (Table 2-2) equal net worth (net assets or net equity).

I owe, I owe, so off to work I go

One reason you continue to work is probably so that you can pay off your bills. But many people today are losing their jobs because their company owes, too!

Debt is one of the biggest financial problems in America today. Companies and individuals holding excessive debt contributed to the stock market's massive decline in 2000 and the U.S. recession in 2001. If individuals managed their personal liabilities more responsibly, the general economy would be much better off.

One reason the United States appeared to be doing so well during the late 1990s was the fact that individuals and organizations went on an unprecedented spending binge, financed mostly by excessive debt. The economy looked unstoppable. However, sooner or later you have to pay the piper. Stock prices may go up and down, but debt stays up until it is either paid down or the debtor files for bankruptcy. As of the 4th quarter of 2004, U.S. debt has surpassed a mind-boggling $37 trillion, which means that consumers, businesses, and governments will continue dealing with challenging times through this decade. Yes, the stock market will be affected!

Table 2-3 shows this equation in action with a net worth of $169,090 — a very respectable number. For many investors, just being in a position where assets exceed liabilities (a positive net worth) is great news. Use Table 2-3 as a model to analyze your own financial situation. Your mission (if you choose to accept it — and you should) is to ensure that your net worth increases from year to year as you progress toward your financial goal.

Table 2-3	Figuring Your Personal Net Worth	
Totals	*Amounts ($)*	*Increase from Year Before*
Total assets (from Table 2-1)	$286,090	+5%
Total liabilities (from Table 2-2)	($117,000)	–2%
Net worth (total assets less total liabilities)	$169,090	+3%

Step 5: Analyzing your balance sheet

Create a balance sheet based on the prior steps in this chapter to illustrate your current finances. Take a close look at it and try to identify any changes you can make to increase your wealth. Sometimes reaching your financial goals can be as simple as refocusing the items on your balance sheet (use the above table as a general guideline). Here are some brief points to consider:

✔ **Is the money in your emergency (or rainy day) fund sitting in an ultra-safe account and earning the highest interest available?** Bank money market accounts or money market funds are recommended. The safest type of account is a U.S. Treasury money market fund. Banks are backed by the Federal Deposit Insurance Corporation (FDIC) while U.S. treasury securities are backed by the "full faith and credit" of the Federal Government.

✔ **Can you replace depreciating assets with appreciating assets?** Say that you have two stereo systems. Why not sell one and invest the proceeds? You may say, "But I bought that unit two years ago for $500, and if I sell it now, I'll only get $300." That's your choice. You need to decide what helps your financial situation more — a $500 item that keeps shrinking in value (a *depreciating asset*) or $300 that can grow in value when invested (an *appreciating asset*).

✔ **Can you replace low-yield investments with high-yield investments?** Maybe you have $5,000 in a bank certificate of deposit earning 3 percent. You can certainly shop around for a better rate at another bank, but you can also seek alternatives that can offer a higher yield, such as U.S. savings bonds or short-term bond funds.

✔ **Can you pay off any high-interest debt with funds from low-interest assets?** If, for example, you have $5,000 earning 2 percent in a taxable bank account, and you have $2,500 on a credit card charging 18 percent (nondeductible), you may as well pay off the credit card balance and save on the interest.

✔ **If you're carrying debt, are you using that money for an investment return that is greater than the interest you're paying?** Carrying a loan with an interest rate of 8 percent is acceptable if that borrowed money is yielding more than 8 percent elsewhere. Suppose that you have $6,000 in cash in a brokerage account. If you qualify, you can actually make a stock purchase greater than $6,000 by using margin (essentially a loan from the broker). You can buy $12,000 of stock using your $6,000 in cash, with the remainder financed by the broker. Of course, you pay interest on that margin loan. But what if the interest rate is 6 percent and the stock you're about to invest in has a dividend that yields 9 percent? In that case, the dividend can help you pay off the margin loan, and you keep the additional income. (For more on buying on margin, see Chapter 17.)

✔ **Can you sell any personal stuff for cash?** You can replace unproductive assets with cash from garage sales and auction Web sites.

> ✔ **Can you use your home equity to pay off consumer debt?** Borrowing against your home has more favorable interest rates, and this interest is still tax deductible. (Be careful about your debt level. See Chapter 23 for warnings on debt and other concerns.)

Paying off consumer debt by using funds borrowed against your home is a great way to wipe the slate clean. What a relief to get rid of your credit card balances! Just don't turn around and run up the consumer debt again. You can get overburdened and experience financial ruin (not to mention home-lessness). Not a pretty picture.

The important point to remember is that you can take control of your finances with discipline (and with the advice I offer in this book).

Funding Your Stock Program

If you're going to invest money in stocks, the first thing you need is . . . money! Where can you get that money? If you're waiting for an inheritance to come through, you may have to wait a long time, considering all the advances being made in healthcare lately. What's that? You were going to invest in healthcare stocks? How ironic. Yet, the challenge still comes down to how to fund your stock program.

Many investors can reallocate their investments and assets to do the trick. *Reallocating* simply means selling some investments or other assets and rein-vesting that money into stocks. It boils down to deciding what investment or asset you can sell or liquidate. Generally, you want to consider those invest-ments and assets that give you a low return on your money (or no return at all). If you have a complicated mix of investments and assets, you may want to consider reviewing your options with a financial planner. Reallocation is just part of the answer; your cash flow is the other part.

Ever wonder why there's so much month left at the end of the money? Consider your cash flow. Your *cash flow* refers to what money is coming in (income) and what money is being spent (outgo). The net result is either a positive cash flow or a negative cash flow, depending on your cash manage-ment skills. Maintaining a positive cash flow (more money coming in than going out) helps you increase your net worth (mo' money, mo' money, mo' money!). A negative cash flow ultimately depletes your wealth and wipes out your net worth if you don't turn it around immediately. The following sec-tions show you how to analyze your cash flow. The first step is to do a cash flow statement.

Dot-com-and-go

If you were publishing a book about negative cash flow, look for the employees of any one of a hundred dot-com companies to write it. Their qualifications include working for a company that flew sky-high in 1999 and crashed in 2000 and 2001. Companies such as eToys.com, Pets.com, and DrKoop.com were given millions, yet they couldn't turn a profit and eventually closed for business. You may as well call them "dot-com-and-go." You can learn from their mistakes. (Actually, they could have learned from you.) In the same way that profit is the most essential single element in a business, a positive cash flow is important for your finances in general and for funding your stock investment program in particular.

Don't confuse a cash flow statement with an income statement (also called a "profit and loss statement" or an "income and expense statement"). A cash flow statement is simple to calculate because you can easily track what goes in and what goes out.

With a cash flow statement (see Table 2-6), you ask yourself three questions:

- ✔ **What money is coming in?** In your cash flow statement, jot down all sources of income. Calculate it for the month and then for the year. Include everything, including salary, wages, interest, dividends, and so on. Add them all up and get your grand total for income.

- ✔ **What is your outgo?** Write down all the things that you spend money on. List all your expenses. If possible, categorize them into essential and nonessential. You can get an idea of all the expenses that you can reduce without affecting your lifestyle. But before you do that, make as complete a list as possible of what you spend your money on.

- ✔ **What's left?** If your income is greater than your outgo, then you have money ready and available for stock investing. No matter how small the amount seems, it definitely helps. I've seen fortunes built when people started to diligently invest as little as $25 to $50 per week or per month. If your outgo is greater than your income, then you better sharpen your pencil. Cut down on nonessential spending and/or increase your income. If your budget is a little tight, hold off on your stock investing until your cash flow improves.

Step 1: Tallying up your income

Using Table 2-4 as a worksheet, list and calculate the money you have coming in. The first column describes the source of the money, the second column indicates the monthly amount from each respective source, and the last column indicates the amount projected for a full year. Include all income, such as wages, business income, dividends, interest income, and so on. Then project these amounts for a year (multiply by 12) and enter those amounts in the third column.

Table 2-4	Listing Your Income	
Item	*Monthly $ Amount*	*Yearly $ Amount*
Salary and wages		
Interest income and dividends		
Business net (after taxes) income		
Other income		
Total income		

This is the amount of money you have to work with. To ensure your financial health, don't spend more than this amount. Always be aware of and carefully manage your income.

Step 2: Adding up your outgo

Using Table 2-5 as a worksheet, list and calculate the money that's going out. What are you spending and on what? The first column describes the source of the expense, the second column indicates the monthly amount, and the third column shows the amount projected for a full year. Include all the money you spend, including credit card and other debt payments; household expenses, such as food, utility bills, and medical expenses; and money spent for nonessential expenses such as video games and elephant-foot umbrella stands.

Table 2-5	Listing Your Expenses (Outgo)	
Item	*Monthly $ Amount*	*Yearly $ Amount*
Payroll taxes		
Rent or mortgage		

Item	Monthly $ Amount	Yearly $ Amount
Utilities		
Food		
Clothing		
Insurance (medical, auto, homeowners, and so on)		
Telephone		
Real estate taxes		
Auto expenses		
Charity		
Recreation		
Credit card payments		
Loan payments		
Other		
Total		

Payroll taxes is just a category in which to lump all the various taxes that the government takes out of your paycheck. Feel free to put each individual tax on its own line if you prefer. The important thing is creating a comprehensive list that is meaningful to you. You may notice that the outgo doesn't include items such as payments to a 401(k) plan and other savings vehicles. Yes, these items do impact your cash flow, but they're not expenses; the amounts that you invest (or your employer invests for you) are essentially assets that benefit your financial situation versus an expense that doesn't help you build wealth. To account for the 401(k), simply deduct it from the gross pay first before you calculate the above worksheet. If, for example, your gross pay is $2,000 and your 401(k) contribution is $300, then use $1,700 as your income figure.

Step 3: Creating a cash flow statement

Okay, you're almost to the end. The last step is creating a cash flow statement so that you can see (all in one place) how your money moves — how much comes in and how much goes out and where it goes.

Plug the amount of your total income (from Table 2-4) and the amount of your total expenses (from Table 2-5) into the Table 2-6 worksheet to see your *cash flow*. Do you have positive cash flow — more coming in than going out — so that you can start investing in stocks (or other investments), or are expenses overpowering your income? Doing a cash flow statement isn't just about finding money in your financial situation to fund your stock program. First and foremost, it's about your financial well-being. Are you managing your finances well or not?

Table 2-6	Looking at Your Cash Flow	
Item	*Monthly $ Amount*	*Yearly $ Amount*
Total income (from Table 2-4)		
Total outgo (from Table 2-5)		
Net inflow/outflow		

2004 was another record year for personal and business bankruptcies. Personal debt and expenses far exceeded whatever income they generated. That announcement is another reminder to watch your cash flow; keep your income growing and your expenses and debt as low as possible.

Step 4: Analyzing your cash flow

Use your cash flow statement to identify sources of funds for your investment program. The more you can increase your income and the more you can decrease your outgo, the better. Scrutinize your data. Where can you improve the results? Here are some questions to ask yourself:

- How can you increase your income? Do you have hobbies, interests, or skills that can generate extra cash for you?

- Can you get more paid overtime at work? How about a promotion or a job change?

- Where can you cut expenses?

- Have you categorized your expenses as either "necessary" or "nonessential"?

> ✔ Can you lower your debt payments by refinancing or consolidating loans and credit card balances?
>
> ✔ Have you shopped around for lower insurance or telephone rates?
>
> ✔ Have you analyzed your tax withholdings in your paycheck to make sure that you are not overpaying your taxes (just to get your overpayment back next year as a refund?)

Finding investment money in tax savings

According to the Tax Foundation, the average U.S. citizen pays more in taxes than in food, clothing, and shelter combined. Sit down with your tax advisor and try to find ways to reduce your taxes. A home-based business, for example, is a great way to gain new income and increase your tax deductions, resulting in a lower tax burden. Your tax advisor can make recommendations that work for you.

One tax strategy to consider is doing your stock investing in a tax-sheltered account such as a traditional Individual Retirement Account (IRA) or a Roth Individual Retirement Account (Roth IRA). Again, check with your tax advisor for deductions and strategies available to you. For more on the tax implications of stock investing, see Chapter 20.

Setting Your Sights on Your Financial Goals

Consider stocks as tools for living, just like any other investment — no more, no less. Stocks are the tools you use (one of many) to accomplish something — to achieve a goal. Yes, successfully investing in stocks is the goal that you're probably shooting for if you're reading this book. However, you must complete the following sentence: "I want to be successful in my stock investing program to accomplish _____." You must consider stock investing as a means to an end. When people buy a computer, they don't (or shouldn't) think of buying a computer just to have a computer. People buy a computer because doing so helps them achieve a particular result, such as being more efficient in business, playing fun games, or having a nifty paperweight (tsk, tsk).

Know the difference between long-term, intermediate-term, and short-term goals and then set some of each. Long-term is a reference to projects or financial goals that need funding five or more years from now. Intermediate-term refers to financial goals that need funding two to five years from now, while short-term goals need funding less than two years from now.

Stocks, in general, are best suited for long-term goals such as these:

- ✔ Achieving financial independence (think retirement funding)
- ✔ Paying for future college costs
- ✔ Paying for any long-term expenditure or project

Some categories of stock (such as conservative or blue-chip) may be suitable for intermediate-term financial goals. If, for example, you will retire four years from now, conservative stocks are appropriate. If you're optimistic about the stock market and confident that stock prices will rise, then go ahead and invest. However, if you're negative about the market (you're *bearish,* or you believe that stock prices will decline), you may want to wait until the economy starts to forge a clear path. For more on investing in bull or bear markets, see Chapter 15.

Stocks generally aren't suitable for short-term investing goals because stock prices can behave irrationally in a short period of time. Stocks fluctuate from day to day, so you don't know what the stock will be worth in the near future. You may end up with less money than you expected. For investors seeking to reliably accrue money for short-term needs, short-term bank certificates of deposit or money market funds are more appropriate.

In recent years, investors have sought quick, short-term profits by trading and speculating in stocks. Lured by the fantastic returns generated by the stock market in the late 1990s, investors saw stocks as a get-rich-quick scheme. It is very important for you to understand the difference between *investing, saving,* and *speculating.* Which one do you want to do? Knowing the answer to this question is crucial to your goals and aspirations. Investors who don't know the difference tend to get burned. Here's some information to help you distinguish among these three actions:

- ✔ *Investing* **is the act of putting your current funds into securities or tangible assets for the purpose of gaining future appreciation, income, or both.** You need time, knowledge, and discipline to invest. The investment can fluctuate in price, but has been chosen for long-term potential.

- ✔ *Saving* **is the safe accumulation of funds for a future use.** Savings don't fluctuate and are generally free of financial risk. The emphasis is on safety and liquidity.

- ✔ *Speculating* **is the financial world's equivalent of gambling.** An investor who speculates is seeking quick profits gained from short-term price movements in that particular asset or investment.

These distinctly different concepts are often confused even among so-called financial experts. I know of one financial advisor who actually put a child's college fund money into an Internet stock fund only to lose over $17,000 in less than ten months! This advisor thought that she was investing, but in reality, she was speculating. I know of another advisor who told a client to avoid savings accounts altogether because the client had a 401(k) plan. This particular advisor didn't catch the crucial difference between "saving" and "investing." The client eventually found out the difference; his 401(k) fell by 40 percent when the bear market of 2000 arrived.

Fortunately, we can learn from these situations and get back on track. That child that lost the $17,000? He is my neighbor and I helped the father to reinvest the remaining funds. The portfolio doubled in value by the following year. It is still growing. The second fellow that lost 40 percent in his 401(k) account? He became my student and he has recouped his losses and his 401(k) plan is up (this occurred within two years). As of 2005, both investors have portfolios that are beating the general market.

Chapter 3

Defining Common Approaches to Stock Investing

In This Chapter

▶ Deciding what time frame fits your investment strategy

▶ Looking at your purpose for investing

▶ Determining your investing style

*R*ead this chapter carefully. Millions of investors are at risk because the market sees as much misinvesting activity in stocks as it does investing. I know it sounds weird, but the situation is similar to your crazy Uncle Bill punching the accelerator rather than the brakes when heading right toward the Grand Canyon — he knows that he needs to do something, but he chooses the wrong mechanism. Stocks are tools you can use to build your wealth. When used wisely, for the right purpose, and in the right environment, they do a great job. But when improperly applied, they can lead to disaster.

In this chapter, I show you how to choose the right investments, based on your short- and long-term financial goals. I also show you how to decide on your purpose for investing (growth or income investing) and the style of investing — conservative or aggressive — that you need to take.

Matching Stocks and Strategies with Your Goals

Various stocks are out there, as well as various investment approaches. The key to success in the stock market is matching the right kind of stock with the right kind of investment situation. You have to choose the stock and the approach that match your goals. (Refer to Chapter 2 for more on defining your financial goals.)

Before investing in a stock, ask yourself, "When do I want to reach my financial goal?" Stocks are a means to an end. Your job is to figure out what that end is — or, more importantly, when it is. Do you want to retire in ten years or next year? Must you pay for your kid's college education next year or 18 years from now? The length of time you have before you need the money you hope to earn from stock investing determines what stocks you should buy. Table 3-1 gives you some guidelines for choosing the kind of stock best suited for the type of investor you are and the goals you have.

Table 3-1	Stock Types, Financial Goals, and Investor Types	
Type of Investor	*Time Frame for Financial Goals*	*Type of Stock Most Suitable*
Conservative (worries about risk)	Long term (over 5 years)	Large-cap stocks and mid-cap stocks
Aggressive (high tolerance to risk)	Long term (over 5 years)	Small-cap stocks and mid-cap stocks
Conservative (worries about risk)	Intermediate term (2 to 5 years)	Large-cap stocks, preferably with dividends
Aggressive (high tolerance to risk)	Intermediate term (2 to 5 years)	Small-cap stocks and mid-cap stocks
Short term	1 to 2 years	Stocks are not suitable for the short-term. Instead, look at vehicles such as savings accounts and money market funds.

Dividends are payments made to an owner (unlike *interest,* which is payment to a creditor). Dividends are a great form of income, and companies that issue dividends tend to have more stable stock prices as well. For more information on dividend-paying stocks, see the section "Investing for a Purpose," later in this chapter, and Chapter 9.

Table 3-1 gives you general guidelines, but keep in mind that not everyone can fit into a particular profile. Every investor has a unique situation, set of goals, and level of risk tolerance. Remember that the terms *large-cap, mid cap,* and *small-cap* refer to the size (or *market capitalization,* also known as *market cap*) of the company. All factors being equal, large companies are safer (less risky) than small companies. For more on market caps, see the section "Investing for Your Personal Style," later in this chapter.

Investing for the Future

Are your goals long term or short term? Answering this question is important because individual stocks can be either great or horrible choices, depending on the time period you want to focus on. Generally, the length of time you plan to invest in stocks can be short term, intermediate term, or long term. The following sections outline what kinds of stocks are most appropriate for each term length.

Investing in stocks becomes less risky as the time frame lengthens. Stock prices tend to fluctuate on a daily basis, but they have a tendency to trend up or down over an extended period of time. Even if you invest in a stock that goes down in the short term, you're likely to see it rise and possibly go above your investment if you have the patience to wait it out and let the stock price appreciate.

Focusing on the short term

Short term generally means one year or less, although some people extend the period to two years or less. You get the point.

Every person has short-term goals. Some are modest, such as setting aside money for a vacation next month or paying for medical bills. Other short-term goals are more ambitious, such as accruing funds for a down payment to purchase a new home within six months. Whatever the expense or purchase, you need a predictable accumulation of cash soon. If this sounds like your situation, stay away from the stock market!

Because stocks can be so unpredictable in the short term, they're a bad choice for short-term considerations. I get a kick out of market analysts on television saying things such as, "At $25 a share, XYZ is a solid investment, and we feel that its stock should hit our target price of $40 within six to nine months." You know that an eager investor hears that and says, "Gee, why bother with 3 percent at the bank when this stock will rise by more than 50 percent? I better call my broker." It may hit that target amount (or surpass it), or it may not. Most of the time, the stock doesn't reach the target price, and the investor is disappointed. The stock could even go down! The reason that target prices are frequently (usually) missed is that the analyst is one person and it's difficult to figure out what millions of investors will do in the short-term. The short-term can be irrational because so many investors have so many reasons for buying and selling that it can be difficult to analyze. If you want to use the money you invest for an important short-term need, you could lose very important cash quicker than you think.

Short-term investing = speculating

If you look at a period of a single year, stocks have a mixed-performance record compared with other investments, such as bonds or bank investments. In 1999, big-company stocks grew an average of 25 percent, and small-company stocks averaged a blistering 50 to 70 percent, but bank accounts and various bonds ranged only from 1.5 to 7 percent. In the year 2000, the picture was much different. Stock investors lost their shirts, and conservative investors who put their money in bank certificates of deposit and treasury bonds watched their money grow.

The bottom line is that investing in stocks for the short term is nothing more than speculating. Your only possible strategy is luck.

Short-term stock investing is very unpredictable. You can better serve your short-term goals with stable, interest-bearing investments (like Certificates of Deposit at your local bank).

During the raging-bull market (see more about bull markets in Chapter 15) of the late 1990s, investors watched as some high-profile stocks went up 20 to 50 percent in a matter of months. Hey, who needs a savings account earning a measly interest when stocks grow like that! Of course, when the bear market hit from 2000 to 2003 and those same stocks fell 50 to 85 percent, a savings account earning a measly interest rate suddenly didn't seem so bad.

Stocks — even the best ones — fluctuate in the short term. In a negative environment, they can be very volatile. No one can accurately predict the price movement (unless you have some inside information), so stocks are definitely inappropriate for any financial goal that you need to reach within one year. Check Table 3-1 for suggestions about your short-term strategies.

Considering intermediate-term goals

Intermediate term refers to your financial goals that you plan to reach within five years. If, for example, you want to accumulate funds to put money down for investment in real estate four years from now, some growth-oriented investments may be suitable.

Although some stocks *may* be appropriate for a two- or three-year period, not all stocks are good intermediate-term investments. Different types and categories of stocks exist. Some stocks are fairly stable and hold their value well, such as the stock of much larger or established dividend-paying companies.

Other stocks have prices that jump all over the place, such as the stocks of untested companies that haven't been in existence long enough to develop a consistent track record.

 If you plan to invest in the stock market to meet intermediate-term goals, consider large, established companies or dividend-paying companies in industries that provide the necessities of life (like food and beverage or electric utilities).

Preparing for the long term

Stock investing is best suited for making money over a long period of time. When you measure stocks against other investments in terms of five to (preferably) ten or more years, they excel. Even investors who bought stocks during the depths of the Great Depression saw profitable growth in their stock portfolios over a ten-year period.

In fact, if you examine any ten-year period over the past 50 years, you see that stocks beat out other financial investments (such as bonds or bank investments) in almost every single ten-year period when measured by total return (taking into account reinvesting and compounding of capital gains and dividends)! Chapters 8 and 9 cover growth and income. As you can see, long-term planning allows stocks to shine. Of course, your work doesn't stop at deciding on a long-term investment. You still have to do your homework and choose stocks wisely because, even in good times, you can lose money if you invest in companies that go out of business. Part III shows you how to evaluate specific companies and industries and alerts you to factors in the general economy that can affect stock behavior. Appendix A provides plenty of resources you can turn to.

 Because you can choose between many different types and categories of stocks, virtually any investor with a long-term perspective should add stocks to his investment portfolio. Whether you want to save for a young child's college fund or for future retirement goals, carefully selected stocks have proven to be a superior long-term investment.

Investing for a Purpose

When the lady was asked why she bungee jumped off the bridge that spanned a massive ravine, she answered, "Because it's fun!" When someone asked the fellow why he dove into a pool that was chock-full of alligators and snakes, he responded, "Because someone pushed me." Your investment in stocks shouldn't happen unless you have a purpose that you understand, like investing for growth or investing for income. Even if an advisor pushes you to invest, be sure that your advisor gives you an explanation of how that stock choice fits your purpose.

I know of a very nice, elderly lady who had a portfolio brimming with aggressive-growth stocks because she had an overbearing broker. Her purpose should've been conservative, and she should've chosen investments that would preserve her wealth rather than grow it. Obviously, the broker's agenda got in the way. Stocks are just a means to an end. Figure out your desired end and then match the means. To find out more about dealing with brokers, go to Chapter 7.

Making loads of money quickly: Growth investing

When investors want their money to grow, they look for investments that appreciate in value. *Appreciate* is just another way of saying "grow." If you have a stock that you bought for $8 per share and now its value is $30 per share, your investment has grown by $22 per share — that's appreciation. I know I would appreciate it.

Appreciation (also known as *capital gain*) is probably the number one reason why people invest in stocks. Few investments have the potential to grow your wealth as conveniently as stocks. If you want the stock market to make you loads of money relatively quickly (and you can assume some risk), head to Chapter 8, which takes an in-depth look at investing for growth.

Stocks are a great way to grow your wealth, but they're not the only way. Many investors seek alternative ways to make money, but many of these alternative ways are more aggressive and carry significantly more risk. You may have heard about people who made quick fortunes in areas such as commodities (like wheat, pork bellies, or precious metals), options, and other more sophisticated investment vehicles. Keep in mind that you should limit risky investments to only a portion of your portfolio, such as 10 percent of your investable funds. Experienced investors, however, can go as high as 20 percent. Chapter 8 goes into greater detail about growth investing.

Steadily making money: Income investing

Not all investors want to take on the risk that comes with making a killing. (Hey . . . no guts, no glory!) Some people just want to invest in the stock market as a means of providing a steady income. They don't need stock values to go through the ceiling. Instead, they need stocks that perform well consistently.

If your purpose for investing in stocks is to create income, you need to choose stocks that pay dividends. Dividends are typically paid quarterly to stockholders on record.

Distinguishing between dividends and interest

Don't confuse dividends with interest. Most people are familiar with interest, because that's how you grow your money over the years in the bank. The important difference is that *interest* is paid to creditors, and *dividends* are paid to owners (meaning *shareholders* — and if you own stock, you're a shareholder, because stocks represent shares in a publicly traded company).

When you buy stock, you buy a piece of that company. When you put money in a bank (or when you buy bonds), you basically loan your money. You become a creditor, and the bank or bond issuer is the debtor, and as such, it must eventually pay your money back to you with interest.

Recognizing the importance of an income stock's yield

Investing for income means that you have to consider your investment's yield. If you want income from a stock investment, you must compare the yield from that particular stock with alternatives. Looking at the yield is a way to compare the income you expect to receive from one investment with the expected income from others. Table 3-2 shows some comparative yields.

Table 3-2	Comparing the Yields of Various Investments				
Investment	**Type**	**Amount**	**Pay Type**	**Payout**	**Yield**
Smith Co.	Stock	$50/share	Dividend	$2.50	5.0%
Jones Co.	Stock	$100/share	Dividend	$4.00	4.0%
Acme Bank	Bank CD	$500	Interest	$25.00	5.0%
Acme Bank	Bank CD	$2,500	Interest	$131.25	5.25%
Acme Bank	Bank CD	$5,000	Interest	$287.50	5.75%
Brown Co.	Bond	$5,000	Interest	$300.00	6.0%

To understand how to calculate yield, you need the following formula:

Yield = Payout ÷ Investment Amount

Yield enables you to compare how much income you would get for a prospective investment compared with the income you would get from other investments. For the sake of simplicity, this exercise is based on an annual percentage yield basis (compounding would increase the yield).

Jones Co. and Smith Co. are both typical dividend-paying stocks, and in the example presented by Table 3-2, presume that both companies are similar in most respects except for their differing dividends. How can you tell whether a $50 stock with a $2.50 annual dividend is better (or worse) than a $100 stock with a $4.00 dividend? The yield tells you.

Even though Jones Co. pays a higher dividend ($4.00), Smith Co. has a higher yield (5 percent). Therefore, if you had to choose between those two stocks as an income investor, you would choose Smith Co. Of course, if you truly want to maximize your income and don't really need your investment to appreciate a lot, you should probably choose Brown Co.'s bond because it offers a yield of 6 percent.

Dividend-paying stocks do have the ability to increase in value. They may not have the same growth potential as growth stocks, but, at the very least, they have a greater potential for capital gain than bank CDs or bonds. Dividend-paying stocks (investing for income) are covered in Chapter 9.

Investing for Your Personal Style

Your investing style isn't a blue-jeans-versus-three-piece-suit debate. It refers to your approach to stock investing. Do you want to be conservative or aggressive? Would you rather be the tortoise or the hare? Your investment personality greatly depends on your purpose and the term over which you're planning to invest (see the previous two sections in this chapter). The following sections outline the two most general investment styles.

Conservative investing

Conservative investing means that you put your money in something proven, tried, and true. You invest your money in safe and secure places, such as banks and government-backed securities. But how does that apply to stocks? (Table 3-1 gives you suggestions.)

Conservative stock investors want to place their money in companies that have exhibited some of the following qualities:

> ✔ **Proven performance:** You want companies that have shown increasing sales and earnings year after year. You don't demand anything spectacular, just a strong and steady performance.

✔ **Market size:** Companies should be large-cap (short for large capitalization). In other words, they should have a market value exceeding $10 billion. Conservative investors surmise that bigger is safer.

✔ **Market leadership:** Companies should be leaders in their industries.

✔ **Perceived staying power:** You want companies with the financial clout and market position to weather uncertain market and economic conditions. It shouldn't matter what happens in the economy or who gets elected.

As a conservative investor, you don't mind if the companies' share prices jump (who would?), but you're more concerned with steady growth over the long term.

Aggressive investing

Aggressive investors can plan long term or look only over the intermediate term, but in any case, they want stocks that resemble jack rabbits — they show the potential to break out of the pack.

Aggressive stock investors want to invest their money in companies that have exhibited some of the following qualities:

✔ **Great potential:** The company must have superior goods, services, ideas, or ways of doing business compared to the competition.

✔ **Capital gains possibility:** You don't even consider dividends. If anything, you dislike dividends. You feel that the money that would've been dispensed in dividend form is better reinvested in the company. This, in turn, can spur greater growth.

✔ **Innovation:** Companies should have technologies, ideas, or innovative methods that make them stand apart from other companies.

Aggressive investors usually seek out small capitalization stocks, known as *small-caps,* because they have plenty of potential for growth. Take the tree example, for instance: A giant redwood may be strong, but it may not grow much more, whereas a brand-new sapling has plenty of growth to look forward to. Why invest in stodgy, big companies when you can invest in smaller enterprises that may become the leaders of tomorrow? Aggressive investors have no problem investing in obscure companies because they hope that such companies will become another IBM or McDonald's. Find out more about growth investing in Chapter 8.

Chapter 4

Recognizing the Risks

In This Chapter

▶ Considering the types of risk

▶ Taking steps to reduce your risk

▶ Balancing risk against return

*I*nvestors face many risks, many of which I cover in this chapter. The simplest definition of risk for investors is "the possibility that your investment will lose some (or all) of its value." Yet you don't have to fear risk if you understand and plan for it. You need to get familiar with the concept of risk. You must understand the oldest equation in the world of investing — risk versus return. This equation states the following:

> If you want a greater return on your money, you need to tolerate more risk. If you don't want to tolerate more risk, you must tolerate a lower rate of return.

This point about risk is best illustrated from a moment in one of my investment seminars. One of the attendees told me that he had his money in the bank but was dissatisfied with the rate of return. He lamented, "The yield on my money is pitiful! I want to put my money somewhere where it can grow." I asked him, "How about investing in common stocks? Or what about growth mutual funds? They have a solid, long-term growth track record." He responded, "Stocks? I don't want to put my money there. It's too risky!" Okay, then. If you don't want to tolerate more risk, then don't complain about earning less on your money. Risk (in all its forms) has a bearing on all your money concerns and goals. That's why it's so important that you understand risk before you invest.

This man — as well as the rest of us — needs to remember that risk is not a four-letter word. Well, it is a four-letter word, but you know what I mean. Risk is present no matter what you do with your money. Even if you simply stick your money in your mattress, risk is involved — several kinds of risk, in fact.

You have the risk of fire. What if your house burns down? You have the risk of theft. What if burglars find your stash of cash? You also have relative risk. (In other words, what if your relatives find your money?)

Be aware of the different kinds of risk, and you can easily plan around them to keep your money growing.

Exploring Different Kinds of Risk

Think about all the ways that an investment can lose money. You can list all sorts of possibilities. So many that you may think, "Holy cow! Why invest at all?"

Don't let risk frighten you. After all, life itself is risky. Just make sure that you understand the different kinds of risk before you start navigating the investment world. Be mindful of risk and find out about the effects of risk on your investments and personal financial goals.

Financial risk

The financial risk of stock investing is that you can lose your money if the company whose stock you purchase loses money or goes belly up. This type of risk is the most obvious because companies do go bankrupt.

You can greatly enhance the chances of your financial risk paying off by doing an adequate amount of research and choosing your stocks carefully (which this book helps you do — see Part III for more details). Financial risk is a real concern even when the economy is doing well. Some diligent research, a little planning, and a dose of common sense help you reduce your financial risk.

In the stock investing mania of the late 1990s, millions of investors (along with many well-known investment "gurus") ignored some obvious financial risks of many then-popular stocks. Investors blindly plunked their money into stocks that were bad choices. Consider investors who put their money in DrKoop.com, a health information Web site, in 1999 and held on during 2000. DrKoop.com went into cardiac arrest as it collapsed from $45 per share to $2 per share by mid-2000. By the time the stock was DOA, investors lost millions. RIP (risky investment play!).

Internet and tech stocks littered the graveyard of stock market catastrophes during 2000–2001 because investors didn't see (or didn't want to see?) the risks involved with companies that didn't offer a solid record of results (profits, sales, and so on). Remember that when you invest in companies that don't have a proven track record, you're not investing, you're speculating.

Investors who did their homework regarding the financial conditions of companies such as the Internet stocks discovered that these companies had the hallmarks of financial risk — high debt, low (or no) earnings, and plenty of competition. They steered clear, avoiding tremendous financial loss. Investors who didn't do their homework were lured by the status of these companies — the poster children of booming Internet fortunes — and lost their shirts.

Of course, the individual investors who lost money by investing in these trendy, high-profile companies don't deserve all the responsibility for their tremendous financial losses; some high-profile analysts and media sources also should have known better. The late 1990s may someday be a case study of how euphoria and the herd mentality (rather than good, old-fashioned research and common sense) ruled the day (temporarily). The excitement of making potential fortunes gets the best of people sometimes, and they throw caution to the wind. Historians may look back at those days and say, "What *were* they thinking?" Achieving true wealth takes diligent work and careful analysis.

In terms of financial risk, the bottom line is . . . well . . . the bottom line! A healthy bottom line means that a company is making money. And if a company is making money, then you can make money by investing in its stock. However, if a company isn't making money, you won't make money if you invest in it. Profit is the lifeblood of any company. (Are you listening, Dr. Koop?)

Interest rate risk

Interest rate risk may sound like an odd type of risk, but in fact, it's a common consideration for investors. Be aware that interest rates change on a regular basis, causing some challenging moments. Banks set interest rates, and the primary institution to watch closely is the Federal Reserve (the Fed), which is, in effect, the country's central bank. The Fed raises or lowers interest rates, actions that, in turn, cause banks to raise or lower interest rates accordingly. Interest rate changes affect consumers, businesses, and, of course, investors.

The scenario outlined in the following paragraphs gives you a generic introduction to the way fluctuating interest rate risk can affect investors in general.

Suppose that you buy a long-term, high-quality corporate bond and get a yield of 6 percent. Your money is safe, and your return is locked in at 6 percent. Whew! That's a guaranteed 6 percent. Not bad, huh? But what happens if, after you commit your money, interest rates increase to 8 percent? You lose the opportunity to get that extra 2 percent interest. The only way to get out of your 6 percent bond is to sell it at current market values and use the money to reinvest at the higher rate.

The only problem with this scenario is that the 6 percent bond is likely to drop in value because interest rates rose. Why? Say that the investor is Bob and the bond yielding 6 percent is a corporate bond issued by Lucin-Muny (LM). According to the bond agreement, LM must pay 6 percent (called the "face rate" or "nominal rate") during the life of the bond and then, upon maturity, pay the principal. If Bob buys $10,000 of LM bonds on the day they are issued, he gets $600 (of interest) every year for as long as he holds the bonds. If he holds on until maturity, he gets back his $10,000 (the principal). So far so good, right? The plot thickens, however.

Say that he decides to sell the bond long before maturity and that, at the time of the sale, interest rates in the market have risen to 8 percent. Now what? The reality is that no one is going to want his 6 percent bond if the market is offering bonds at 8 percent. What's Bob to do? He can't change the face rate of 6 percent, and he can't change the fact that only $600 is paid each year for the life of the bond. What has to change so that current investors get the *equivalent* yield of 8 percent? If you said, "The bond's value has to go down," . . . bingo! In this example, the bond's market value needs to drop to $7,500 so that investors buying the bond get an equivalent yield of 8 percent. (For simplicity sake, I left out the time it takes for the bond to mature.) Here's how that figures:

New investors still get $600 annually. However, $600 is equal to 8 percent of $7,500. Therefore, even though investors get the face rate of 6 percent, they get a yield of 8 percent because the actual investment amount is $7,500. In this example, no financial risk is present, but you see how interest rate risk presents itself. Bob finds out that you can have a good company with a good bond, yet you still lose $2,500 because of the change in the interest rate. Of course, if Bob doesn't sell, he doesn't realize that loss. (For more on when to sell, see Chapter 17.)

You can lose money in an apparently sound investment because of something that sounds as harmless as "interest rates have changed."

Understanding the adverse effects of rising interest rates

Rising and falling interest rates offer a special risk to stock investors. Historically, rising interest rates have had an adverse effect on stock prices. I outline several reasons why in the following sections.

Hurting a company's financial condition

Rising interest rates have a negative impact on companies that carry a large current debt load or that need to take on more debt because when interest rates rise, the cost of borrowing money rises, too. Ultimately, the company's profitability and ability to grow are reduced. When a company's profits (or earnings) drop, its stock becomes less desirable, and its stock price falls.

Affecting a company's customers

A company's success comes when it sells its products or services. But what happens if increased interest rates negatively impact its customers (specifically, other companies that buy from it)? The financial health of its customers directly affects the company's ability to grow sales and earnings.

For a good example of this situation, consider what happened to Cisco Systems in 2000. Because a huge part of its sales went to the telecommunications industry, Cisco's profitability depended on the health of that entire industry. The telecom industry's debt ballooned to $700 billion. This debt became the telecom industry's financial Achilles heel, which, in turn, became a pain in the neck to Cisco. Because telecom companies bought less (especially from Cisco), Cisco's profits shrank. From March 2000 to March 2001, Cisco's stock fell by nearly 70 percent! As of September 2001, Cisco's stock price continued to decline because the companies that were Cisco's customers were hurting financially.

Impacting investors' decision-making considerations

When interest rates rise, investors start to rethink their investment strategies, resulting in one of two outcomes:

- ✓ Investors may sell any shares in interest-sensitive stocks that they hold. Interest-sensitive industries include electric utilities, real estate, and the financial sector. Although increased interest rates can hurt these sectors, the reverse is also generally true: Falling interest rates boost the same industries. Keep in mind that interest rate changes affect some industries more than others.

- ✓ Investors who favor increased current income (versus waiting for the investment to grow in value to sell for a gain later on) are definitely attracted to investment vehicles that offer a higher rate of return. Higher interest rates can cause investors to switch from stocks to bonds or bank certificates of deposit.

Hurting stock prices indirectly

High or rising interest rates can have a negative impact on any investor's total financial picture. What happens when an investor struggles with burdensome debt, such as a second mortgage, credit card debt, or *margin debt* (debt from borrowing against stock in a brokerage account)? He may sell some stock in order to pay off some of his high-interest debt. Selling stock to service debt is a common practice that, when taken collectively, can hurt stock prices.

As this book goes to press, the stock market and the U.S. economy face perhaps the greatest challenge since the Great Depression — debt. In terms of Gross Domestic Product (GDP), the size of the economy is about $11.5 trillion (give or take $100 billion), but the debt level is about $37 trillion. This already enormous amount does not include $44 trillion of liabilities such as Social

Security and Medicare. Additionally (Yikes! There's more?!), some of our financial institutions hold over $50 trillion worth of derivatives. These can be very complicated and sophisticated investment vehicles that can backfire. Derivatives have, in fact, sunk some large organizations (such as Enron), and investors should be aware of them. Just check out the company's financial reports. (Find out more in Chapter 11.)

Because of the effects of interest rates on stock portfolios, both direct and indirect, successful investors regularly monitor interest rates in both the general economy and in their personal situations. Although stocks have proven to be a superior long-term investment (the longer the term, the better), every investor should maintain a balanced portfolio that includes other investment vehicles, such as money market funds, savings bonds, and/or bank investments.

A diversified investor has some money in vehicles that do well when interest rates rise. These vehicles include money market funds, U.S. savings bonds (EE), and other variable-rate investments whose interest rates rise when market rates rise. These types of investments add a measure of safety from interest rate risk to your stock portfolio.

Market risk

People talk about *the market* and how it goes up or down, making it sound like a monolithic entity instead of what it really is — a group of millions of individuals making daily decisions to buy or sell stock. No matter how modern our society and economic system, you can't escape the laws of supply and demand. When masses of people want to buy a particular stock, it becomes in demand, and its price rises. That price rises higher if the supply is limited. Conversely, if no one's interested in buying a stock, its price falls. Supply and demand is the nature of market risk. The price of the stock you purchase can rise and fall on the fickle whim of market demand.

Millions of investors buying and selling each minute of every trading day affect the share price of your stock. This fact makes it impossible to judge which way your stock will move tomorrow or next week. This unpredictability and seeming irrationality is why stocks aren't appropriate for short-term financial growth.

In April 2001, a news program reported that in 2000, a fellow with $80,000 in the bank decided to take his money and invest it in the stock market. Because he was getting married in 2001, he wanted his money to grow faster and higher so that he could afford a nice wedding and a down payment on the couple's future home. What happened? His money shrank to $11,000, and he had to change his plans. Sometimes, "market risk" begets "romantic" risk.

Losing money is only one headache you face when you lose money this way; the idea of postponing a joyful event, such as a wedding or a home purchase, just adds to the pain. The gent in the preceding story could have easily minimized his losses with some knowledge and discipline.

Markets are volatile by nature; they go up and down, and investments need time to grow. This poor guy (literally, now) should have been aware of the fact that stocks in general aren't suitable for short-term (one year or less) goals (see Chapter 2 for more on short-term goals). Despite the fact that the companies he invested in may have been fundamentally sound, all stock prices are subject to the gyrations of the marketplace and need time to trend upward.

Investing requires diligent work and research before putting your money in quality investments with a long-term perspective. Speculating is attempting to make a relatively quick profit by monitoring the short-term price movements of a particular investment. Investors seek to minimize risk, whereas speculators don't mind risk because it can also magnify profits. Speculating and investing have clear differences, but investors frequently become speculators and ultimately put themselves and their wealth at risk. Don't go there!

Consider the married couple nearing retirement who decided to play with their money to see about making their pending retirement more comfortable. They borrowed a sizable sum by tapping into their home equity to invest in the stock market. (Their home, which they had paid off, had enough equity to qualify for this loan.) What did they do with these funds? You guessed it; they invested in the high-flying stocks of the day, which were high-tech and Internet stocks. Within eight months, they lost almost all their money.

Understanding market risk is especially important for people who are tempted to put their nest eggs or emergency funds into volatile investments such as growth stocks (or mutual funds that invest in growth stocks or similar aggressive investment vehicles). Remember, you can lose everything.

Inflation risk

Inflation is the artificial expansion of the quantity of money so that too much money is used in exchange for goods and services. To consumers, inflation shows up in the form of higher prices for goods and services. Inflation risk is also referred to as *purchasing power risk*. This term just means that your money doesn't buy as much as it used to. For example, a dollar that bought you a sandwich in 1980 barely bought you a candy bar a few years later. For you, the investor, this risk means that the value of your investment (a bond, for example) may not keep up with inflation.

Say that you have money in a bank savings account currently earning 4 percent. This account has flexibility — if the market interest rate goes up, the rate you earn in your account goes up. Your account is safe from both financial risk and interest rate risk. But what if inflation is running at 5 percent? At that point you're losing money.

Tax risk

Taxes (such as income tax or capital gains tax) don't affect your stock investment directly. Taxes can obviously affect how much of your money you get to keep. Because the entire point of stock investing is to build wealth, you need to understand that taxes take away a portion of the wealth that you're trying to build. Taxes can be risky because if you make the wrong move with your stocks (selling them at the wrong time, for example), you can end up paying higher taxes than you need to. Because tax laws change so frequently, tax risk is part of the risk-versus-return equation, as well.

It pays to gain knowledge about how taxes can impact your wealth-building program before you make your investment decisions. Chapter 20 covers in greater detail the impact of taxes.

Political and governmental risks

If companies were fish, politics and government policies (such as taxes, laws, and regulations) would be the pond. In the same way that fish die in a toxic or polluted pond, politics and government policies can kill companies. Of course, if you own stock in a company exposed to political and governmental risks, you need to be aware of these risks. For some companies, a single new regulation or law is enough to send them into bankruptcy. For other companies, a new law could help them increase sales and profits.

What if you invest in companies or industries that become political targets? You may want to consider selling them (you can always buy them back later) or consider putting in stop loss orders on the stock (see Chapter 17). For example, tobacco companies were the targets of political firestorms that battered their stock prices. Whether you agree or disagree with the political machinations of today is not the issue. As an investor, you have to ask yourself, "How do politics affect the market value and the current and future prospects of my chosen investment?" (See Chapter 14 for more on how politics can affect the stock market.)

Personal risks

Frequently, the risk involved with investing in the stock market may not be directly involved with the investment or factors directly related to the investment; sometimes the risk is with the investor's circumstances.

Suppose that investor Ralph puts $15,000 into a portfolio of common stocks. Imagine that the market experiences a drop in prices that week and Ralph's stocks drop to a market value of $14,000.

Because stocks are good for the long term, this type of decrease is usually not an alarming incident. Odds are that this dip is temporary, especially if Ralph carefully chose high-quality companies. Incidentally, if a portfolio of high-quality stocks *does* experience a temporary drop in price, it can be a great opportunity to get more shares at a good price. (Chapter 17 covers orders you can place with your broker to help you do that.)

Over the long term, Ralph would probably see the value of his investment grow substantially. But, what if during a period when his stocks are declining, Ralph experiences financial difficulty and needs quick cash? He may have to sell his stock to get some money.

This problem occurs frequently for investors who don't have an emergency fund or a rainy day fund to handle large, sudden expenses. You never know when your company may lay you off or when your basement may flood, leaving you with a huge repair bill. Car accidents, medical emergencies, and other unforeseen events are part of life's bag of surprises — for anyone. Be sure to set money aside for sudden expenses before you buy stocks. Then you aren't forced to prematurely liquidate your stock investments to pay emergency bills (Chapter 2 provides more guidance on having liquid assets for emergencies).

You probably won't get much comfort from knowing that stock losses are tax deductible — a loss is a loss (see Chapter 20 regarding taxes). However, you can avoid the kind of loss that results from prematurely having to sell your stocks if you maintain an emergency cash fund. A good place for your emergency cash fund is in either a bank savings account or a money market fund.

Emotional risk

What does emotional risk have to do with stocks? Emotions are important risk considerations because the main decision makers are human beings. Logic and discipline are critical factors in investment success, but even the best investor can let emotions take over the reins of money management and cause loss. For stock investing, you're likely to be sidetracked by three main emotions: greed, fear, and love. You need to understand your emotions and what kinds of risk they can expose you to. If you get too attached to a sinking stock, then you don't need a stock investing book — you need Dr. Phil!

Paying the price for greed

In the 1998–2000 period, millions of investors threw caution to the wind and chased highly dubious, risky dot-com stocks. The dollar signs popped up in their eyes (just like slot machines) when they saw that easy street was lined with dot-com stocks that were doubling and tripling in a very short time. Who cares about price/earnings (P/E) ratios and earnings when you can just buy stock, make a fortune, and get out with millions? (Of course, *you* care about making money with stocks, so you can flip to Chapter 10 and Appendix B to find out more about P/E ratios.)

Investment lessons from September 11

September 11, 2001, was a horrific day that is burned in our minds and won't be forgotten in our lifetime. The acts of terrorism that day took over 3,000 lives and caused untold pain and grief. A much less important aftereffect was the hard lessons that investors learned that day. Terrorism reminds us that risk is more real than ever and that we should never let our guard down. What lessons can investors learn from the worst acts of terrorism to ever happen on U.S. soil? Here are a few pointers:

✓ **Diversify your portfolio.** Of course, the events of September 11 were certainly surreal and unexpected. But before the events occurred, investors should have made it a habit to assess their situations and see whether they had any vulnerabilities. Stock investors with no money outside the stock market are always more at risk. Keeping your portfolio diversified is a time-tested strategy that is more relevant than ever before.

✓ **Review and re-allocate.** September 11 triggered declines in the overall market, but specific industries, such as airlines and hotels, were hit particularly hard. In addition, some industries, such as defense and food, saw stock prices rise. Monitor your portfolio and ask yourself whether it is overly reliant on or exposed to events in specific sectors. If so, reallocate your investments to decrease your risk exposure.

✓ **Check for signs of trouble.** Techniques such as trailing stops (which I explain in Chapter 17) come in very handy when your stocks plummet because of unexpected events. Even if you don't use these techniques, you can make it a regular habit to analyze your stocks and check for signs of trouble, such as debts or P/E ratios that are too high. If you see signs of trouble (check out Chapter 21), consider selling anyway.

Unfortunately, the lure of the easy buck can easily turn healthy attitudes about growing wealth into unhealthy greed that blinds investors and discards common sense (such as investing for quick short-term gains in dubious "hot stocks," rather than doing your homework and buying stocks of solid companies with strong fundamentals and a long-term focus).

Recognizing the role of fear

Greed can be a problem, but fear is the other extreme. People who are fearful of loss frequently avoid suitable investments and end up settling for a low rate of return. If you have to succumb to one of these emotions, at least fear exposes you to less loss.

Looking for love in all the wrong places

Stocks are dispassionate, inanimate vehicles, but people can look for love in the strangest places. Emotional risk occurs when investors fall in love with a stock and refuse to sell it even when the stock is plummeting and shows all the symptoms of getting worse. Emotional risk also occurs when investors are drawn to bad investment choices just because they sound good, are popular, or are pushed by family or friends. Love and attachment are great in relationships with people, but can be horrible with investments.

Minimizing Your Risk

Now, before you go crazy thinking that stock investing carries so much risk that you may as well not get out of bed, take a breath. Minimizing your risk in stock investing is easier than you think. Although wealth building through the stock market doesn't take place without some amount of risk, you can practice the following tips to maximize your profits and still keep your money secure.

Gaining knowledge

Some people spend more time analyzing a restaurant menu to choose a $10 entrée than analyzing where to put their next $5,000. Lack of knowledge constitutes the greatest risk for new investors, but diminishing that risk starts with gaining knowledge. The more familiar you are with the stock market — how it works, factors that affect stock value, and so on — the better you can navigate around its pitfalls and maximize your profits. The same knowledge that enables you to grow your wealth also enables you to minimize your risk. Before you put your money anywhere, you want to know as much as you can. This book is a great place to start — check out Chapter 6 for a rundown of the kinds of information you want to know before you buy stocks, as well as the resources that can give you the information you need to invest successfully.

Staying out . . . for now

If you don't understand stocks, don't invest! Yeah, I know this book is about stock investing, and I think that some measure of stock investing is a good idea for most people. But that doesn't mean you should be 100 percent invested 100 percent of the time. If you don't understand a particular stock (or don't understand stocks, period), stay away until you do understand. Instead, give yourself an imaginary sum of money, such as $100,000, give yourself reasons to invest, and just make believe. Pick a few stocks that you think will increase in value and then track them for a while and see how they perform. Begin to understand how the price of a stock goes up and down, and watch what happens to the stocks you chose when various events take place. As you find out more and more about stock investing, you get better and better at picking individual stocks, and you haven't risked — or lost — any money during your learning period. A good place to do your "imaginary" investing is at Web sites such as Marketocracy (www.marketocracy.com). You can design a stock portfolio and track its performance with thousands of other investors to see how well you do.

Getting your financial house in order

Advice on what to do before you invest could be a whole book all by itself. The bottom line is that you want to make sure that you are, first and foremost, financially secure before you take the plunge into the stock market. If you're not sure about your financial security, look over your situation with a financial planner. (You can find more on financial planners in Appendix A.)

Before you buy your first stock, here are a few things you can do to get your finances in order:

✓ **Have a cushion of money.** Set aside three to six months' worth of your gross living expenses somewhere safe, such as in a bank account or treasury money market fund, in case you suddenly need cash for an emergency.

✓ **Reduce your debt.** Overindulging in debt was the worst personal economic problem for many Americans in the late 1990s. The year 2001 was a record year for bankruptcy, with nearly 1.5 million people filing for bankruptcy.

✓ **Make sure that your job is as secure as you can make it.** Are you keeping your skills up to date? Is the company you work for strong and growing? Is the industry that you work in strong and growing?

✓ **Make sure that you have adequate insurance.** You need enough insurance to cover you and your family's needs in case of illness, death, disability, and so on.

Diversifying your investments

Diversification is a strategy for reducing risk by spreading your money across different investments. It's a fancy way of saying, "Don't put all your eggs in one basket." But how do you go about divvying up your money and distributing it among different investments? The easiest way to understand proper diversification may be to look at what you should *not* do:

✓ **Don't put all your money in just one stock.** Sure, if you choose wisely and select a hot stock, you may make a bundle, but the odds are tremendously against you. Unless you're a real expert on a particular company, it's a good idea to have small portions of your money in several different stocks. As a general rule, the money you tie up in a single stock should be money you can do without.

✓ **Don't put all your money in one industry.** I know people who own several stocks, but the stocks are all in the same industry. Again, if you're an expert in that particular industry, it could work out. But just understand that you're not properly diversified. If a problem hits an entire industry, you may get hurt.

✔ **Don't put all your money in just one type of investment.** Stocks may be a great investment, but you need to have money elsewhere. Bonds, bank accounts, treasury securities, real estate, and precious metals are perennial alternatives to complement your stock portfolio. Some of these alternatives can be found in mutual funds or exchange traded funds (ETFs).

Okay, now that you know what you *shouldn't* do, what *should* you do? Until you become more knowledgeable, follow this advice:

✔ **Only keep 20 percent (or less) of your investment money in a single stock.**

✔ **Invest in four or five different stocks that are in different industries.** Which industries? Choose industries that offer products and services that have shown strong, growing demand. To make this decision, use your common sense (which isn't as common as it used to be). Think about the industries that people need no matter what happens in the general economy, such as food, energy, and other consumer necessities. See Chapter 12 for more information about analyzing industries.

Weighing Risk Against Return

How much risk is appropriate for you, and how do you handle it? Before you try to figure out what risks accompany your investment choices, analyze yourself. Here are some points to keep in mind when weighing risk versus return in your situation:

✔ **Your financial goal:** In five minutes with a financial calculator, you can easily see how much money you're going to need to become financially independent (presuming that financial independence is your goal). Say that you need $500,000 in ten years for a worry-free retirement and that your financial assets (such as stocks, bonds, and so on) are currently worth $400,000. In this scenario, your assets need to grow by only 2.25 percent to hit your target. Getting investments that grow by 2.25 percent safely is easy to do because that is a relatively low rate of return.

The important point is that you don't have to knock yourself out trying to double your money with risky, high-flying investments; some run-of-the-mill bank investments will do just fine. All too often, investors take on more risk than is necessary. Figure out what your financial goal is so that you know what kind of return you realistically need.

✔ **Your investor profile:** Are you nearing retirement, or are you fresh out of college? Your life situation matters when it comes to looking at risk versus return. If you're just beginning your working years, you can certainly tolerate greater risk than someone facing retirement. Even if you lose big time, you still have a long time to recoup your money and get back on track. However, if you're approaching retirement, risky or aggressive investments can do much more harm than good. If you lose money, you don't have as much time to recoup your investment, and the odds are that you'll need the investment money (and its income-generating capacity) to cover your living expenses after you are no longer employed.

✔ **Asset allocation:** I never tell retirees to put a large portion of their retirement money into a high-tech stock or other volatile investment. But if they still want to speculate, I don't see a problem as long as they limit such investments to 5 percent of their total assets. As long as the bulk of their money is safe and sound in secure investments (such as U.S. treasury bonds), I know I can sleep well (knowing that *they* can sleep well!).

Asset allocation beckons back to diversification. For people in their 20s and 30s, having 75 percent of their money in a diversified portfolio of growth stocks (such as mid-cap and small-cap stocks) is acceptable. For people in their 60s and 70s, it's not acceptable. They may, instead, consider investing no more than 20 percent of their money in stocks (mid-caps and large-caps are preferable). Check with your financial advisor to find the right mix for your particular situation.

Better luck next time

A little knowledge can be very risky. Consider the true story of one "lucky" fellow who played the California lottery in 1987. He discovered that he had a winning ticket, with the first prize of $412,000. He immediately ordered a Porsche, booked a lavish trip to Hawaii for his family, and treated his wife and friends to a champagne dinner at a posh Hollywood restaurant. When he finally went to collect his prize, he found out that he had to share first prize with over 9,000 other lottery players who also had the same winning numbers. His share of the prize was actually only $45! Hopefully, he invested that tidy sum based on his increased knowledge about risk.

Chapter 5

Say Cheese: Getting a Snapshot of the Market

"**H**ow's the market doing today?" is the most common question that interested parties ask about the stock market. "What did the Dow do?" "How about Nasdaq?" Invariably, people asking those questions expect an answer regarding how well the market has performed that day. "Well, the Dow fell 57 points to 9,500, while Nasdaq was unchanged at 1,882." You can use indexes as general gauges of stock market activity. From them, you get a basic idea of how well (or how poorly) the overall market is doing. In this chapter, I focus my attention on stock market indexes.

Knowing How Indexes Are Measured

An *index* is a statistical measure that represents the value of a batch of stocks. Investors use this measure like a barometer to track the overall progress of the market (or a segment of it).

The oldest stock market index is the Dow Jones Industrial Average (DJIA or simply "The Dow"). In 1896, Charles Dow (of Dow Jones fame) created the Dow Jones Industrial Average; it covered only 12 stocks then (the number increased to 30 stocks in 1928, and it remains the same to this day). Because Dow worked long before the age of computers, he kept calculating a stock market index simple and did it arithmetically by hand. Dow added up the stock prices of the 12 companies and then divided the sum by 12. Technically, this number is an *average* and not an index (hence the word "average" in the name). For simplicity sake, we'll refer to it as an index.

Nowadays, the number gets tweaked to also account for things such as stock splits. (For more on stock splits see Chapter 19.)

However, indexes get calculated differently. The primary difference between an "index" and an "average" is the concept of weighting. *Weighting* is the relative importance of the items when they are computed within the index. Several kinds of indexes exist, including:

- **Price-weighted index:** This kind of index tracks changes based on the change in the individual stock's price per share.

  To give you an example, suppose that you own two stocks: Stock A worth $20 per share and Stock B worth $40 per share. A price-weighted index allocates a greater proportion of the index to the stock at $40 than to the one at $20. Therefore, if we had only these two stocks in an index, the index number would reflect the $40 stock as being 67 percent (two-thirds of the number), while the $20 stock would be 33 percent (one-third of the number).

- **Market-value weighted index:** This kind of index tracks the proportion of a stock based on its market capitalization (or market value, also called market cap).

  Say that in your portfolio, you have 10 million shares of a $20 stock (Stock A) and 1 million shares of a $40 stock (Stock B). Stock A's market cap is $200 million, while Stock B's market cap is $40 million. Therefore, in a market-value weighted index, Stock A represents 83 percent of the index's value because of its much larger market cap.

- **Broad-based index:** The sample portfolios in the preceding bullets show only two stocks — obviously not a good representative index. Most investing professionals (especially money managers and mutual fund firms) use a broad-based index as a benchmark to compare their progress. A broad-based index has the purpose to provide a "snapshot" of the entire market, such as the S&P 500 or the Wilshire 5000. (See descriptions of both indexes later in this chapter.)

- **Composite index:** This is an index or average that is a combination of several averages or indexes. An example is the New York Stock Exchange (NYSE) Composite, which tracks all the stocks on the NYSE.

Checking Out the Indexes

Although most people consider the Dow, Nasdaq, and Standard & Poor's 500 to be the stars of the financial press, you may find other indexes equally important to follow because they cover other significant facets of the market, such as small-cap and mid-cap stocks.

You can check out other less-sexy indexes that cover specific sectors and industries. If you're investing in an Internet stock, you should also check the Internet Stock Index to compare what your stock is doing when measured against the index. You can find indexes that cover industries such as transportation, brokerage firms, retailers, computer companies, and real estate firms. For a comprehensive list of indexes, go to www.djindexes.com (a Dow Jones & Co. Web site). The most reliable and most widely respected indexes are produced not only by Dow Jones but also Standard & Poor's and the major exchanges/markets themselves such as the New York Stock Exchange (NYSE), the American Stock Exchange (AMEX), and Nasdaq. There are also indexes issued or provided by smaller exchanges (such as the Philadelphia Exchange).

The Dow Jones Industrial Average

The most famous stock market barometer is my first example — the Dow Jones Industrial Average (DJIA). When someone asks how the market is doing, most investors quote the DJIA (simply referred to as "the Dow"). The Dow is price weighted and tracks a basket of 30 of the largest and most influential public companies in the stock market. The following list shows the current roster of 30 stocks tracked on the DJIA (in alphabetical order by company with their stock symbols in parentheses).

Alcoa (AA)

Altria (MO)

American Express Co. (AXP)

American International Group (AIG)

Boeing (BA)

Caterpillar (CAT)

Citigroup (C)

Coca-Cola (KO)

Disney (DIS)

DuPont (DD)

Exxon Mobil (XOM)

General Electric (GE)

General Motors (GM)

Hewlett-Packard (HPQ)

Home Depot (HD)

Honeywell International Inc. (HON)

Intel (INTC)

International Business Machines (IBM)

Johnson & Johnson (JNJ)

J.P. Morgan Chase (JPM)

McDonald's (MCD)

Merck (MRK)

Microsoft (MSFT)

Minnesota Mining and Manufacturing (3M) (MMM)

Pfizer (PFE)

Procter & Gamble (PG)

SBC Communications (SBC)

United Technologies (UTX)

Verizon (VZ)

Wal-Mart Stores (WMT)

The Dow has survived as a popular gauge of stock market activity for over a century. Although it's an important indicator of the market's progress, the Dow does have one major drawback: It tracks only 30 companies. Regardless of their status in the market, the companies in the Dow represent a limited sampling, so they don't communicate the true pulse of the market. For example, when the Dow surpassed the record 10,000 and 11,000 milestones during 1999 and 2000, the majority of (nonindex) companies showed lackluster or declining stock price movement. (See the "Dow Jones milestones" sidebar, later in this chapter, for more information.)

The roster of the Dow has changed many times during the 100-plus years of its existence. The only original company from 1896 is General Electric. Dow Jones made most of the changes because of company mergers and bankruptcy. However, they made some changes to simply reflect the changing times. In 2004, AT&T, International Paper, and Eastman Kodak were removed from the Dow and replaced with AIG Corp., Pfizer, and Verizon.

The Dow isn't a pure gauge of industrial activity because it also includes a hodgepodge of nonindustrial companies such as J.P. Morgan Chase and Citigroup (banks), Home Depot (retailing), and Microsoft (software). Because of these changes, it doesn't adequately reflect industrial activity. During the late 1990s and right up to 2005, true industrial sectors such as manufacturing had difficult times, yet the Dow rose to record levels.

Serious investors look at the following indexes:

- **Broad-based indexes:** Indexes such as the S&P 500 and the Wilshire 5000 are more realistic gauges of the stock market's performance than the Dow.

- **Industry or sector indexes:** These indexes are better gauges of the growth (or lack of growth) of specific industries and sectors. If you buy a gold stock, then you should track the index for the precious metals industry.

Dow Jones has several averages, including the Dow Jones Transportation Average (DJTA) and the Dow Jones Utilities Average (DJUA). Dow Jones manages both of these indexes more strictly than the Dow. The DJUA sticks to utilities, so it tends to be a more accurate barometer of the market it represents. (The same goes for the DJTA.)

Dow Jones milestones

This table shows when the Dow Jones Industrial Average reached each of eleven 1,000-point milestones and how long it took to reach that point:

Milestone	Date	How long it took
1,000	Nov. 14, 1972	76 years
2,000	Jan. 8, 1987	14 years
3,000	April 17, 1991	4 years
4,000	Feb. 23, 1995	4 years
5,000	Nov. 21, 1995	9 months
6,000	Oct. 14, 1996	11 months
7,000	Feb. 13, 1997	4 months
8,000	July 16, 1997	5 months
9,000	April 6, 1998	9 months
10,000	March 29, 1999	12 months
11,000	May 3, 1999	1 month

As you can see, the Dow took 76 years to hit its first milestone. But as each succeeding milestone came along, it took less and less time to hit the next one, due to the fact that the higher the Dow is in a relative sense, the easier it is to jump 1,000 points. For example, it went from 6,000 to 7,000 in only four months.

The Dow moved between 1,000 and 11,000 mostly during modern times. As the table indicates, most of the milestones happened during the 1982–1999 bull market. But the Dow didn't reach a new milestone from 2000–2004. That fact alone tells you that the Dow either stalled or declined when the bear market of 2000 arrived. Although the Dow had an up year in 2004, the long-term bear market is actually still in effect. The Dow hit its high of 11,722 in January 2000, and it traded around 10,500 in September 2005.

Nasdaq indexes

Nasdaq became a formalized market in 1971. The name used to stand for "National Association of Securities Dealers Automated Quote" system, but now it's simply "Nasdaq" (as if it's a name like Ralph or Eddie). Nasdaq indexes are similar to other indexes in style and structure. The only difference is that, well, they cover companies traded on the Nasdaq. The Nasdaq has two indexes (both reported in the financial pages):

- ✔ **Nasdaq Composite Index:** Most frequently quoted on the news, the Nasdaq Composite Index covers the more than 5,000 companies that trade on Nasdaq. The companies encompass a variety of industries, but the index's concentration has primarily been technology, telecom, and Internet industries. The Nasdaq Composite Index hit an all-time high of 5,048 in March 2000 before the worst bear market in its history occurred. The index dropped a whopping 60 percent by 2003 to approximately 2,000.

- ✔ **Nasdaq 100 Index:** The Nasdaq 100 tracks the 100 largest companies in Nasdaq. This index is for investors who want to concentrate on the largest companies, which tend to be especially weighted in technology issues, which means it provides extra representation of technology-related companies such as Microsoft, Adobe, and Symantec.

In either case, although these indexes track growth-oriented companies, the stocks of these companies are also very volatile and carry commensurate risk. The indexes themselves bear this risk out; in the bear market of 2000 and 2001 (and even extending into 2002), they fell more than 60 percent.

Standard & Poor's 500

The Standard & Poor's 500 (S&P 500) tracks the 500 largest (measured by market value) publicly traded companies. The publishing firm Standard & Poor's created this index. (I bet you could've guessed that.) Because it contains 500 companies, the S&P 500 represents overall market performance better than the DJIA's 30 companies. Money managers and financial advisors actually watch the S&P 500 stock index more closely than the DJIA. Most mutual funds especially like to measure their performance against the S&P 500 rather than against any other index. Mutual funds that concentrate on small-cap stocks usually prefer an index that has more small-cap stocks in it, such as the Russell 2000.

The S&P 500 doesn't attempt to cover the 500 "biggest" companies. Instead, it includes companies that are widely held and widely followed. The companies are also industry leaders in a variety of industries, including energy, technology, healthcare, and finance. It's a market-value weighted index (which I explain in the section "Knowing How Indexes Are Measured," earlier in this chapter).

Although it's a reliable indicator of the market's overall status, the S&P 500 also has some limitations. Despite the fact that it tracks 500 companies, the top 50 companies encompass 50 percent of the index's market value. This situation can be a drawback because those 50 companies have a greater influence on the S&P 500 index's price movement than any other segment of companies. In other words, 10 percent of the companies have an equal impact to 90 percent of the companies on the same index. Therefore, although the index better represents the market than the DIJA, the index may not offer an accurate representation of the general market.

S&P doesn't set the 500 companies they track in stone. S&P can add or remove companies when market conditions change. They can remove a company if it isn't doing well or goes bankrupt, and they can replace a company in the index with another company that is doing better.

Russell 3000 Index

The Russell 3000 Index is a great example of an index that seeks more comprehensive inclusion of U.S. companies. It includes the 3,000 largest publicly traded companies (nearly 98 percent of publicly traded stocks). The Russell 3000 is important because it includes many mid-cap and small-cap stocks. Most companies covered in the Russell 3000 have an average market value of a billion dollars or less.

The Frank Russell Company created the Russell 3000 Index and actually computes a series of indexes such as the Russell 1000 and the Russell 2000. The Russell 2000, for example, contains the smallest 2,000 companies from the Russell 3000, while the Russell 1000 contains the largest 1,000 companies. The Russell indexes don't cover *micro cap stocks* (companies with a market capitalization under $250 million).

Wilshire Total Market Index

The Wilshire 5000 Equity Index, often referred to as the Wilshire Total Market Index, is probably the largest stock index in the world. Wilshire Associates started out in 1980 tracking 5,000 stocks. Since then, the Wilshire 5000 has ballooned to cover more than 7,500 stocks. The advantage of the Wilshire

5000 is that it's very comprehensive, covering nearly the entire market. For investors and analysts that seek the greatest representation/ performance of the general market, they would check out this index. (At the very least, the Wilshire 5000 tracks the largest publicly traded stocks.) It includes all the stocks that are on the major stock exchanges (NYSE, AMEX, and the largest issues on Nasdaq), which by default also include all the stocks covered by the S&P 500. The Wilshire 5000 is a market-value weighted index, which I discuss in the section "Knowing How Indexes Are Measured," earlier in this chapter.

International indexes

Investors need to remember that the whole world is a vast marketplace that interacts with and exerts tremendous influence on individual national economies and markets. Whether you have one stock or one mutual fund, keep tabs on how world markets affect your portfolio. The best way to get a snapshot of international markets is, of course, with indexes. Here are some of the more widely followed international indexes:

- ✔ **Nikkei (Japan):** This index is considered Japan's version of the Dow. If you're invested in Japanese stocks or in stocks that do business with Japan, you want to know what's up with the Nikkei.

- ✔ **FTSE-100 (Great Britain):** Usually referred to as the "footsie," this market-value weighted index includes the top 100 public companies in the United Kingdom.

- ✔ **CAC-40 (France):** This index tracks the 40 public stocks that trade on the Paris Stock Exchange.

- ✔ **DAX (Germany):** This index tracks the 30 largest and most active stocks that trade on the Frankfurt Exchange.

- ✔ **Halter USX China Index (China):** This index tracks a basket of 50 U.S. public companies that derive most of their revenues from China.

You can track these international indexes (among others) at major financial Web sites, such as www.bloomberg.com and www.marketwatch.com. You may find international indexes useful in your analysis as you watch your stock's progress. What if you have stock in a company that has most of its customers in Japan? Then the Nikkei can help you get a general snapshot of how well the major companies are doing in Japan, which in turn can be a general barometer of its economy's well-being. If your company's business partners or customers are in the Nikkei, and it's plunging, then you know it's probably "sayonara" for the company's stock price.

Using the Indexes

You may be wondering what to do with all the indexes out there and which one or ones you should be checking out. The sections below give you some idea of how to put all the pieces together.

Tracking the indexes

The bottom line is that investors get an instant snapshot of how well the market is doing from indexes. Indexes offer a quick way to compare the performance of one investor's stock portfolio or mutual funds with the rest of the market. If the Dow goes up 10 percent in a year and your portfolio shows a cumulative gain of 12 percent, then you know that you're doing well. Appendix A in the back of this book lists resources to help you keep up with various indexes.

The problem with indexes is that they can be misleading if you take them too literally as an accurate barometer of stock success. The Dow, for example, has changed its roster of companies many times since 1896. Had it not, the Dow's general upward trajectory in the past few decades would have been much different. Laggard stocks have been dropped and replaced with other stocks that have shown more promise. Many of the original companies that were in the DJIA in 1896 did go out of business, or other companies, that aren't reflected in the index, bought them out.

Investing in indexes

Can you invest directly in indexes? If the market is doing well but your specific stock is not, can you find a way to invest in the index itself? With investments based on indexes, you can invest in the general market or a particular industry.

Say that you want to invest in the DJIA. After all, why try to "beat the market" if just matching it is sufficient to grow your wealth? Why not have a portfolio that directly mirrors the DJIA? Well, it's too impractical and expensive to invest in all 30 stocks that are in the DJIA. Fortunately, there are alternatives that can accomplish the act of "investing in indexes." Here are the best ways:

- ✔ **Index mutual funds:** An index mutual fund is much like a regular mutual fund except that it will only invest in securities (in this case, stocks) that match as closely as possible the basket of stocks that are in that particular index. There are index mutual funds, for example, that track the DJIA and the S&P 500. Find out more about index mutual funds at places such as the Investment Company Institute (www.ici.org).

✔ **Exchange Traded Funds (ETFs):** This is a particular favorite of mine. ETFs have similar characteristics to a mutual fund except for a few key differences. An ETF can reflect a basket of stocks that mirror a particular index, but the ETF can be traded like a stock itself. You can transact ETFs like stocks in that you can buy, sell, or go short. You can put stop losses on them and you can even purchase them on margin. ETFs can give you the diversification of mutual funds coupled with the versatility of stocks. Examples of ETFs that track indexes are the DJIA ETF (symbol DIA) and the ETF for Nasdaq (QQQ). You can find out more about ETFs at the American Stock Exchange (www.amex.com).

Part II
Before You Start Buying

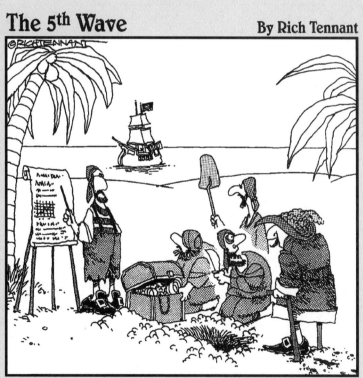

The 5th Wave · By Rich Tennant

"Growth Stock? Income Stock? I say we stick the money in the ground like always, and then feed this guy to the sharks."

In this part . . .

When you're about to begin investing in stocks, you should know that different types of stocks exist for different objectives. If you can at least get a stock that "fits" your situation, you're that much ahead in the game. In this part, you can find out where to start gathering information and discover what stockbrokers can do for you.

Chapter 6

Gathering Information

● ●

In This Chapter

▶ Using stock exchanges to get investment information

▶ Applying accounting and economic know-how to your investments

▶ Exploring financial issues

▶ Deciphering stock tables

▶ Interpreting dividend news

▶ Recognizing good (and bad) advice when you hear it

● ●

Knowledge and information are two critical success factors in stock investing. (Isn't that true about most things in life?) People who plunge headlong into stocks without sufficient knowledge of the stock market in general, and current information in particular, quickly learn the lesson of the eager diver who didn't find out ahead of time that the pool was only an inch deep (ouch!). In their haste to avoid missing so-called golden investment opportunities, investors too often end up losing money.

Opportunities to *make* money in the stock market will always be there, no matter how well or how poorly the economy and the market are performing in general. There's no such thing as a single (and fleeting) magical moment, so don't feel that if you let an opportunity pass you by, you'll always regret that you missed your one big chance.

For the best approach to stock investing, you want to build your knowledge and find quality information first. Then buy stocks and make your fortunes more assuredly. Basically, before you buy stock, you need to know that the company you're investing in is

✔ Financially sound and growing

✔ Offering products and services that are in demand by consumers

✔ In a strong and growing industry (and general economy)

Where do you start and what kind of information do you want to acquire? Keep reading.

Looking to Stock Exchanges for Answers

Before you invest in stocks, you need to be completely familiar with the basics of stock investing. At its most fundamental, stock investing is about using your money to buy a piece of a company that will give you value in the form of appreciation or income. Fortunately, many resources are available to help you find out about stock investing. Some of my favorite places are the stock exchanges themselves.

Stock exchanges are organized marketplaces for the buying and selling of stocks (and other securities). The New York Stock Exchange (NYSE), the premier stock exchange, provides a framework for stock buyers and sellers to make their transactions. The NYSE makes money not only from a piece of every transaction but also from fees (such as listing fees) charged to companies and brokers that are members of its exchanges.

The main exchanges for most stock investors are the NYSE and the American Stock Exchange (AMEX). Nasdaq is technically not an exchange but it is a formal market that effectively acts as an exchange. These three encourage and inform people about stock investing. Since these exchanges/markets benefit from increased popularity of stock investing and continued demand for stocks, they offer a wealth of free (or low-cost) information and resources for stock investors. Go to their Web sites and you find useful resources such as:

- ✔ Tutorials on how to invest in stocks, common investment strategies, and so on

- ✔ Glossaries and free information to help you understand the language, practice, and purpose of stock investing

- ✔ A wealth of news, press releases, financial data, and other information about companies listed at the exchange or market, accessed usually through an onsite search engine

- ✔ Industry analysis & news

- ✔ Stock quotes and other market information related to the daily market movements of stocks including data such as volume, new highs, new lows, and so on

- ✔ Free tracking of your stock selections (You can input a sample portfolio, or the stocks you are following, to see how well you are doing.)

What each exchange/market offers keeps changing or is updated, so go explore each at their Web sites:

- ✔ New York Stock Exchange: www.nyse.com

- ✔ American Stock Exchange: www.amex.com

- ✔ Nasdaq: www.nasdaq.com

Understanding Stocks and the Companies They Represent

Stocks represent ownership in companies. Before you buy individual stocks, you want to understand the companies whose stock you're considering and find out about their operations. It may sound like a daunting task, but you'll digest the point more easily when you realize that companies work very similarly to how you work. They make decisions on a day-to-day basis just as you do.

Think about how you grow and prosper as an individual or as a family, and you see the same issues with companies and how they grow and prosper. Low earnings and high debt are examples of financial difficulties that can affect both people and companies. You'll understand companies' finances when you take the time to pick up some information in two basic disciplines: accounting and economics. These two disciplines play a significant role in understanding the performance of a company's stock.

Accounting for taste and a whole lot more

Accounting. Ugh! But face it: Accounting is the language of business, and believe it or not, you're already familiar with the most important accounting concepts! Just look at the following three essential principles:

- **Assets minus liabilities equal net worth.** In other words, take what you own (your assets), subtract what you owe (your liabilities), and the rest is yours (net worth)! Your own personal finances work the same way as Microsoft's (except yours have fewer zeros at the end). See Chapter 2 to figure out how to calculate your own net worth.

    A company's balance sheet shows you its net worth at a specific point of time (such as December 31). The net worth of a company is the bottom line of a company's asset and liability picture, and it tells you whether the company is *solvent* (has the ability to pay its debts without going out of business). The net worth of a successful company is regularly growing. To see whether your company is successful, compare its net worth with the net worth from the same point a year earlier. A company that has a $4 million net worth on December 31, 2005, and a $5 million net worth on December 31, 2006, is doing well; its net worth has gone up 25 percent ($1 million) in one year.

- **Income less expenses equal net income.** In other words, take what you make (your income), subtract what you spend (your expenses), and the remainder is your *net income* (or net profit or net earnings — your gain).

    A company's profitability is the whole point of investing in its stock. As it profits, the company becomes more valuable, and in turn, its stock price becomes more valuable. To discover a company's net income, look at its income statement. Try to determine whether the company uses its gains wisely, either reinvesting it for continued growth or paying down debt.

✔ **Do a comparative financial analysis.** That's a mouthful, but it's just a fancy way of saying how a company is doing now, compared with something else (like a prior period or a similar company).

If you know that a company you're looking at had a net income of $50,000 for the year, you may ask, "Is that good or bad?" Obviously, making a net profit is good, but you also need to know whether it's good compared to something else. If the company had a net profit of $40,000 the year before, you know that the company's profitability is improving. But if a similar company had a net profit of $100,000 the year before and in the current year is making $50,000, then you may want to either avoid that company or see what went wrong (if anything) with it.

Accounting can be this simple. If you understand these three basic points, you're ahead of the curve (in stock investing as well as in your personal finances). For more information on how to use a company's financial statements to pick good stocks, see Chapter 11.

Understanding how economics affects stocks

Economics. Double ugh! No, you aren't required to understand "the inelasticity of demand aggregates" (thank heavens!) or "marginal utility" (say what?). But a working knowledge of basic economics is crucial (and I mean crucial) to your success and proficiency as a stock investor. The stock market and the economy are joined at the hip. The good (or bad) things that happen to one have a direct effect on the other.

Getting the hang of the basic concepts

Alas, many investors get lost on basic economic concepts (as do some so-called experts that you see on television). I owe my personal investing success to my status as a student of economics. Understanding basic economics helped me (and will help you) filter the financial news to separate relevant information from the irrelevant in order to make better investment decisions. Be aware of these important economic concepts:

✔ **Supply and demand:** How can anyone possibly think about economics without thinking of the ageless concept of supply and demand? *Supply and demand* can be simply stated as the relationship between what's available (the supply) and what people want and are willing to pay for (the demand). This equation is the main engine of economic activity and is extremely important for your stock investing analysis and decision-making process. I mean, do you really want to buy stock in a company that makes elephant-foot umbrella stands if you find out that the company has an oversupply and nobody wants to buy them anyway?

✔ **Cause and effect:** If you pick up a prominent news report and read, "Companies in the table industry are expecting plummeting sales," do you rush out and invest in companies that sell chairs or manufacture tablecloths? Considering cause and effect is an exercise in logical thinking, and believe you me, logic is a major component of sound economic thought.

When you read business news, play it out in your mind. What good (or bad) can logically be expected given a certain event or situation? If you're looking for an effect ("I want a stock price that keeps increasing"), you also want to understand the cause. Here are some typical events that can cause a stock's price to rise:

- **Positive news reports about a company:** The news may report that a company is enjoying success with increased sales or a new product.

- **Positive news reports about a company's industry:** The media may be highlighting that the industry is poised to do well.

- **Positive news reports about a company's customers:** Maybe your company is in industry A, but its customers are in industry B. If you see good news about industry B, that may be good news for your stock.

- **Negative news reports about a company's competitors:** If they are in trouble, their customers may seek alternatives to buy from, including your company.

✔ **Economic effects from government actions:** Political and governmental actions have economic consequences. As a matter of fact, nothing (and I mean nothing!) has a greater effect on investing and economics than government. Government actions usually manifest themselves as taxes, laws, or regulations. They also can take on a more ominous appearance, such as war or the threat of war. Government can willfully (or even accidentally) cause a company to go bankrupt, disrupt an entire industry, or even cause a depression. It controls the money supply, credit, and all public securities markets.

What happens to the elephant-foot, umbrella stand industry if the government passes a 50 percent sales tax for that industry? Such a sales tax certainly makes a product uneconomical and encourages consumers to seek alternatives to elephant-foot umbrella stands. It may even boost sales for the wastepaper basket industry.

The opposite can be true as well. What if the government passes a tax credit that encourages the use of solar power in homes and businesses? That obviously has a positive impact on industries that manufacture or sell solar power devices. Just don't ask me what happens to solar-powered elephant-foot umbrella stands.

Gaining insight from past mistakes

Because most investors ignored some basic observations about economics in the late 1990s, they subsequently lost trillions in their stock portfolios. In the late 1990s, the United States experienced the greatest expansion of debt in history, coupled with a record expansion of the money supply. The Federal Reserve (or "the Fed"), the U.S. government's central bank, controls both. This growth of debt and money supply resulted in more consumer (and corporate) borrowing, spending, and investing. This activity hyperstimulated the stock market and caused stocks to rise 25 percent per year for five straight years.

Of course, you should always be happy to earn 25 percent per year with your investments, but such a return can't be sustained and encourages speculation. This artificial stimulation by the Fed resulted in the following:

- More and more people depleted their savings. After all, why settle for 3 percent in the bank when you can get 25 percent in the stock market?

- More and more people bought on credit. If the economy is booming, why not buy now and pay later? Consumer credit hit record highs.

- More and more people borrowed against their homes. Why not borrow and get rich now? I can pay off my debt later.

- More and more companies sold more goods as consumers took more vacations and bought SUVs, electronics, and so on. Companies then borrowed to finance expansion, open new stores, and so on.

- More and more companies went public and offered stock to take advantage of more money that was flowing to the markets from banks and other financial institutions.

In the end, spending started to slow down because consumers and businesses became too indebted. This slowdown in turn caused the sales of goods and services to taper off. However, companies had too much overhead, capacity, and debt because they expanded too eagerly. At this point, companies were caught in a financial bind. Too much debt and too many expenses in a slowing economy mean one thing: Profits shrink or disappear. Companies, to stay in business, had to do the logical thing — cut expenses. What is usually the biggest expense for companies? People! To stay in business, many companies started laying off employees. As a result, consumer spending dropped further because more people were either laid off or had second thoughts about their own job security.

As people had little in the way of savings and too much in the way of debt, they had to sell their stock to pay their bills. This trend was a major reason that stocks started to fall in 2000. Earnings started to drop because of shrinking sales from a sputtering economy. As earnings fell, stock prices also fell.

The lessons from the 1990s are important ones for investors today:

Know thyself

If you're reading this book, you're probably doing so because you want to become a successful investor. Granted, to be a successful investor, you have to select great stocks, but having a realistic understanding of your own financial situation and goals is equally important. I recall one investor who lost $10,000 in a speculative stock. The loss wasn't that bad because he had most of his money safely tucked away elsewhere. He also understood that his overall financial situation was secure and that the money he lost was "play" money whose loss wouldn't have a drastic effect on his life. But many investors often lose even more money, and the loss does have a major, negative effect on their lives. You may not be like the investor who could afford to lose $10,000. Take time to understand yourself, your own financial picture, and your personal investment goals before you decide to buy stocks.

- ✔ Stocks are not a replacement for savings accounts. Always have some money in the bank.

- ✔ Stocks should never occupy 100 percent of your investment funds.

- ✔ When anyone (including an expert) tells you that the economy will keep growing indefinitely, be skeptical and read diverse sources of information.

- ✔ If stocks do well in your portfolio, consider protecting your stocks (both your original investment and any gains) with stop-loss orders. (See Chapter 18 for more on these strategies.)

- ✔ Keep debt and expenses to a minimum.

- ✔ Remember that if the economy is booming, a decline is sure to follow as the ebb and flow of the economy's business cycle continues.

Staying on Top of Financial News

Reading the financial news can help you decide where or where not to invest. Many newspapers, magazines, and Web sites offer great coverage of the financial world. Obviously, the more informed you are, the better, but you don't have to read everything that's written. The information explosion in recent years has gone beyond overload, and you can easily spend so much time reading that you have little time left for investing.

The most obvious publications of interest to stock investors are *The Wall Street Journal* and *Investor's Business Daily.* These excellent publications report the news and stock data as of the prior trading day. Some of the more obvious Web sites are MarketWatch (www.marketwatch.com) and Bloomberg (www.bloomberg.com). These Web sites can actually give you news and stock data within 15 to 20 minutes after an event occurs. (Don't forget the exchanges' Web sites!)

Appendix A of this book provides more information on these resources along with a treasure trove of some of the best publications, resources, and Web sites to assist you.

Figuring out what a company's up to

Before you invest, you need to know what's going on with a company. When you read about a company, either from the company's literature (its annual report, for example) or from media sources, be sure to get answers to some pertinent questions:

- ✔ **Is the company making more net income than it did last year?** You want to invest in a company that is growing.

- ✔ **Are the company's sales greater than they were the year before?** Remember, you won't make money if the company isn't making money.

- ✔ **Is the company issuing press releases on new products, services, inventions, or business deals?** All these achievements indicate a strong, vital company.

Knowing how the company is doing, no matter what's happening with the general economy, is obviously important. To better understand how companies tick, see Chapter 12.

Discovering what's new with an industry

As you consider investing in a stock, make it a point to know what's going on in that company's industry. If the industry is doing well, your stock is likely to do well, too. But then again, the reverse is also true.

Yes, I have seen investors pick successful stocks in a failing industry, but those cases are exceptional. By and large, it's easier to succeed with a stock when the entire industry is doing well. As you're watching the news, reading the financial pages, or viewing financial Web sites, check out the industry to see that it's strong and dynamic. See Chapter 13 for information on analyzing industries.

Knowing what's happening with the economy

No matter how well or how poorly the overall economy is performing, you want to stay informed about its general progress. It's easier for the value of stock to keep going up when the economy is stable or growing. The reverse is also true; if the economy is contracting or declining, the stock has a tougher time keeping its value. Some basic items to keep tabs on include the following:

- ✔ **Gross domestic product (GDP):** This is roughly the total value of output for a particular nation, measured in the dollar amount of goods and services. GDP is reported quarterly, and a rising GDP bodes well for your stock. When the GDP is rising 3 percent or more on an annual basis, that's solid growth. If it rises at more than zero but less than 3 percent, that's generally considered less than stellar (or mediocre). GDP under zero (or negative) means that the economy is shrinking (heading into recession).

- ✔ **The index of leading economic indicators (LEI):** The LEI is a snapshot of a set of economic statistics covering activity that precedes what's happening in the economy. Each statistic helps you understand the economy in much the same way that barometers (and windows!) help you understand what's happening with the weather. Economists don't just look at an individual statistic; they look at a set of statistics to get a more complete picture of what's happening with the economy. Chapter 14 goes into greater detail on ways the economy affects stock prices.

Seeing what the politicians and government bureaucrats are doing

Being informed about what public officials are doing is vital to your success as a stock investor. Because federal, state, and local governments pass literally thousands of laws every year, monitoring the political landscape is critical to your success. The news media report what the president and Congress are doing, so always ask yourself, "How does a new law, tax, or regulation affect my stock investment?"

Because government actions have a significant effect on your investments, it's a good idea to see what's going on. Laws being proposed or enacted by the Federal government can be found through the Thomas legislative search engine, which is run by the Library of Congress (www.loc.gov). Also, some great organizations inform the public about tax laws and their impact, such as the National Taxpayers Union (www.ntu.org).

Checking for trends in society, culture, and entertainment

As odd as it sounds, trends in society, popular culture, and entertainment affect your investments, directly or indirectly. For example, headlines such as "The graying of America — more people than ever before will be senior citizens" give you some important information that can make or break your stock portfolio. With that particular headline, you know that as more and more people age, companies that are well positioned to cater to this growing market's wants and needs will do well — meaning a successful stock for you.

Keep your eyes open to emerging trends in society at large. What trends are evident now? Can you anticipate the wants and needs of tomorrow's society? Being alert, staying a step ahead of the public, and choosing stock appropriately gives you a profitable edge over other investors. If you own stock in a solid company with growing sales and earnings, other investors eventually notice. As more investors buy up your company's stocks, you're rewarded as the stock price increases.

Reading (And Understanding) Stock Tables

The stock tables in major business publications, such as *The Wall Street Journal* and *Investor's Business Daily,* are loaded with information that can help you become a savvy investor — *if* you know how to interpret them. You need the information in the stock tables for more than selecting promising investment opportunities. You also need to consult the tables after you invest to monitor how your stocks are doing. If you bought HokySmoky common stock last year at $12 per share and you want to know what it's worth today, check out the stock tables.

If you look at the stock tables without knowing what or why you're looking, it's the equivalent of reading *War and Peace* backwards through a kaleidoscope. Nothing makes sense. But I can help you make sense of it all (well, at least the stock tables!). Table 6-1 shows a sample stock table for you to refer to as you read the sections that follow.

Table 6-1		Deciphering Stock Tables						
52-Wk High	52-Wk Low	Name (Symbol)	Div	Vol	Yld	P/E	Day Last	Net Chg
21.50	8.00	SkyHighCorp (SHC)	3,143		76	21.25	+.25	
47.00	31.75	LowDownInc (LDI)	2.35	2,735	5.9	18	41.00	−.50
25.00	21.00	ValueNowInc (VNI)	1.00	1,894	4.5	12	22.00	+.10
83.00	33.00	DoinBadlyCorp (DBC)		7,601			33.50	−.75

Every newspaper's financial tables are a little different, but they give you basically the same information. Updated daily, this section is not the place to start your search for a good stock; this section is usually where your search ends. The stock tables are the place to look when you already know what you want to buy and you're just checking to see the most recent price, or to look when you already own it and you want to check the latest stock price.

Each item gives you some clues about the current state of affairs for that particular company. The sections that follow describe each column to help you understand what you're looking at.

52-week high

The column labeled "52-Wk High" (refer to Table 6-1) gives you the highest price that particular stock has reached in the most recent 52-week period. Knowing this price lets you gauge where the stock is now versus where it has been recently. SkyHighCorp's (SHC) stock has been as high as $21.50, while its last (most recent) price is $21.25, the number listed in the "Day Last" column. (Flip to the "Day Last" section for more on understanding this information.) SkyHighCorp's stock is trading very high right now because it's hovering right near its overall 52-week high figure.

Now, take a look at DoinBadlyCorp's (DBC) stock price. It seems to have tumbled big time. Its stock price has had a high in the past 52 weeks of $83, but it's currently trading at $33.50. Something just doesn't seem right here. During the past 52 weeks, DBC's stock price fell dramatically. If you're thinking about investing in DBC, find out why the stock price fell. If the company is a strong company, it may be a good opportunity to buy stock at a lower price. If the company is having tough times, avoid it. In any case, research the company and find out why its stock has declined.

52-week low

The column labeled "52-Wk Low" gives you the lowest price that particular stock reached in the most recent 52-week period. Again, this information is crucial to your ability to analyze stock over a period of time. Look at DBC in Table 6-1, and you can see that its current trading price of $33.50 is close to its 52-week low.

Keep in mind that the high and the low prices just give you a range of how far that particular stock's price has moved within the past 52 weeks. They could alert you that a stock has problems, or they could tell you that a stock's price has fallen enough to make it a bargain. Simply reading the 52-Wk High and 52-Wk Low columns isn't enough to determine which of those two scenarios is happening. They basically tell you to get more information before you commit your money.

Name and symbol

The "Name (Symbol)" column is the simplest in Table 6-1. It tells you the company name (usually abbreviated) and the stock symbol assigned to the company. When you have your eye on a stock for potential purchase, get familiar with its symbol. Knowing the symbol makes it easier for you to find your stock in the financial tables, which list stocks in alphabetical order by the company's name. Stock symbols are the language of stock investing, and you need to use them in all stock communications, from getting a stock quote at your broker's office to buying stock over the Internet.

Dividend

Dividends (shown under the "Div" column in Table 6-1) are basically payments to owners (stockholders). If a company pays a dividend, it's shown in the dividend column. The amount you see is the annual dividend quoted for one share of that stock. If you look at LowDownInc (LDI) in Table 6-1, you can see that you get $2.35 as an annual dividend for each share of stock that you own. Companies usually pay the dividend in quarterly amounts. If I own 100 shares of LDI, the company pays me a quarterly dividend of $58.75 ($235 total per year). A healthy company strives to maintain or upgrade the dividend for stockholders from year to year. In any case, the dividend is very important to investors seeking income from their stock investment. For more about investing for income, see Chapter 9. Investors buy stock in companies that don't pay dividends primarily for growth. For more information on growth stocks, see Chapter 8.

Volume

Normally, when you hear the word *volume* on the news, it refers to how much stock is bought and sold for the entire market. ("Well, stocks were very active today. Trading volume at the New York Stock Exchange hit 2 billion shares.") Volume is certainly important to watch because the stocks that you're investing in are somewhere in that activity. For the "Vol" column in Table 6-1, though, the volume refers to the individual stock.

Volume tells you how many shares of that particular stock were traded that day. If only 100 shares are traded in a day, then the trading volume is 100. SHC had 3,143 shares change hands on the trading day represented in Table 6-1. Is that good or bad? Neither, really. Usually the business news media only mention volume for a particular stock when it's unusually large. If a stock normally has volume in the 5,000 to 10,000 range and all of a sudden has a trading volume of 87,000, then it's time to sit up and take notice.

Keep in mind that a low trading volume for one stock may be high trading volume for another stock. You can't necessarily compare one stock's volume against that of any other company. The large-cap stocks like IBM or Microsoft typically have trading volumes in the millions of shares almost every day, while less active, smaller stocks may have average trading volumes in far, far smaller numbers.

The main point to remember is that trading volume that is far in excess of that stock's normal range is a sign that something is going on with that stock. It may be negative or positive, but something newsworthy is happening with that company. If the news is positive, the increased volume is a result of more people buying the stock. If the news is negative, the increased volume is probably a result of more people selling the stock. What are typical events that cause increased trading volume? Some positive reasons include the following:

- ✔ **Good earnings reports:** A company announces good (or better-than-expected) earnings.
- ✔ **A new business deal:** A company announces a favorable business deal, such as a joint venture, or lands a big client.
- ✔ **A new product or service:** A company's research and development department creates a potentially profitable new product.
- ✔ **Indirect benefits:** A company may benefit from a new development in the economy or from a new law passed by Congress.

Some negative reasons for an unusually large fluctuation in trading volume for a particular stock include the following:

- ✔ **Bad earnings reports:** Profit is the lifeblood of a company. When a company's profits fall or disappear, you see more volume.
- ✔ **Governmental problems:** The stock is being targeted by government action (such as a lawsuit or Securities and Exchange Commission probe).
- ✔ **Liability issues:** The media report that a company has a defective product or similar problem.
- ✔ **Financial problems:** Independent analysts report that a company's financial health is deteriorating.

Check out what's happening when you hear about heavier than usual volume (especially if you already own the stock).

Yield

In general, yield is a return on the money you invest. However, in the stock tables, *yield* ("Yld" in Table 6-1) is a reference to what percentage that particular dividend is to the stock price. Yield is most important to income investors.

It's calculated by dividing the annual dividend by the current stock price. In Table 6-1, you can see that the yield du jour of ValueNowInc (VNI) is 4.5 percent (a dividend of $1 divided by the company's stock price of $22). Notice that many companies have no yield reported; because they have no dividends, yield is zero.

Keep in mind that the yield reported in the financial pages changes daily as the stock price changes. Yield is always reported as if you're buying the stock that day. If you buy VNI on the day represented in Table 6-1, your yield is 4.5 percent. But what if VNI's stock price rises to $30 the following day? Investors who buy stock at $30 per share obtain a yield of just 3.3 percent. (The dividend of $1 is then divided by the new stock price, $30.) Of course, because you bought the stock at $22, you essentially locked in the prior yield of 4.5 percent. Lucky you. Pat yourself on the back.

P/E

The P/E ratio is the ratio between the price of the stock and the company's earnings. P/E ratios are widely followed and are important barometers of value in the world of stock investing. The P/E ratio (also called the "earnings multiple" or just "multiple") is frequently used to determine whether a stock is expensive (a good value). Value investors (such as yours truly) find P/E ratios to be essential to analyzing a stock as a potential investment. As a general rule, the P/E should be 10 to 20 for large-cap or income stocks. For growth stocks, a P/E no greater than 30 to 40 is preferable.

In the P/E ratios reported in stock tables, *price* refers to the cost of a single share of stock. *Earnings* refers to the company's reported earnings per share as of the most recent four quarters. The P/E ratio is the price divided by the earnings. In Table 6-1, VNI has a reported P/E of 12, which is considered a low P/E. Notice how SHC has a relatively high P/E (76). This stock is considered too pricey because you're paying a price equivalent to 76 times earnings. Also notice that DBC has no available P/E ratio. Usually this lack of a P/E ratio indicates that the company reported a loss in the most recent four quarters.

Day last

The "Day Last" column tells you how trading ended for a particular stock on the day represented by the table. In Table 6-1 , LDC ended the most recent day of trading at $41. Some newspapers report the high and low for that day in addition to the stock's ending price for the day.

Net change

The information in the "Net Chg" column answers the question "How did the stock price end today compared with its trading price at the end of the prior trading day?" Table 6-1 shows that SHC stock ended the trading day up 25 cents (at $21.25). This column tells you that SHC ended the prior day at $21. On a day when VNI ends the day at $22 (up 10 cents), you can tell that the prior day it ended the trading day at $21.90.

Using News about Dividends

Reading and understanding the news about dividends is essential if you're an *income investor* (someone who invests in stocks as a means of generating regular income). See Chapter 9 on investing for income.

Looking at important dates

In order to understand how buying stocks that pay dividends can benefit you as an investor, you need to know how companies report and pay dividends. Some important dates in the life of a dividend are as follows:

- **Date of declaration:** This is the date when a company reports a quarterly dividend and the subsequent payment dates. On January 15, for example, a company may report that it "is pleased to announce a quarterly dividend of 50 cents per share to shareholders of record as of February 10." That was easy. The date of declaration is really just the announcement date. If you buy the stock before, on, or after the date of declaration, it won't matter in regard to receiving the stock's quarterly dividend. The date that matters is the date of record (see that bullet later in this list).

- **Date of execution:** This is the day you actually initiate the stock transaction (buying or selling). If you call up a broker (or contact her online) today to buy a particular stock, then today is the date of execution, or the date on which you execute the trade. You don't own the stock on the date of execution; it's just the day you put in the order. For an example, skip to the section "Understanding why these dates matter," later in this chapter.

- **Closing date (settlement date):** The closing or settlement date is the date on which the trade is finalized, which usually happens three business days after the date of execution. The closing date for stock is similar in concept to a real estate closing. On the closing date, you're officially the proud new owner (or happy seller) of the stock.

✔ **Date of record:** The date of record is used to identify which stockholders qualify to receive the declared dividend. Because stock is bought and sold every day, how does the company know which investors to pay? The company establishes a cut-off date by declaring a date of record. All investors who are official stockholders as of the declared date of record receive the dividend on the payment date even if they plan to sell the stock any time between the date of declaration and the date of record.

✔ **Ex-dividend date:** *Ex-dividend* means *without dividend.* Because it takes three days to process a stock purchase before you become an official owner of the stock, you have to qualify (that is, you have to own or buy the stock) *before* the three-day period. That three-day period is referred to as the "ex-dividend period." When you buy stock during this short time frame, you aren't on the books of record, because the closing (or settlement) date falls after the date of record. See the section, "Understanding why these dates matter" to see the effect that the ex-dividend date can have on an investor.

✔ **Payment date:** The date on which a company issues and mails its dividend checks to shareholders. Finally!

For typical dividends, the events in Table 6-2 happen four times per year.

Table 6-2	The Life of the Quarterly Dividend	
Event	*Sample Date*	*Comments*
Date of declaration	January 15	The date that the company declares the quarterly dividend
Ex-dividend date	February 7	Starts the three-day period during which, if you buy the stock, you don't qualify for the dividend
Record date	February 10	The date by which you must be on the books of record to qualify for the dividend
Payment date	February 27	The date that payment is made (a dividend check is issued and mailed to stockholders who were on the books of record as of February 10)

Understanding why these dates matter

Remember that three business days pass between the date of execution and the closing date. Three business days are also between the ex-dividend date and the date of record. This information is important to know if you want to qualify to receive an upcoming dividend. Timing is important, and if you understand these dates, you know when to purchase stock and whether you qualify for a dividend.

As an example, say that you want to buy ValueNowInc (VNI) in time to qualify for the quarterly dividend of 25 cents per share. Assume that the date of record (the date by which you have to be an official owner of the stock) is February 10. You have to execute the trade (buy the stock) no later than February 7 to be assured of the dividend. If you execute the trade right on February 7, the closing date occurs three days later, on February 10 — just in time for the date of record.

But what if you execute the trade on February 8, a day later? Well, the trade's closing date is February 11, which occurs *after* the date of record. Because you aren't on the books as an official stockholder on the date of record, you aren't getting that quarterly dividend. In this example, the February 7–10 period is called the *ex-dividend period.*

Fortunately, for those people who buy the stock during this brief ex-dividend period, the stock actually trades at a slighter lower price to reflect the amount of the dividend. If you can't get the dividend, you may as well save on the stock purchase. How's that for a silver lining?

Evaluating (Avoiding?) Investment Tips

Psssst. Have I got a stock tip for you! Come closer. You know what it is? Research! What I'm trying to tell you is to never automatically invest just because you get a hot tip from someone. Good investment selection means looking at several sources before you decide on a stock. No shortcut exists. That said, getting opinions from others never hurts — just be sure to carefully analyze the information you get. In the following list, I present some important points to bear in mind as you evaluate tips and advice from others:

   ✔ **Consider the source.** Frequently, people buy stock based on the views of some market strategist or market analyst. People may see an analyst being interviewed on a television financial show and take that person's opinions and advice as valid and good. The danger here is that the analyst may be biased because of some relationship that isn't disclosed on the show.

It happens on TV all too often. The show's host interviews Analyst U.R. Kiddingme from the investment firm Foollum & Sellum. The analyst says, "Implosion Corp. is a good buy with solid, long-term, upside potential." You later find out that the analyst's employer gets investment banking fees from Implosion Corp. Do you really think that analyst would ever issue a negative report on a company that's helping to pay the bills? It's not likely.

✔ **Get multiple views.** Don't base your investment decisions on just one source unless you have the best reasons in the world for thinking that a particular, single source is outstanding and reliable. A better approach is to scour current issues of independent financial publications, such as *Barron's, Money Magazine, SmartMoney,* and other publications (and Web sites) listed in Appendix A.

✔ **Gather data from the SEC.** When you want to get more objective information about a company, why not take a look at the reports that companies must file with the Securities and Exchange Commission (SEC)? These reports are the same reports that the pundits and financial reporters read. Arguably, the most valuable report you can look at is the 10K. The 10K is a report that all publicly traded companies must file with the SEC. It provides valuable information on the company's operations and financial data, and it's likely to be less biased than the information a company includes in other corporate reports, such as an annual report.

To access 10K reports, go to the SEC's Web site (www.sec.gov). From there, you can find the SEC's extensive database of public filings called EDGAR (Electronic Data Gathering, Analysis, and Retrieval system). By searching EDGAR, you can find companies' balance sheets, income statements, and other related information so that you can verify what others say and get a fuller picture of what a company is doing and what its financial condition is.

Chapter 7

Going for Brokers

*W*hen you're ready to dive in and start investing in stocks, you first have to choose a broker. It's kind of like buying a car: You can do all the research in the world and know exactly what kind of car you want to buy; still, you need a venue to do the actual transaction. Similarly, when you want to buy stock, your task is to do all the research you can to select the company you want to invest in. Still, you need a broker to actually buy the stock, whether you buy over the phone or online. In this chapter, I set out to introduce you to the intricacies of the investor/broker relationship.

For information on various types of orders you can place with a broker, such as market orders, stop-loss orders, and so on, flip to Chapter 17.

Defining the Broker's Role

The broker's primary role is to serve as the vehicle through which you either buy or sell stock. When I talk about brokers, I'm referring to organizations such as Charles Schwab, Merrill Lynch, E*TRADE, and many other organizations that can buy stock on your behalf. Brokers can also be individuals who work for such firms. Although you can buy some stocks directly from the company that issues them (I discuss direct purchase plans in Chapter 18), to purchase most stocks, you still need a broker.

Although the primary task of brokers is the buying and selling of securities (keep in mind that the word *securities* refers to the world of financial or paper investments, and that stocks are only a small part of that world), such as stocks, they can perform other tasks for you, including the following:

- **Providing advisory services:** Investors pay brokers a fee for investment advice. Customers also get access to the firm's research.

- **Offering limited banking services:** Brokers can offer features such as interest-bearing accounts, check writing, direct deposit, and credit cards.

- **Brokering other securities:** Brokers can also buy bonds, mutual funds, options, Exchange Traded Funds (ETFs), and other investments on your behalf.

Personal stockbrokers make their money from individual investors like you and me through various fees, including the following:

- **Brokerage commissions:** This fee is for buying and/or selling stocks and other securities.

- **Margin interest charges:** This interest is charged to investors for borrowing against their brokerage account for investment purposes.

- **Service charges:** These charges are for performing administrative tasks and other functions. Brokers charge fees to investors for Individual Retirement Accounts (IRAs) and for mailing stocks in certificate form.

Any broker you deal with should be registered with the National Association of Securities Dealers (NASD) and the Securities and Exchange Commission (SEC). In addition, to protect your money after you've deposited it into a brokerage account, that broker should be a member of the Securities Investor Protection Corporation (SIPC). SIPC doesn't protect you from market losses; it protects your money in case the brokerage firm goes out of business. To find out whether the broker is registered with these organizations, contact the NASD, SEC, and SIPC. (See Appendix A for information on these three organizations.)

The distinction between personal stockbrokers and institutional stockbrokers is important. Institutional brokers make money from institutions and companies through investment banking and securities placement fees (such as initial public offerings and secondary offerings), advisory services, and other broker services. Personal stockbrokers generally offer the same services to individuals and small businesses.

Distinguishing between Full-Service and Discount Brokers

Stockbrokers fall into two basic categories: full-service and discount. The type you choose really depends on what type of investor you are. In a nutshell, full-service brokers are suitable for investors who need some guidance, while discount brokers are better for those investors who are sufficiently confident and knowledgeable about stock investing to manage with minimal help.

Full-service brokers

Full-service brokers are just what the name indicates. They try to provide as many services as possible for investors who open accounts with them. When you open an account at a brokerage firm, a representative is assigned to your account. This representative is usually called an *account executive,* a *registered rep,* or a *financial consultant* by the brokerage firm. This person usually has a securities license and is knowledgeable about stocks in particular and investing in general.

What they can do for you

Your account executive is responsible for assisting you, answering questions about your account and the securities in your portfolio, and transacting your buy and sell orders. Here are some things that full-service brokers can do for you:

- **Offer guidance and advice.** The greatest distinction between full-service brokers and discount brokers is the personal attention you receive from your account rep. You get to be on a first-name basis with a full-service broker, and you disclose much information about your finances and financial goals. The rep is there to make recommendations about stocks and funds that are hopefully suitable for you.

- **Provide access to research.** Full-service brokers can give you access to their investment research department, which can give you in-depth information and analysis on a particular company. This information can be very valuable, but be aware of the pitfalls. (See the section "Judging Brokers' Recommendations," later in this chapter.)

- **Help you achieve your investment objectives.** Beyond advice on specific investments, a good rep gets to know you and your investment goals and *then* offers advice and answers your questions about how specific investments and strategies can help you accomplish your wealth-building goals.

✔ **Make investment decisions on your behalf.** Many investors don't want to be bothered when it comes to investment decisions. Full-service brokers can actually make decisions for your account with your authorization. This service is fine, but be sure to require them to explain their choices to you.

What to watch out for

Although the full-service brokers, with their seemingly limitless assistance, can make life easy for an investor, you need to remember some important points to avoid problems:

✔ Brokers and account reps are still salespeople. No matter how well they treat you, they're still compensated based on their ability to produce revenue for the brokerage firm. They generate commissions and fees from you on behalf of the company. (In other words, they're paid to sell you things.)

✔ Whenever your rep makes a suggestion or recommendation, be sure to ask why and request a complete answer that includes the reasoning behind the recommendation. A good advisor is able to clearly explain the reasoning behind every suggestion. If you don't fully understand and agree with the advice, don't take it.

✔ Working with a full-service broker costs more than working with a discount broker. Discount brokers are paid simply for performing the act of buying or selling stocks for you. Full-service brokers do that and more. Additionally, they provide advice and guidance. Because of that, full-service brokers are more expensive (through higher brokerage commissions and advisory fees). Also, most full-service brokers expect you to invest at least $5,000 to $10,000 just to open an account.

✔ Handing over decision-making authority to your rep can be a possible negative because letting others make financial decisions for you is always dicey — especially when they're using *your* money. If they make poor investment choices that lose you money, you may not have any recourse because you authorized them to act on your behalf.

✔ Some brokers engage in an activity called churning. *Churning* is basically buying and selling stocks for the sole purpose of generating commissions. Churning is great for brokers but bad for customers. If your account shows a lot of activity, ask for justification. Commissions, especially by full-service brokers, can take a big bite out of your wealth, so don't tolerate churning or other suspicious activity.

Before you deal with any broker, full-service or otherwise, get a free report on the broker from the National Association of Securities Dealers by calling 800-289-9999 or visiting the NASD Regulation Web site at www.nasdr.com. The report can indicate whether any complaints or penalties have been filed against that brokerage firm or the individual rep.

Examples of full-service brokers are Merrill Lynch and Morgan Stanley. Of course, all brokers now have full-featured Web sites to give you further information about their services. Get as informed as possible before you open your account. A full-service broker is there to help you build wealth, not make you . . . uh . . . broker.

Discount brokers

Perhaps you don't need any hand-holding from a broker. You know what you want, and you can make your own investment decisions. All you want is someone to transact your buy/sell orders. In that case, go with a discount broker. They don't offer advice or premium services — just the basics required to perform your stock transactions.

Discount brokers, as the name implies, are cheaper to engage than full-service brokers. Because you're advising yourself (or getting advice from third parties such as newsletters or independent advisors), you can save on costs that you incur when you pay for a full-service broker.

If you choose to work with a discount broker, you must know as much as possible about your personal goals and needs. You have a greater responsibility for conducting adequate research to make good stock selections, and you must be prepared to accept the outcome, whatever that may be.

For a while, the regular investor had two types of discount brokers to choose from: conventional discount brokers and Internet discount brokers. But the two are so similar now that the differences are hardly worth mentioning. Conventional discount brokers primarily conducted business through regular offices and over the phone, while Internet discount brokers conducted business primarily through Web sites. But through industry consolidation, most of the conventional discount brokers today have fully featured Web sites, while Internet discount brokers adapted by adding more telephone and face-to-face services.

Charles Schwab and TD Waterhouse are examples of conventional discount brokers that have adapted well to the Internet era. Internet brokers such as E*TRADE.com, Ameritrade.com, Scottrade.com, and Thinkorswim.com have added more conventional services.

What they can do for you

Discount brokers offer some significant advantages over full-service brokers, such as:

- ✔ **Lower cost:** This lower cost is usually the result of lower commissions, and it's the primary benefit of using discount brokers.

- ✔ **Unbiased service:** Discount brokers offer you the ability to just transact your stock buy and sell orders only. Since they don't offer advice, they have no vested interest in trying to sell you any particular stock.

- ✔ **Access to information:** Established discount brokers offer extensive educational materials at their offices or on their Web sites.

What to watch out for

Of course, doing business with discount brokers also has its downside, including the following:

- ✔ **No guidance:** Because you've chosen a discount broker, you *know* not to expect guidance, but the broker should make this fact clear to you anyway. If you're a knowledgeable investor, the lack of advice is considered a positive thing — no interference.

- ✔ **Hidden fees:** Discount brokers may shout about their lower commissions, but commissions aren't their only way of making money. Many discount brokers charge extra for services that you may think are included, such as issuing a stock certificate or mailing a statement. Ask whether they assess fees for maintaining IRAs or fees for transferring stocks and other securities (such as bonds) in or out of your account, and find out what interest rates they charge for borrowing through brokerage accounts.

- ✔ **Minimal customer service:** If you deal with an Internet brokerage firm, find out about its customer service capability. If you can't transact business at its Web site, find out where you can call for assistance with your order.

Choosing a Broker

Before you choose a broker, you need to analyze your personal investing style. After you know yourself and the way you invest, then you can proceed to finding the kind of broker that fits your needs. It's almost like choosing shoes; if you don't know your size, you can't get a proper fit. (And you can be in for a really uncomfortable future.)

When it's time to choose a broker, keep the following points in mind:

✔ Match your investment style with a brokerage firm that charges the least amount of money for the services you're likely to use most frequently.

✔ Compare all the costs of buying, selling, and holding stocks and other securities through a broker. Don't compare only commissions. Compare other costs, too, such as margin interest and other service charges.

✔ Use broker comparison services such as Gomez Advisors at www.gomez.com and read articles that compare brokers in publications such as *SmartMoney* and *Barron's*. Check out Appendix A for a list of sources that compare brokers.

Finding brokers is easy. They're listed in the Yellow Pages as well as in many investment publications and on many financial Web sites. Start your search by using the sources in Appendix A, which includes a list of the major brokerage firms.

Discovering Various Types of Brokerage Accounts

When you decide to start investing in the stock market, you have to somehow actually *pay* for the stocks you buy. Most brokerage firms offer investors several different types of accounts, each serving a different purpose. I present three of the most common types in the following sections. The basic difference boils down to how particular brokers view your "creditworthiness" when it comes to buying and selling securities. If your credit isn't great, your only choice is a cash account. If your credit is good, you can open either a cash account or a margin account. Once you qualify for a margin account, you can (with additional approval) upgrade it to do options trades.

To open an account, you have to fill out an application and submit a check or money order for at least the minimum amount required to establish an account.

Cash accounts

A *cash account* (also referred to as a *Type 1* account) means just what you think it means. You must deposit a sum of money along with the new account application to begin trading. The amount of your initial deposit varies from broker to broker. Some brokers have a minimum of $10,000, while others let you open an account for as little as $500. Once in a while you may see a broker offering cash accounts with no minimum deposit, usually as part of a promotion. Use the resources in Appendix A to help you shop around. Qualifying for a cash account is usually easy as long as you have cash and a pulse.

With a cash account, your money has to be deposited in the account before the closing (or settlement) date for any trade you make. The closing occurs three business days after the date you make the trade (the date of execution). You may be required to have the money in the account even before the date of execution. See Chapter 6 for details on these and other important dates.

In other words, if you call your broker on Monday, October 10, and order 50 shares of CashLess Corp. at $20 per share, then on Thursday, October 13, you better have $1,000 in cash sitting in your account (plus commission). Otherwise, the purchase doesn't go through.

If you have cash in a brokerage account, see whether the broker will pay you interest on the uninvested cash in it. Some offer a service in which uninvested money earns money market rates and you can even make a choice about whether the venue is a regular money market account or a tax-free municipal money market account.

Margin accounts

A *margin account* (also called a *Type 2* account) gives you the ability to borrow money against the securities in the account to buy more stock. Because you have the ability to borrow in a margin account, you have to be qualified and approved by the broker. After you're approved, this newfound credit gives you more leverage so that you can buy more stock or do short-selling. (You can read more about buying on margin and short-selling in Chapter 17.)

For stock trading, the margin limit is 50 percent. For example, if you plan to buy $10,000 worth of stock on margin, you need at least $5,000 in cash (or securities owned) sitting in your account. The interest rate that you pay varies depending on the broker, but most brokers generally charge a rate that's several points higher than their own borrowing rate.

Why use margin? Margin is to stocks what mortgage is to buying real estate. You can buy real estate with all cash, but many times, using borrowed funds makes sense since you may not have enough money to make a 100% cash purchase or you prefer not to pay all cash. With margin, you could, for example, be able to buy $10,000 worth of stock with as little as $5,000. The balance of the stock purchase is acquired using a loan (margin) from the brokerage firm.

Option accounts

An *option account* (also referred to as a *Type 3* account) gives you all the capabilities of a margin account (which in turn also gives you the capabilities of a cash account) plus the ability to trade options on stocks and stock indexes. To upgrade your margin account to an options account, the broker usually asks you to sign a statement that you're knowledgeable about options and familiar with the risks associated with them.

Options can be a very effective addition to a stock investor's array of wealth-building investment tools. A more comprehensive review of options is available in the book *Stock Options For Dummies* by Alan R. Simon (Wiley).

Judging Brokers' Recommendations

In recent years, Americans have become enamored with a new sport: the rating of stocks by brokers on the television financial shows. Frequently these shows feature a dapper market strategist talking up a particular stock. Some stocks have been known to jump significantly right after an influential analyst issues a buy recommendation. Analysts' speculation and opinions make for great fun, and many people take their views very seriously. However, most investors should be very wary when analysts, especially the glib ones on TV, make a recommendation. It's often just showbiz.

Brokers issue their recommendations (advice) as a general idea of how much regard they have for a particular stock. The following list presents the basic recommendations (or ratings) and what they mean to you:

- ✓ *Strong buy* **and** *buy:* Hot diggity dog! These ratings are the ones to get. The analyst loves this pick, and you would be very wise to get a bunch of shares. The thing to keep in mind, however, is that *buy* recommendations are probably the most common because (let's face it) brokers sell stocks.

- ✓ *Accumulate* **and** *market perform:* An analyst who issues these types of recommendations is positive, yet unexcited, about the pick. This rating is akin to asking a friend whether he likes your new suit and getting the response "it's nice" in a monotone voice. It's a polite reply, but you wish his opinion had been more enthusiastic.

- ✓ *Hold* **or** *neutral:* Analysts use this language when their backs are to the wall, but they still don't want to say, "Sell that loser!" This recommendation reminds me of my mother telling me to be nice and either say something positive or keep my mouth shut. In this case, this rating is the analyst's way of keeping his mouth shut.

- ✔ *Sell:* Many analysts should have issued this recommendation during 2000 and 2001, but few actually uttered it. What a shame. So many investors lost money because some analysts were too nice or just afraid to be honest and sound the alarm and urge people to sell.

- ✔ *Avoid like the plague:* I'm just kidding about this one, but I wish that this recommendation was available. I've seen plenty of stocks that I thought were dreadful investments — stocks of companies that made no money and were in terrible financial condition that should never have been considered at all. Yet investors gobble up billions of dollars' worth of stocks that eventually become worthless.

Don't get me wrong. An analyst's recommendation is certainly a better tip than what you'd get from your barber or your sister-in-law's neighbor, but you want to view recommendations from analysts with a healthy dose of reality. Analysts have biases because their employment depends on the very companies that are being presented. What investors need to listen to when a broker talks up a stock is the reasoning behind the recommendation. In other words, why is the broker making this recommendation?

Keep in mind that analysts' recommendations can play a useful role in your personal stock investing research. If you find a great stock and *then* you hear analysts give glowing reports on the same stock, you're on the right track! Here are some questions and points to keep in mind:

- ✔ **How does the analyst arrive at a rating?** The analyst's approach to evaluating a stock can help you round out your research as you consult other sources such as newsletters and independent advisory services.

- ✔ **What analytical approach is the analyst using?** Some analysts use *fundamental analysis* (looking at the company's financial condition and factors related to its success, such as its standing within the industry and the overall market). Other analysts use *technical analysis* (looking at the company's stock price history and judging past stock price movements to derive some insight regarding the stock's future price movement). Many analysts use a combination of the two. Is this analyst's approach similar to your approach or to those of sources that you respect or admire?

- ✔ **What is the analyst's track record?** Has the analyst had a consistently good record through both bull and bear markets? Major financial publications, such as *Barron's* and *Hulbert Financial Digest,* and Web sites, such as `MarketWatch.com`, regularly track recommendations from well-known analysts and stock pickers.

✔ **How does the analyst treat important aspects of the company's performance, such as sales and earnings?** How about the company's balance sheet? The essence of a healthy company is growing sales and earnings coupled with strong assets and low debt.

✔ **Is the industry that the company is in doing well?** Do the analysts give you insight on this important information? A strong company in a weak industry can't stay strong for long.

✔ **What research sources does the analyst cite?** Does the analyst quote the federal government or industry trade groups to support her thesis? These sources are important because they help give a more complete picture regarding the company's prospects for success. Imagine that you decide on the stock of a strong company. But what if the federal government (through agencies such as the SEC) is penalizing the company for fraudulent activity? Or what if the company's industry is shrinking or has ceased to grow (making it tougher for the company to continue growing)? The astute investor looks at a variety of sources before buying stock.

✔ **Is the analyst rational when citing a target price for a stock?** When she says, "We think the stock will hit $100 per share within 12 months," is she presenting a rational model, such as basing the share price on a projected price/earnings ratio? The analyst must be able to provide a logical scenario about why the stock has a good chance of achieving the cited target price within the time frame mentioned. You may not necessarily agree with the analyst's conclusion, but the explanation can help you decide whether the stock choice was well thought out.

✔ **Does the company that is being recommended have any ties to the analyst or the analyst's firm?** During 2000–2002, the financial industry got bad publicity because many analysts gave positive recommendations on stocks of companies that were doing business with the very firms that employed those analysts. This conflict of interest is probably the biggest reason that analysts were so wrong in their recommendations during that period. Ask your broker to disclose any conflict of interest.

The bottom line with brokerage recommendations is that you shouldn't use them to buy or sell a stock. Instead, use them to confirm your own research. I know that if I buy a stock based on my own research and later discover the same stock being talked up on the financial shows, that's just the icing on the cake. The experts may be great to listen to, and their recommendations can augment your own opinions; however, they're no substitute for your own careful research.

Chapter 8

Investing for Growth

*W*hat's the number one reason people invest in stocks? To grow their wealth (also referred to as capital appreciation). Yes, some people invest for income (in the form of dividends), but that's a different matter handled in Chapter 9. Investors seeking growth would rather see the money that could have been distributed as dividends be reinvested in the company so that (hopefully) a greater gain is achieved by seeing the stock's price rise or appreciate. People interested in growing their wealth see stocks as one of the convenient ways to do it. Growth stocks tend to be riskier than other categories of stocks, but they offer excellent long-term prospects for making the big bucks. If you don't believe me, then just ask Warren Buffett, Peter Lynch, and other successful investors. Although someone like Warren Buffett is not considered a "growth" investor, his long-term, value-oriented approach has been a successful growth strategy. If you're the type of investor who has enough time to let somewhat-risky stocks trend upward, or who has enough money so that a loss won't devastate you financially, then growth stocks are definitely for you. As they say, no guts, no glory. The challenge is to figure out which stocks will make you richer quicker.

Short of starting your own business, stock investing is the best way to profit from a business venture. I want to emphasize that to make money in stocks consistently over the long haul, you must remember that you're investing in a company; buying the stock is just a means for you to participate in the company's success (or failure).

What does it matter that you think of stock investing as buying a *company* versus buying a *stock?* Invest in a stock only if you're just as excited about it as you would be if you were the CEO and in charge of running the company. If you're the sole owner of the company, do you act differently than one of a legion of obscure stockholders? Of course you do. As the owner of the company, you have a greater interest in the company. You have a strong desire to know how the enterprise is doing. As you invest in stocks, make believe that you're the owner, and take an active interest in the company's products, services, sales, earnings, and so on. This attitude and discipline can enhance your goals as a stock investor. This approach is especially important if your investment goal is growth.

Becoming a Value-Oriented Growth Investor

A stock is considered a growth stock when it's growing faster and higher than the overall stock market. Basically, a growth stock performs better than its peers in categories such as sales and earnings. Value stocks are stocks that are priced lower than the value of the company and its assets — you can identify a value stock by analyzing the company's fundamentals and looking at key financial ratios, such as the price-to-earnings ratio. (For more on the topic of ratios, see Appendix B.) Growth stocks tend to have better prospects for growth for the immediate future (from one to four years), but value stocks tend to have less risk and more steady growth over a longer term.

Over the years, a debate has quietly raged in the financial community about growth versus value investing. Some people believe that growth and value are mutually exclusive. They maintain that large numbers of people buying stock with growth as the expectation tend to drive up the stock price relative to the company's current value. Growth investors, for example, aren't put off by price to earnings (P/E) ratios of 30, 40, or higher. Value investors, meanwhile, are too nervous buying a stock at those P/E ratio levels.

However, you *can* have both. A value-oriented approach to growth investing serves you best. Long-term growth stock investors spend time analyzing the company's fundamentals to make sure that the company's growth prospects lie on a solid foundation. But what if you have to choose between a growth stock and a value stock? Which do you choose? Seek value when you are buying the stock and analyze the company's prospects for growth. Growth includes but is not limited to the health and growth of the company's specific industry and the economy at large (see Chapters 12, 13, and 14).

The bottom line is that growth is much easier to achieve when you seek solid, value-oriented companies in growing industries. To better understand industries and how they affect stock value, see Chapter 12.

Being a value-oriented growth investor probably has the longest history of success versus most other stock investing philosophies. The track record for those people who use value-oriented growth investing is enviable. Warren Buffett, Benjamin Graham, John Templeton, and Peter Lynch are a few of the more well-known practitioners. Each may have his own spin on the concepts, but all have successfully applied the basic principles of value-oriented growth investing over many years.

Getting Tips for Choosing Growth Stocks

Although the information in the previous section can help you shrink your stock choices from thousands of stocks to maybe a few dozen or a few hundred (depending on how well the general stock market is doing), the purpose of this section is to help you cull the so-so growth stocks to unearth the go-go ones. It's time to dig deeper for the biggest potential winners. Keep in mind that you probably won't find a stock to satisfy all the criteria presented here. Just make sure that your selection meets as many criteria as realistically possible. But hey, if you do find a stock that meets all the criteria cited, *buy as much as you can!*

When choosing growth stocks, you should consider investing in a company only *if* it makes a profit and *if* you understand *how* it makes that profit and from *where* it generates sales. Part of your research means looking at the industry (Chapter 12) and economic trends in general.

Making the right comparison

You have to measure the growth of a company against something to figure out whether it's a growth stock. Usually, you compare the growth of a company with growth from other companies in the same industry or with the stock market in general. In practical terms, when you measure the growth of a stock against the stock market, you're actually comparing it against a generally accepted benchmark, such as the Dow Jones Industrial Average (DJIA) or the Standard & Poor's 500 (S&P 500). For more on DJIA or S&P 500, see Chapter 5.

If a company has earnings growth of 15 percent per year over three years or more, and the industry's average growth rate over the same time frame is 10 percent, then this stock qualifies as a growth stock.

A growth stock is called that not only because the company is growing but also because the company is performing well with some consistency. Having a single year where your earnings do well versus the S&P 500's average doesn't cut it. Growth must be consistently accomplished.

Checking out a company's fundamentals

When you hear the word *fundamentals* in the world of stock investing, it refers to the company's financial condition and related data. When investors (especially value investors) do *fundamental analysis,* they look at the company's fundamentals — its balance sheet, income statement, cash flow, and other operational data, along with external factors such as the company's market position, industry, and economic prospects. Essentially, the fundamentals indicate the company's financial condition. Chapter 10 goes into greater detail about analyzing a company's financial condition. However, the main numbers you want to look at include the following:

- ✔ **Sales:** Are the company's sales this year surpassing last year's? As a decent benchmark, you want to see sales at least 10 percent higher than last year. Although it may differ depending on the industry, 10 percent is a reasonable, general "yardstick."

- ✔ **Earnings:** Are earnings at least 10 percent higher than last year? Earnings should grow at the same rate as sales (or, hopefully, better).

- ✔ **Debt:** Is the company's total debt equal to or lower than the prior year? The death knell of many a company has been excessive debt.

A company's financial condition has more factors than I mention here, but these numbers are the most important. I also realize that using the 10 percent figure may seem like an oversimplification, but you don't need to complicate matters unnecessarily. I know someone's computerized financial model may come out to 9.675 percent or maybe 11.07 percent, but keep it simple for now.

Looking for leaders and megatrends

A strong company in a growing industry is a common recipe for success. If you look at the history of stock investing, this point comes up constantly. Investors need to be on the alert for megatrends because they help ensure your success.

What is a megatrend? A *megatrend* is a major development that has huge implications for much (if not all) of society for a long time to come. Good examples are the advent of the Internet and the aging of America. Both of these trends offer significant challenges and opportunities for our economy. Take the Internet, for example. Its potential for economic application is still being developed. Millions are flocking to it for many reasons. And census data tells us that senior citizens (over 65) will be the fastest growing segment of our population during the next 20 years. How does the stock investor take advantage of a megatrend?

In the wake of the 2000–2002 stock bear market, two megatrends hit their stride: rising energy prices and an overheated housing market. As of 2005, these two issues became major news items with tremendous ripple effects across the national economy. For the growth investor, strategy became clear. Find value-oriented companies with solid fundamentals that are well-positioned to benefit from these megatrends. What's the result? From 2002–2005, many energy-related and housing-related stocks skyrocketed. As oil surpassed $65 a barrel and gasoline hit $3 a gallon, most oil and oil services companies saw their stocks go up 50 percent, 100 percent, and more during that three-year time frame. Housing stocks were even more impressive. In addition, companies that cater to these industries also prospered. Mortgage firms that were publicly traded also posted impressive gains.

Considering a company with a strong niche

Companies that have established a strong niche are consistently profitable. Look for a company with one or more of the following characteristics:

- ✔ **A strong brand:** Companies such as Coca-Cola and Microsoft come to mind. Yes, other companies out there can make soda or software, but a business needs a lot more than a similar product to topple companies that have established an almost irrevocable identity with the public.

- ✔ **High barriers to entry:** United Parcel Service and Federal Express have set up tremendous distribution and delivery networks that competitors can't easily duplicate. High barriers to entry offer an important edge to companies that are already established.

- ✔ **Research and development (R&D):** Companies such as Pfizer and Merck spend a lot of money researching and developing new pharmaceutical products. This investment becomes a new product with millions of consumers who become loyal purchasers, so the company's going to grow.

Noticing who's buying and/or recommending the stock

You can invest in a great company and still see its stock go nowhere. Why? Because what makes the stock go up is demand — having more buyers than sellers of the stock. If you pick a stock for all the right reasons, and the market notices the stock as well, that attention causes the stock price to climb. The things to watch for include the following:

- ✔ **Institutional buying:** Are mutual funds and pension plans buying up the stock you're looking at? If so, this type of buying power can exert tremendous upward pressure on the stock's price. Some resources and publications track institutional buying and how that affects any particular stock. (You can find these resources in Appendix A.) Frequently, when a mutual fund buys a stock, others soon follow. In spite of all the talk about independent research, a herd mentality still exists.

- ✔ **Analysts' attention:** Are analysts talking about the stock on the financial shows? As much as you should be skeptical about an analyst's recommendation (given the stock market debacle of 2000–2002), it offers some positive reinforcement for your stock. Don't ever buy a stock solely on the basis of an analyst's recommendation. Just know that if you buy a stock based on your own research, and analysts subsequently rave about it, your stock price is likely to go up. A single recommendation by an influential analyst can be enough to send a stock skyward.

- ✔ **Newsletter recommendations:** Independent researchers usually publish newsletters. If influential newsletters are touting your choice, that praise is also good for your stock. Although some great newsletters are out there (find them in Appendix A), and they offer information that's as good or better than the research departments of some brokerage firms, don't use a single tip to base your investment decision on. But it should make you feel good if the newsletters tout a stock that you've already chosen.

- ✔ **Consumer publications:** No, you won't find investment advice here. This one seems to come out of left field, but it's a source that you should notice. Publications such as *Consumer Reports* regularly look at products and services and rate them for consumer satisfaction. If a company's offerings are well received by consumers, that's a strong positive for the company. This kind of attention ultimately has a positive effect on that company's stock.

Learning investing lessons from history

A growth stock isn't a creature like the Loch Ness monster — always talked about but rarely seen. Growth stocks have been part of the financial scene for nearly a century. Examples abound that offer rich information that you can apply to today's stock market environment. Look at past market winners, especially those of the 1970s and 1980s, and ask yourself, "What made them profitable stocks?" I mention these two decades because they offer a stark contrast to one another. The '70s were a tough, bearish decade for stocks, while the '80s were booming bull times. (See Chapter 15 for details on bear and bull markets.) Being aware and acting logically are as vital to successful stock investing as they are to any other pursuit. Over and over again, history gives you the formula for successful stock investing:

✔ Pick a company that has strong fundamentals, including signs such as rising sales and earnings and low debt. (See Chapter 10.)

✔ Make sure that the company is in a growing industry. (See Chapter 12.)

✔ Be fully invested in stocks during a bull market, when prices are rising in the stock market and in the general economy. (See Chapter 15.)

✔ During a bear market, switch more of your money out of growth stocks (such as technology) and into defensive stocks (such as utilities).

✔ Monitor your stocks. Hold on to stocks that continue to grow, and sell those stocks that are declining. (See Chapter 21 for some warning signals to watch out for.)

Evaluating the management of a company

The management of a company is crucial to its success. Before you buy stock in a company, you want to know that the company's management is doing a great job. But how do you do that? If you call up a company and ask, it may not even return your phone call. How do you know whether management is running the company properly? The best way is to check the numbers. The following sections tell you the numbers you need to check. If the company's management is running the business well, the ultimate result is a rising stock price.

Return on equity

Although you can measure how well management is doing in several ways, you can take a quick snapshot of a management team's competence by checking the company's return on equity (ROE). You calculate the ROE simply by dividing earnings by equity. The resulting percentage gives you a good idea whether the company is using its equity (or net assets) efficiently and profitably. Basically, the higher the percentage, the better, but you can consider the ROE solid if the percentage is 10 percent or higher. Keep in mind that not all industries have identical ROEs.

To find out a company's earnings, check out the company's income statement. The *income statement* is a simple financial statement that expresses the equation: sales less expenses equal net earnings (or net income or net profit).

You can see an example of an income statement in Table 8-1. (I give more details on income statements in Chapter 10.)

Table 8-1	Grobaby, Inc., Income Statement	
	2005 Income Statement	*2006 Income Statement*
Sales	$82,000	$90,000
Expenses	–$75,000	–$78,000
Net earnings	$7,000	$12,000

To find out a company's equity, check out that company's balance sheet. (See Chapter 10 for more details on balance sheets.) The balance sheet is actually a simple financial statement that illustrates total assets minus total liabilities equal net equity. For public stock companies, the net assets are called "shareholders' equity" or simply "equity." Table 8-2 shows a balance sheet for Grobaby, Inc.

Table 8-2	Grobaby, Inc., Balance Sheet	
	Balance Sheet for December 31, 2005	*Balance Sheet for December 31, 2006*
Total assets (TA)	$55,000	$65,000
Total liabilities (TL)	–$20,000	–$25,000
Equity (TA less TL)	$35,000	$40,000

Table 8-1 shows that Grobaby's earnings went from $7,000 to $12,000. In Table 8-2, you can see that Grobaby increased the equity from $35,000 to $40,000 in one year. The ROE for the year 2005 is 20 percent ($7,000 in earnings divided by $35,000 in equity), which is a solid number. The following year, the ROE is 30 percent ($12,000 in earnings divided by $40,000 equity), another solid number.

Equity and earnings growth

Two additional barometers of success are a company's growth in earnings and growth of equity. Look at the growth in earnings in Table 8-1. The earnings grew from $7,000 (in 2005) to $12,000 (in 2006), or a percentage increase of 71 percent ($12,000 less $7,000 equals $5,000, and $5,000 divided by $7,000 is 71 percent), which is excellent. In Table 8-2, Grobaby's equity grew by

$5,000 (from $35,000 to $40,000), or 14 percent, which is very good — management is doing good things here.

Insider buying

Watching management as it manages the business is important, but another indicator of how well the company is doing is to see whether management is buying stock in the company as well. If a company is poised for growth, who knows better than management? And if management is buying up the company's stock en masse, then that's a great indicator of the stock's potential. See Chapter 19 for more details on insider trading.

TECHNICAL STUFF

Protecting your downside

I become a Johnny-one-note on one topic: trailing stops. (See Chapter 17 for a full explanation of trailing stops.) *Trailing stops* are stop losses that you regularly manage with the stock you invest in. I always advocate using them, especially if you're new to the game of buying growth stocks. Trailing stops can help you, no matter how good or bad the economy is (or how good or bad the stock you're investing in is).

Suppose that you had invested in Enron, a classic example of a phenomenal growth stock that went bad. In 1999 and 2000, when its stock soared, investors were as happy as chocoholics at Hershey. Along with many investors who forgot that sound investing takes discipline and research, Enron investors thought, "Downside risk? What downside risk?"

Here's an example of how a stop-loss order would have worked if you had invested in Enron. Suppose that you bought Enron in 2000 at $50 per share and put in a stop-loss order with your broker at $45. (Remember to make it a *GTC* or good-till-canceled order. If you do, the stop-loss order stays on indefinitely.) As a general rule, I like to place the stop-loss order at 10 percent below the market value. As the stock went up, you kept the stop-loss trailing upward like a tail. (Now you know why it's called a "trailing" stop;

it trails the stock's price.) When Enron hit $70, your stop-loss was changed to, say, $63, and so on. At $84, your new stop-loss was at $76. Then what?

When Enron started its perilous descent, you got out at $76. The new price of $76 triggered the stop-loss, and the stock was automatically sold — you stopped the loss! Actually, in this case, you could call it a "stop and cash in the gain" order. Because you bought the stock at $50 and sold at $76, you pocketed a nice capital gain of $26 (52 percent appreciation — a do-Enron-ron a do-en-ron!). Then you safely stepped aside and watched the stock continue its plunge.

But what if the market is doing well? Are trailing stops a good idea? Because these stops are placed below the stock price, you're not stopping the stock from rising upward indefinitely. All you're doing is protecting your investment from loss. That's discipline! The stock market of 2004–2005 was fairly good to stock investors as the bear market that started in 2000 took a break. If a bear market continues, trailing stop strategies will again become very useful because a potential decline in the stock price will become a greater risk.

Making sure a company continues to do well

A company's financial situation does change, and you, as a diligent investor, need to continue to look at the numbers for as long as the stock is in your portfolio. You may have chosen a great stock from a great company with great numbers in 2003, but chances are pretty good that the numbers have changed since then.

Great stocks don't always stay that way. A great selection that you're drawn to today may become tomorrow's pariah. Information, both good and bad, moves like lightning. In late 2000, analysts considered Enron a cream-of-the-crop stock, and they fell over themselves extolling its virtues. Even the then-celebrated market strategist Abby Joseph Cohen called Enron her number one choice in the energy sector as late as September 2001. Yet Enron shocked investors when it filed for bankruptcy in December 2001. Its stock price fell from $84 in December 2000 to a staggering 26 cents a share (yikes!) in October 2001! Keep an eye on your stock company's numbers!

Exploring Small-caps and Speculative Stocks

Everyone wants to get in early on a hot new stock. Why not? You buy Shlobotky, Inc., at $1 per share and hope it zooms to $98 before lunchtime. Who doesn't want to buy a stock that could become the next IBM or Microsoft? This possibility is why investors are attracted to small-cap stocks.

Small-cap (or small-capitalization) is a reference to the company's market size. *Small-cap stocks* are stocks that have a market value under $1 billion. Investors may face more risk with small-caps, but they also have the chance for greater gains.

Out of all the types of stocks, small-cap stocks continue to exhibit the greatest amount of growth. In the same way that a tree planted last year has more opportunity for growth than a mature 100-year-old redwood, small-caps have greater growth potential than established large-cap stocks. Of course, a small-cap doesn't exhibit spectacular growth just because it's small. It grows when it does the right things, such as increasing sales and earnings by producing goods and services that customers want.

Don't rush to buy IPO stock

When a company goes public, it means that it undergoes an initial public offering (IPO). The *IPO* is the process by which a private firm seeks the assistance of an investment banking firm to gain financing by issuing stock that the public purchases. IPOs generate a lot of excitement, and many investors consider the IPO to be that proverbial ground-floor opportunity. After all, some people find it appealing to get a stock before its price skyrockets after investors subsequently flock to it. Why wouldn't people find IPOs appealing?

IPOs actually have a poor track record of success in their first year. Studies periodically done by the brokerage industry have revealed that IPOs (more times than not) actually decline in price during the first 12 months 60 percent of the time. In other words, an IPO has a better than even chance of dropping in price. The lesson for investors is that they're better off waiting to see how the stock and the company perform. Don't worry about missing that great opportunity; if it's a bona fide opportunity, you'll still do well after the IPO.

For every small company that becomes a Fortune 500 firm, hundreds of companies don't grow at all or go out of business. When you try to guess the next great stock before any evidence of growth, you're not investing — you're speculating. Have you heard that one before? (If not, flip to Chapter 2 for details.) Of course you have, and you'll hear it again. Don't get me wrong — there's nothing wrong with speculating. But it's important to *know* that you're speculating when you're doing it. If you're going to speculate in small stocks hoping for the next Cisco Systems, then use the guidelines I present in the following sections to increase your chances of success.

Avoid IPOs, unless . . .

Initial public offerings (IPOs) are the birthplace of public stocks, or the proverbial ground floor. The *IPO* is the first offering to the public of a company's stock. The IPO is also referred to as "going public." Because a company's going public is frequently an unproven enterprise, investing in an IPO can be risky. Here are the two types of IPOs:

✔ **Start-up IPO:** This is a company that didn't exist before the IPO. In other words, the entrepreneurs get together and create a business plan. To get the financing they need for the company, they decide to go public immediately by approaching an investment banker. If the investment banker thinks that it's a good concept, the banker will seek funding (selling the stock to investors) via the IPO.

✔ **A private company that decides to go public:** In many cases, the IPO is done for a company that already exists and is seeking expansion capital. The company may have been around for a long time as a smaller private concern, but it decides to seek funding through an IPO to grow even larger (or to fund a new product, promotional expenses, and so on).

Which of the two IPOs do you think is less risky? That's right! The private company going public. Why? Because it's already a proven business, which is a safer bet than a brand-new start-up. Some great examples of successful IPOs in recent years are United Parcel Service and Google (they were both established companies *before* they went public).

Great stocks started as small companies going public. You may be able to recount the stories of Federal Express, Dell, AOL, Home Depot, and hundreds of other great successes. But do you remember an IPO by the company Lipschitz & Farquar? No? I didn't think so. It's among the majority of IPOs that don't succeed. For investors, the lesson is clear: Wait until a track record appears before you invest in a company. If you don't, you're simply rolling the dice (in other words, you're speculating, not investing!).

If it's a small-cap stock, make sure it's making money

I emphasize two points when investing in stocks:

✔ Make sure that a company is established. (Being in business for at least three years is a good minimum.)

✔ Make sure that a company is profitable.

These points are especially important for investors in small stocks. Plenty of start-up ventures lose money but hope to make a fortune down the road. A good example is a company in the biotechnology industry. Biotech is an exciting area, but it's esoteric, and at this early stage, companies are finding it difficult to use the technology in profitable ways. You may say, "But shouldn't I jump in now in anticipation of future profits?" You may get lucky, but understand that when you invest in unproven, small-cap stocks, you're speculating.

Investing in small-cap stocks requires analysis

The only difference between a small-cap stock and a large-cap stock is a few zeros in their numbers and the fact that you need to do more research with small-caps. By sheer dint of size, small-caps are riskier than large-caps, so you offset the risk by accruing more information on yourself and the stock in question. Plenty of information is available on large-cap stocks because they're widely followed. Small-cap stocks don't get as much press, and fewer analysts issue reports on them. Here are a few points to keep in mind:

✔ **Understand your investment style.** Small-cap stocks may have more potential rewards, but they also carry more risk. No investor should devote a large portion of his capital to small-cap stocks. If you're considering retirement money, you're better off investing in large-cap stocks, Exchange-Traded Funds (ETFs), investment-grade bonds, bank accounts, and mutual funds. For example, retirement money should be in investments that are either very safe or have proven track records of steady growth over an extended period of time (five years or longer).

✔ **Check with the SEC.** Get the financial reports that the company must file with the SEC (such as its 10Ks and 10Qs — see Chapter 6 for more details). These reports offer more complete information on the company's activities and finances. Go to the SEC Web site at www.sec.gov and check its massive database of company filings at EDGAR (Electronic Data Gathering, Analysis, and Retrieval system). You can also check to see whether any complaints have been filed against the company.

✔ **Check other sources.** See whether brokers and independent research services, such as Value Line, follow the stock. If two or more different sources like the stock, it's worth further investigation. Check the resources in Appendix A for further sources of information before you invest.

Chapter 9

Investing for Income

*I*nvesting for income means investing in stocks that provide you with regular money payments (dividends). Income stocks may not offer stellar growth, but they're good for a steady infusion of money. What type of person is best suited to income stocks? Income stocks can be appropriate for many investors, but they're especially well suited for the following individuals:

✔ **Conservative and novice investors:** Conservative investors like to see a slow-but-steady approach to growing their money while getting regular dividend checks. Novice investors who want to start slowly also benefit from income stocks.

✔ **Retirees:** Growth investing is best suited for long-term needs, while income investing is best suited to current needs. Retirees may want some growth in their portfolios, but they're more concerned with regular income that can keep pace with inflation.

✔ **Dividend reinvestment plan (DRP) investors:** For those investors who like to compound their money with DRPs, income stocks are perfect. For more information on DRPs, see Chapter 18.

If you have a low tolerance for risk or if your investment goal is anything less than long-term, income stocks are your best bet.

Getting your stock portfolio to yield more income is easier than you think. Many income investors increase income using proven techniques such as Covered call writing. Covered call writing is an option strategy that is covered more fully in sources such as *Stock Options For Dummies* (Wiley). You can also find great educational material on this option strategy (and many others) at places such as the Chicago Board Options Exchange (www.cboe.com).

Understanding Income Stocks

When people talk about gaining income from stocks, they're usually talking about dividends. A *dividend* is nothing more than money paid out to the owner of stock. You purchase dividend stocks primarily for income — not for spectacular growth potential.

A dividend is quoted as an annual number but is usually paid on a quarterly basis. For example, if the stock pays a dividend of $4, you're probably paid $1 every quarter. If, in this example, you have 200 shares, you're paid $800 every year (if the dividend doesn't change during that period), or $200 per quarter. Getting that regular dividend check every three months (for as long as you hold the stock) can be a nice perk.

A good income stock is a stock that has a higher-than-average dividend (typically 4 percent or higher).

Dividend rates aren't guaranteed — they can go up or down, or, in some extreme cases, the dividend can be discontinued. Fortunately, most companies that issue dividends continue them indefinitely and actually increase dividend payments from time to time. Historically, dividend increases have equaled (or exceeded) the rate of inflation.

Advantages of income stocks

Income stocks tend to be among the least volatile of all stocks, and many investors view them as defensive stocks. *Defensive stocks* are stocks of companies that sell goods and services that are generally needed no matter what shape the economy is in. (Don't confuse defensive stocks with *defense stocks,* which specialize in goods and equipment for the military.) Food, beverage, and utility companies are great examples of defensive stocks. Even when the economy is experiencing tough times, people still need to eat, drink, and turn the lights on. Companies that offer relatively high dividends also tend to be large firms in established, stable industries.

Some industries in particular are known for high-dividend stocks. Utilities (such as electric, gas, and water), real estate investment trusts (REITs), and the energy sector (oil and gas) are places where you definitely find income stocks. Yes, you can find high-dividend stocks in other industries, but you find a high concentration of them in these industries. For more details, see the sections highlighting these industries later in this chapter.

Disadvantages of income stocks

Before you say, "Income stocks are great! I'll get my checkbook and buy a batch right now," take a look at some potential disadvantages (ugh!). Income stocks do come with some fine print.

What goes up . . .

Income stocks can go down as well as up, just as any stock can. Obviously, you don't mind your income stock going up in value, but it can go down just as easily. The factors that affect stocks in general — politics, economic trends (Chapter 14), industry changes (Chapter 12), and so on — affect income stocks, too. Fortunately, income stocks don't get hit as hard as other stocks when the market is declining because high dividends tend to act as a support to the stock price. Therefore, income stocks' prices usually fall less dramatically than the prices of other stocks in a declining market.

Interest-rate sensitivity

Income stocks can be sensitive to rising interest rates. When interest rates go up, other investments (such as corporate bonds, U.S. treasury securities, and bank certificates of deposit) are more attractive. When your income stock is yielding 4 percent and interest rates are going to 5 percent, 6 percent, or higher, you may think, "Hmmm. Why settle for a 4 percent yield when I can get 5 percent or better elsewhere?" As more and more investors sell their low-yield stock, the prices for those stocks fall.

Another point to remember is that rising interest rates may hurt the company's financial strength. If the company has to pay more interest, that may affect the company's earnings, which in turn may affect the dividend.

Dividend-paying companies that are experiencing consistent, falling revenues tend to cut dividends. In this case, "consistent" means beyond just a year.

Inflation eats into dividends

Although many companies raise their dividends on a regular basis, some don't. Or, if they do raise their dividends, the increases may be small. If income is your primary consideration, you want to be aware of this fact. If you're getting the same dividend year after year and this income is important to you, rising inflation becomes a problem. Say that you have XYZ stock at $10 per share with an annual dividend of 30 cents (the yield is 30 cents divided by $10, or 3 percent). If you have a yield of 3 percent two years in a row, how do you feel when inflation rises 6 percent one year and 7 percent the next year? Because inflation means that your costs are rising, inflation shrinks the value of the dividend income you receive.

Playing it safe

If you're an investor seeking income and you're very nervous about potential risks with income stocks, here are some non-stock alternatives:

✔ **U.S. Treasury securities:** Issued by the federal government, these securities are considered the safest investments in the world. Examples of treasury securities are U.S. savings bonds and treasury bonds. They pay interest and are an ideal addition to any income investor's portfolio.

✔ **Bank certificates of deposit (CDs):** These investments are backed up by the Federal Deposit Insurance Corporation (FDIC) and are considered very safe.

✔ **Income mutual funds:** Many mutual funds, such as treasury bond mutual funds and corporate bond funds, are designed for income investors. They offer investors diversification and professional management, and investors can usually invest with as little as $1,000.

As you can see, even conservative income investors can be confronted with different types of risk. (Chapter 4 covers the topic of risk in greater detail.) Fortunately, the rest of this chapter helps you carefully choose income stocks so that you can minimize these potential disadvantages.

Don't forget Uncle Sam

The government usually taxes dividends as ordinary income. Fortunately, recent tax legislation has favored dividend-paying stock. See Chapter 20 for more information on taxes for stock investors.

Analyzing Income Stocks

Look at income stocks in the same way you do growth stocks when assessing the financial strength of a company. Getting nice dividends comes to a screeching halt if the company can't afford to pay them. If your budget depends on dividend income, then monitoring the company's financial strength is that much more important. You can apply the same techniques I list in Chapter 8 for assessing the financial strength of growth stocks to your assessment of income stocks.

Understanding your needs first

You choose income stocks primarily because you want or need income now. As a secondary point, income stocks have the potential for steady, long-term appreciation. So if you're investing for retirement needs that won't occur for another 20 years, maybe income stocks aren't suitable for you — better to invest in growth stocks because they're more likely to grow your money faster over your stated lengthy investment term.

If you're certain that you want income stocks, do a rough calculation to figure out how big a portion of your portfolio you want income stocks to occupy. Suppose that you need $25,000 in investment income to satisfy your current financial needs. If you have bonds that give you $20,000 in interest income and you want the rest to come from dividends from income stocks, you need to choose stocks that pay you $5,000 in annual dividends. If you have $80,000 left to invest, you know that you need a portfolio of income stocks that provide $5,000 in dividend income or a yield of 6.25 percent ($5,000 divided by $80,000 equals a yield of 6.25 percent).

Use the following table as a general guideline for understanding your need for income.

Item	*Your Amounts*	*Sample Amounts*
A. How much annual income do you need?		$10,000
B. The value of your portfolio (or money available for investment)		$150,000
C. Yield necessary to achieve income (divide item A by item B)		6.7%

With this simple table, you know that if you have $150,000 in income stocks yielding 6.7 percent, you receive income of $10,000 — meeting your stated financial need. You may ask, "Why not just buy $150,000 of bonds (for instance) that yield at least 6.7 percent?" Well, if you're satisfied with that $10,000, and inflation for the foreseeable future is zero, then you have a point. Unforturnately, inflation will probably be with us for a long time. Fortunately, steady growth that income stocks provide are a benefit to you.

If you have income stocks and don't have any immediate need for the dividends, consider reinvesting the dividends in the company's stock. For more details on this kind of reinvesting, see Chapter 18.

Every investor is different. If you're not sure about your current or future needs, your best choice is to consult with a financial planner.

Minding your dividends and interest

Dividends are sometimes confused with interest. However, *dividends* are payouts to owners, while *interest* is a payment to a creditor. A stock investor is considered a part owner of the company he invests in and is entitled to dividends when they're issued. A bank, on the other hand, considers you a creditor when you open an account. The bank borrows your money and pays you interest on it.

Checking out yield

Because income stocks pay out dividends — income — you need to assess which stocks can give you the highest income. How do you decide which stocks will pay the most money? The main thing to look for in choosing income stocks is *yield* (the percentage rate of return paid on a stock in the form of dividends). Looking at a stock's dividend yield is the quickest way to find out how much money you'll earn from a particular income stock versus other dividend-paying stocks (or even other investments such as a bank account). Table 9-1 illustrates this point. Dividend yield is calculated in the following way:

Dividend yield = dividend income ÷ stock investment

The next two sections use the information in Table 9-1 to compare the yields from different investments and to see how evaluating yield can help you choose the stock that will earn you the most money.

Don't stop scrutinizing stocks after you acquire them. You may have made a great choice that gives you a great dividend, but that doesn't mean that the stock stays that way indefinitely. Monitor the company's progress for as long as it's in your portfolio. Use resources such as www.bloomberg.com and www.marketwatch.com (see Appendix A for more resources) to track your stock and to monitor how well that particular company continues to perform.

Table 9-1		Comparing Yields		
Investment	*Type*	*Investment Amount*	*Annual Investment Income (Dividend)*	*Yield (Annual Investment Income ÷ Investment Amount)*
Smith Co.	Common stock	$20 per share	$1.00 per share	5%
Jones Co.	Common stock	$30 per share	$1.50 per share	5%

Investment	Type	Investment Amount	Annual Investment Income (Dividend)	Yield (Annual Investment Income ÷ Investment Amount)
Wilson Bank	Savings account	$1,000 deposit	$40	4%

Examining yield

Most people have no problem understanding yield when it comes to bank accounts. If I tell you that my bank certificate of deposit (CD) has an annual yield of 3.5 percent, you can easily figure out that if I deposit $1,000 in that account, a year later I'll have $1,035 (slightly more if you include compounding). The CD's market value in this example is the same as the deposit amount — $1,000. That makes it easy to calculate.

How about stocks? When you see a stock listed in the financial pages, the dividend yield is provided along with the stock's price and annual dividend. The dividend yield in the financial pages is always calculated as if you bought the stock on that given day. Just keep in mind that, based on supply and demand, stock prices change virtually every day (every minute!) that the market is open. Therefore, because the stock price changes every day, the yield changes as well. So, keep the following two things in mind when examining yield:

✔ **The yield listed in the financial pages may not represent the yield you're receiving.** What if you bought stock in Smith Co. (see Table 9-1) a month ago at $20 per share? With an annual dividend of $1, you know that your yield is 5 percent. But what if today Smith Co. is selling for $40 per share? If you look in the financial pages, the yield quoted would be 2.5 percent. Gasp! Did the dividend get cut in half?! No, not really. You're still getting 5 percent because you bought the stock at $20 rather than the current $40 price; the quoted yield is for investors who purchase Smith Co. today. Investors who buy Smith Co. stock today pay $40 and get the $1 dividend, and they're locked into the current yield of 2.5 percent. Although Smith Co. may have been a good income investment for you a month ago, it's not such a hot pick today because the price of the stock doubled, cutting the yield in half. Even though the dividend hasn't changed, the yield changed dramatically because of the stock price change.

✔ **Stock price affects how good of an investment the stock may be.** Another way to look at yield is by looking at the amount of investment. Using Smith Co. in Table 9-1 as the example, the investor who bought, say, 100 shares of Smith Co. when they were $20 per share only paid $2,000 (100 shares times $20 — leave out commissions to make the example simple). If the same stock is purchased later at $40 per share, the total investment amount is $4,000 (100 shares times $40). In either case, the investor gets a total dividend income of $100 (100 shares times $1 dividend per share). From a yield perspective, which investment is yielding more — the $2,000 investment or the $4,000 investment? Of course, it's better to get the income ($100 in this case) with the smaller investment (a 5 percent yield is better than a 2.5 percent yield).

Comparing yield between different stocks

All things being equal, choosing Smith Co. or Jones Co. is a coin toss. It's looking at your situation and each company's fundamentals and prospects that will sway you. What if Smith Co. is an auto stock (similar to General Motors in 2005) and Jones Co. is a utility serving the Las Vegas metro area. Now what? In 2005, the automotive industry struggled, while utilities were generally in much better shape. In that scenario, Smith Co.'s dividend would be in jeopardy while Jones Co.'s dividend would be more secure. Another issue would be the payout ratio (see later in this chapter). Therefore, having the same yield is not the same as the same risk. Different companies have different risks associated with them.

Checking the stock's payout ratio

You can use the payout ratio to figure out what percentage of the company's earnings are being paid out in the form of dividends. Keep in mind that companies pay dividends from their net earnings. Therefore, the company's earnings should always be higher than the dividends the company pays out. Here's how to figure a payout ratio:

Dividend (per share) divided by Earnings (per share) = Payout Ratio

Say that the company CashFlow Now, Inc., (CFN) has annual earnings of $1 million dollars. (Remember that earnings are what you get when you subtract expenses from sales.) Total dividends are to be paid out of $500,000, and the company has 1 million outstanding shares. Using those numbers, you know that CFN has earnings per share (EPS) of $1.00 ($1 million in earnings divided by 1 million shares) and that it pays an annual dividend of 50 cents per share ($500,000 divided by 1 million shares). The dividend payout ratio is 50 percent (the 50-cent dividend is 50 percent of the $1.00 EPS). This number is a healthy dividend payout ratio because even if the company's earnings fall by 10 percent or 20 percent, it still has plenty of room to pay dividends. People concerned about the safety of their dividend income should regularly watch the payout ratio. The maximum acceptable payout ratio should be 80 percent and a good range is 50–70 percent. A payout ratio of 60 percent and lower is considered very safe.

When a company suffers significant financial difficulties, its ability to pay dividends is compromised. So if you need dividend income to help you pay your bills, you better be aware of the dividend payout ratio. Generally, a dividend payout ratio of 60 percent or less is safe. Obviously, the lower the percentage is, the safer the dividend.

Diversifying your stocks

If most of your dividend income comes from stock in a single company or from a single industry, consider reallocating your investment to avoid having all your eggs in one basket. Concerns for diversification apply to income stocks as well as growth stocks. If all your income stocks are in the electric utility industry, then any problems in the electric utility industry are potential problems for your portfolio as well. See Chapter 4 for more on diversification.

Examining the company's bond rating

Bond rating? Huh? What's that got to do with dividend-paying stocks? Actually, the company's bond rating is very important to income stock investors. The bond rating offers insight into the company's financial strength. Bonds get rated for quality for the same reasons that consumer agencies rate products such as cars or toasters. Standard & Poor's (S&P) is the major independent rating agency that looks into bond issuers. It looks at the issuer of a bond and asks the question "Does the bond issuer have the financial strength to pay back the bond and the interest as stipulated in the bond indenture?" To understand why this rating is important, consider the following:

- ✔ If the bond rating is good, that means the company is strong enough to pay its obligations. These obligations include expenses, payments on debts, and dividends that are declared. If a bond rating agency gives the company a high rating (or if it raises the rating), that's a great sign for anyone holding the company's debt or receiving dividends.

- ✔ If a bond rating agency lowers the rating of a bond, that means that the company's financial strength is deteriorating — a red flag for anyone who owns the company's bonds or stock. A lower bond rating today may mean trouble for the dividend later on.

- ✔ If the bond rating isn't good, that means that the company is having difficulty paying its obligations. If the company can't pay all its obligations, then it has to choose which ones to pay. More times than not, a financially troubled company chooses to cut dividends or (in a worst case scenario) not pay dividends at all.

The highest rating issued by S&P is AAA. The grades AAA, AA, and A are considered "investment grade" or of high quality. Bs and Cs indicate a poor grade, while anything lower than that is considered very risky (the bonds are referred to as "junk bonds"). So if you see a XXX rating, then . . . gee . . . you better stay away! (You may even get an infection.)

Exploring Some Typical Income Stocks

Although virtually every industry has stocks that pay dividends, some industries have more dividend-paying stocks than others. You won't find too many dividend-paying income stocks in the computer or biotech industry! The reason is that these types of companies need a lot of money to finance expensive research and development (R&D) projects to create new products. Without R&D, the company can't create new products to fuel sales, growth, and future earnings. Computer, biotech, and other innovative industries are better for growth investors.

Utilities

Utilities generate a large cash flow. (If you don't believe me, look at your gas and electric bills!) Cash flow includes money from income (sales of products and/or services) and other items (such as the selling of assets, for example). This cash flow is needed to cover things such as expenses, loan payments, and dividends. Utilities are considered the most common type of income stocks, and many investors have at least one in their portfolios. Investing in your own local utility isn't a bad idea. At least it makes paying the utility bill less painful. Before you invest in a public utility, consider the following:

- **The utility company's financial condition:** Is the company making money, and are its sales and earnings growing from year to year? Make sure that the utility's bonds are rated A or higher. I cover bond ratings in the "Examining the company's bond rating" section, earlier in this chapter.

- **The company's dividend payout ratio:** Because utilities tend to have a good cash flow, don't be too concerned if the ratio reaches 70 percent. Again, from a safety point of view, however, the lower the rate the better. See the "Checking the stock's payout ratio" section, earlier in this chapter, for more on payout ratios.

- **The company's geographic location:** If the utility covers an area that's doing well and offers an increasing population base and business expansion, that bodes well for your stock.

Real estate investment trusts (REITs)

Real estate investment trusts (REITs) are a special breed of stock. A *REIT* is an investment that has the elements of both a stock and a *mutual fund* (a pool of money received from investors that's managed by an investment company).

It's like a stock in that it's a company whose stock is publicly traded on the major stock exchanges, and it has the usual features that you expect from a stock — it can be bought and sold easily through a broker, income is given to investors as dividends, and so on. A REIT resembles a mutual fund in that it doesn't make its money selling goods and services; it makes its money by buying, selling, and managing an investment portfolio — in the case of a REIT, the portfolio is full of real estate investments. It generates revenue from rents and property leases as any landlord does. In addition, some REITs own mortgages, and they gain income from the interest.

REITs are called trusts only because they meet the requirements of the Real Estate Investment Trust Act of 1960. This act exempts REITs from corporate income tax and capital gains taxes as long as they meet certain criteria, such as dispensing 95 percent of their net income to shareholders. Other criteria exist, but income investors are interested in this one. This provision is the reason why REITs generally issue generous dividends. Beyond this status, REITs are, in a practical sense, like any other publicly traded company.

The main advantages to investing in REITs include the following:

✔ Unlike other types of real estate investing, REITs are easy to buy and sell. You can buy a REIT by making a phone call to a broker or visiting a broker's Web site, just as you can to purchase any stock.

✔ REITs have higher-than-average yields. Because they must distribute at least 95 percent of their income to their shareholders, their dividends usually yield a return of 5 to 12 percent.

✔ REITs involve a lower risk than the direct purchase of real estate. Because you're investing in a company that buys the real estate, you don't have to worry about managing the properties — the company's management does that on a full-time basis. Usually, the REIT doesn't just manage one property; it's diversified in a portfolio of different properties.

✔ Investing in a REIT is affordable for small investors. REIT shares usually trade in the $10 to $40 range, meaning that you can invest with very little money.

REITs do have disadvantages. They have the same inherent risks as investing in real estate directly. Real estate investing reached manic record-high levels during 2000–2004, which means that a downturn is likely. Whenever you invest in an asset (real estate and therefore REITs) that has already skyrocketed due to artificial stimulants (in the case of real estate, very low interest rates and too much credit and debt), the potential losses can offset any potential (unrealized) income.

When you're looking for a REIT to invest in, analyze it the way you'd analyze a property. Look at the location and type of the property. If shopping malls are booming in California and your REIT buys and sells shopping malls in California, then you'll do well. However, if your REIT invests in office buildings across the country and the office building market is overbuilt and having tough times, so will you.

Royalty trusts

In recent years, the oil and gas sector has generated much interest as people and businesses experience much higher energy prices. Due to a variety of bullish factors, such as increased international demand from China and other emerging industrialized nations, oil and gas prices have zoomed to record highs. Some income investors have capitalized on this price increase by investing in energy stocks called royalty trusts.

Royalty trusts are companies that hold assets such as oil-rich and/or gas-rich land and generate high fees from companies that seek access to these properties for exploration. The fees paid to the Royalty trusts are then disbursed as high dividends to their shareholders. By the second half of 2005, dividend-rich royalty trusts sported yields in the 8–12 percent range, which is very enticing given how low the yields have been in this decade for other investments such as bank accounts and bonds. You can research royalty trusts in generally the same venues as regular stocks (see Appendix A).

Although energy has been a hot field in recent years and royalty trusts have done well, keep in mind that their payout ratios are very high (often in the 90–100 percent range) so dividends will suffer should their cash flow shrink.

Chapter 10

Using Basic Accounting to Choose Winning Stocks

In This Chapter

▶ Determining a company's value

▶ Using accounting principles to understand a company's financial condition

Successful stock picking sometimes seems like plucking a rabbit out of a hat or watching the Amazing Kreskin do some Houdini trick. In other words, it seems like you need sleight of hand to choose a stock. Perhaps stock picking is more art than science. The other guy seems to always pick winners while you're stuck with losers. What does it take? A crystal ball or some system from a get-rich-quick-with-stocks book? Well, with the book in your hands now and a little work on your part, I think you'll succeed. This chapter takes the mystery out of the numbers behind the stock. The most tried-and-true method for picking a good stock starts with picking a good company. Picking the company means looking at its products, services, industry, and financial strength ("the numbers"). Doing some research regarding the company's "financials" is easier than ever before, thanks to the current information age.

Recognizing Value When You See It

If you pick a stock based on the value of the company that's issuing it, you're a *value investor* — an investor who looks at a company's value and judges whether he can purchase the stock at a good price. Companies have values the same way many things have value, such as eggs or elephant-foot umbrella stands. And there's such a thing as a fair price to buy them at, too. Eggs, for example, have value. You can eat them and have a tasty treat while getting nutrition as well. But would you buy an egg for $1,000 (and, no, you're not a starving millionaire on a deserted island)? No, of course not. But what if you could buy an egg for 5 cents? At that point, it has value *and* a good price. This kind of deal is a value investor's dream.

Value investors analyze a company's fundamentals (earnings, assets, and so on) and see if the information justifies purchasing the stock. They see if the stock price is low relative to these verifiable, quantifiable factors. Therefore, value investors use "fundamental analysis" while other investors may use "technical analysis". *Technical analysis* looks at stock charts and statistical data, such as trading volume and historical stock prices. There are also investors that use a combination of both.

History has shown us that the most successful long-term investors have typically been value investors using fundamental analysis as their primary investing approach.

When you look at a company from a value-oriented perspective, here are some of the most important items to consider:

- ✔ **The balance sheet to figure out the company's net worth:** A value investor doesn't buy a company's stock because it's cheap; he buys it because it's *undervalued* (the company is worth more than the price its stock reflects — its market value is as close as possible to its book value).

- ✔ **The income statement to figure out the company's profitability:** A company may be undervalued from a simple comparison of the book value and the market value, but that doesn't mean it's a screaming buy. For example, what if you find out that a company is in trouble and losing money this year? Do you buy its stock then? No, you don't. Why invest in the stock of a losing company? (If you do, you aren't investing — you're gambling or speculating.) The heart of a company's value, besides its net worth, is its ability to generate profit.

- ✔ **Ratios that let you analyze just how well (or not so well) the company is doing:** Value investors basically look for a bargain. That being the case, they generally don't look at companies that everyone is talking about, because by that point, the stock of those companies ceases to be a bargain. The value investor searches for a stock that will eventually be discovered by the market and then watches as the stock price goes up. But before you bother digging into the fundamentals to find that bargain stock, first make sure that the company is making money.

See the section, "Accounting for Value," later in this chapter, for more on using balance sheets, income statements, and ratios to help you analyze stock values.

Value investors can find thousands of companies that have value, but they can probably buy only a handful at a truly good price. The number of stocks that can be bought at a good price is relative to the market. In mature bull markets, a good price is hard to find because most stocks have probably seen significant price increases, but in bear markets, good companies at bargain prices are easier to come by.

Understanding different types of value

Value may seem like a murky or subjective term, but it's the essence of good stock picking. You can measure value in different ways, so you need to know the difference and understand the impact that value has on your investment decisions.

Market value

When you hear someone quoting a stock at $47 per share, that price reflects the stock's market value. The total market valuation of a company's stock is also referred to as its *market cap* or *market capitalization*. How do you determine a company's market cap? With the following simple formula:

Market capitalization = share price × number of shares outstanding

If Bolshevik Corp's stock is $35 per share and it has 10 million shares outstanding (or shares available for purchase), then its market cap is $350 million. Granted, $350 million dollars may sound like a lot of money, but Bolshevik Corp is considered a small-cap stock. For more information about small-cap stocks, dip into Chapter 8.

Who sets the market value of stock? The market — millions of investors directly and through intermediaries such as mutual funds — determines the market value of stock. If the market perceives that the company is desirable, investor demand for the company's stock pushes up the share price.

The problem with market valuation is that it's not always a good indicator of a good investment. In recent years, plenty of companies have had astronomical market values, yet they proved to be terrible companies and subsequently terrible investments. For example, WorldCom was a multi-billion-dollar stock, yet the company eventually went bankrupt, and the stock became worthless. Investors (and analysts) misunderstood the difference between the fleeting market value of the stock and the true value of the underlying company.

Book value

Book value (also referred to as *accounting value*) looks at a company from a balance sheet perspective (assets minus liabilities equal net worth or *stockholders' equity*). It's a way of judging a company by its net worth to see whether the stock's market value is reasonable compared to the company's intrinsic value.

Generally, market value usually tends to be higher than book value. If market value is substantially higher than book value, the value investor becomes more reluctant to buy that particular stock because it's overvalued. The closer the stock's market capitalization is to the book value, the safer the investment.

I like to be cautious with a stock whose market value is more than twice the company's book value. If the market value is $1 billion and the book value is $500 million or more, that's a good indicator that the company may be overvalued, or valued at a higher price than the company's book value and ability to generate a profit. Just understand that the farther the market value is from the company's book value, the more you will pay for the company's real potential value.

Earnings and sales value

A company's intrinsic value is directly tied to its ability to make money. In that case, many analysts like to value stocks from the perspective of the company's income statement. Two common barometers of value are expressed in ratios: the price to sale ratio and the price-to-earnings ratio. In both instances, the price is a reference to the company's market value (as reflected in its share price). Sales and earnings are references to the company's ability to make money. These two ratios are covered more fully in the section "Tooling around with ratios," later in this chapter.

For investors, the general approach is clear. The closer the market value is to the company's intrinsic value, the better. And, of course, if the market value is lower than the company's intrinsic value, then you have a potential bargain worthy of a closer look. Part of looking closer means examining the company's income statement, also called the *profit and loss statement,* or simply, the *P&L.* A low price to sales ratio (PSR) is 1, a medium PSR is between 1 and 2, and a high PSR is 3 or higher.

Putting the pieces together

The more ways that you can look at a company and see value, the better. The first thing I look at (sorry, it's a habit) is the PE ratio. Does the company have one? (It sounds dumb, but if it's losing money, it may not have one.) Does it look reasonable or is it in triple-digit, nose-bleed territory? Is it reasonable or too high? Next, look at the company's debt load. Is it less than the company's equity? Are sales healthy and increasing from the prior year? Does the company compare favorably in these categories versus other companies in the same industry?

Simplicity to me is best. You'll notice that the number "10" comes up frequently as I measure the company's performance juxtaposing all the numbers that you need to be aware of. If net income is rising by 10 percent or more, that's fine. If the company is in the top 10 percent of its industry, that's great. If the industry is growing by 10 percent or better (sales, and so on), that's great. If sales are up 10 percent or more from the prior year, that's great. A great company doesn't have to have all of these things going for it. But it should have as many of these things happening to ensure greater potential success.

Does every company/industry have to neatly fit this criteria? No. Of course not. But it won't hurt you to be as picky as possible. You only need to find a handful of stocks from thousands of choices. (Hey, this approach has worked for me, my clients, and my students for over two decades.) Nuff said.

Accounting for Value

Profit is for a company what oxygen is for you and me. That's neither good nor bad; it just is. Without profit, a company can't survive, much less thrive. Without profit, it can't provide jobs, pay taxes, and invest in new products, equipment, or innovation. Without profit, the company eventually goes bankrupt, and the value of its stock evaporates.

In the heady days leading up to the bear market of 2000–2002, many investors lost a lot of money simply because they invested in stocks of companies that weren't making a profit. Lots of public companies ended up like bugs that just didn't see the windshield coming their way. Companies such as Enron, WorldCom, and Global Crossing entered the graveyard of rather-be-forgotten stocks. Stock investors as a group lost trillions of dollars investing in glitzy companies that sounded good but weren't making money. When their brokers were saying, "buy, buy, buy," their hard-earned money was saying, "bye, bye, bye!" What were they thinking?

Stock investors need to pick up some rudimentary knowledge of accounting to round out their stock-picking prowess and to be sure that they're getting a good value for their investment dollars. Accounting is the language of business. If you don't understand basic accounting, then you'll have difficulty being a successful investor. Investing without accounting knowledge is like traveling without a map. However, if you can run a household budget, using accounting analysis to evaluate stocks will be easier than you think.

Crash-test dummy candidate?

From 2001–2003, consumers were buying up SUVs . . . uh . . . ASAP. Demand was very high for those popular gas-guzzling vehicles and auto giant General Motors (GM) was racking up record sales. Investors noticed GM's success, and its stock surpassed $76 in 2001. However, the numbers (and the times) were catching up with GM. Their zero-interest financing program started to sputter. Debts and human resource liabilities (such as employee health & retirement commitments) started accelerating. Energy costs rose, making SUVs less attractive. The red flags came out. GM's 2004 year-end balance sheet showed debt of over $451 billion while total shareholder equity was only $27.7 billion. GM's net income fell to just 1 percent of net sales, and its price-to-earnings (PE) ratio (see the "Tooling around with ratios" section, later in this chapter) ballooned to a lofty 39. The stock price hit $25 by April 2005. Although the price rebounded to the mid-$30s by July 2005, investors had skid marks on their portfolio as the stock lost nearly two thirds of its value during that time frame. By September 2005, GM reported a net loss (goodbye PE ratio). In my reckoning, GM is no longer an investment; it is now a speculation. At this rate, it may go from SUV to DOA ASAP.

As a contrasting point, look at Exxon Mobil (XOM) during that same time frame. Its stock price went from about $35 in early 2001 to $60 in July 2005 (it had a 2-for-1 stock split in mid-2001). XOM's net income was a healthy 8 percent of sales and the PE ratio was only 14. In its 2004 year-end balance sheet, total shareholder equity of $101.7 billion comfortably exceeded its total liabilities of $89.5 billion. A sound company with sound numbers. (Ya hear me?)

The point here is that the stock price ultimately reflects the financial health and vitality of the company, and you can easily find and evaluate that information. You don't need luck or a crystal ball. Again, just a little work in the form of fundamental analysis is sufficient.

Walking on a wire: The balance sheet

A company's balance sheet gives you a financial snapshot of what the company looks like in terms of the following equation:

> Assets – liabilities = net worth

Analyze the following items that you find on the balance sheet:

- ✔ **Assets:** Have they increased from the prior year? If not, was it due to the sale of an asset or a write-off (uncollectible accounts receivable, for example)?

- ✔ **Inventory:** Is inventory higher or lower than last year? If sales are flat but inventory is growing, that may be a potential problem.

✔ **Debt:** Debt is the biggest weakness on the corporate balance sheet. Make sure that debt isn't a growing item and that it's under control. In recent years, debt has become a huge problem.

✔ **Derivatives:** A *derivative* is a speculative and complex financial instrument that doesn't constitute ownership of an asset (such as a stock, bond, or commodity), but a promise to convey ownership. Some derivatives are quite acceptable because they are used as protective or hedging vehicles (this is not my primary concern). However, they are frequently used to generate income and can then carry risks that can increase liabilities. Options and futures are examples of derivatives. Find out whether the company dabbles in these complicated, dicey, leveraged financial instruments. Find out (from the company's 10K report) whether it has derivatives and, if so, the total amount. If a company has derivatives that are valued higher than the company's net equity, it may cause tremendous problems. Derivatives problems sank many organizations ranging from stodgy banks (Barings Bank of England) to affluent counties (Orange County, California) to once-respected hedge funds (LTCM) to infamous corporations (Enron).

✔ **Equity:** Equity is the company's net worth (what's left in the event that all the assets are used to pay off all the company debts). The stockholders' equity should be increasing steadily by at least 10 percent per year. If not, find out why.

By looking at a company's balance sheet, you can address the following questions:

✔ **What does the company own (assets)?** The company can own assets, which can be financial, tangible, and/or intangible. *Assets* can be anything that has value or that can be converted to or sold for cash. Financial assets can be cash, investments, or accounts receivable. Assets can be tangible things such as inventory, equipment, and/or buildings. They can also be intangible things such as licenses, trademarks, or copyrights.

✔ **What does the company owe (liabilities)?** *Liabilities* are anything of value that the company must ultimately pay to someone else. Liabilities can be invoices (accounts payable) or short-term or long-term debt.

✔ **What is the company's net equity (net worth)?** After you subtract the liabilities from the assets, the remainder is called either *net worth, net equity,* or *net stockholders' equity.* This number is also critical when calculating a company's book value.

As you can see, a balance sheet isn't difficult to understand. It's an important document that you should look at carefully to make sure the company is in a strong financial position. Finding the relevant financial data on a company isn't difficult in the age of information. Web sites, such as www.nasdaq.com, can give you the most recent balance sheets and income statements of most public companies.

The assets and liabilities relationship for a company has the same logic as the assets and liabilities in your own household. When you look at a snapshot of your own finances (your personal balance sheet), how can you tell if you're doing well? Odds are that you'd start by comparing some numbers. If your net worth is $5,000, you may say, "That's great!" But a more appropriate remark is something like, "That's great compared to, say, a year ago."

Compare a company's balance sheet at a recent point in time to a past time. You should do this comparative analysis with all the key items on the balance sheet. You do this analysis to see the company's progress. Is it growing its assets and/or shrinking its debt? Most importantly, is the company's net worth growing? Is it growing by at least 10 percent from a year ago? All too often, investors stop doing their homework after they make an initial investment. You should continue to look at the company's numbers on a regular basis so that you can be ahead of the curve. If the company starts having problems, you can get out before the rest of the market starts getting out (which causes the stock price to fall).

To judge the financial strength of a company, ask yourself the following questions:

- ✔ Are the company's assets greater in value than they were three months ago, a year ago, or two years ago? Compare current asset size to the most recent two years to make sure that the company is growing in size and financial strength.

- ✔ How do the individual items compare with prior periods? Some particular assets that you want to take note of are cash, inventory, and accounts receivable.

- ✔ Are liabilities such as accounts payable and debt about the same, lower, or higher compared to prior periods? Are they growing at a similar, faster, or slower rate than the company's assets? Remember that debt that rises faster and higher than items on the other side of the balance sheet is a warning sign of pending financial problems.

- ✔ Is the company's net worth or equity greater than the previous year? And is that year's equity greater than the year before? In a healthy company, the net worth is constantly rising. As a general rule, in good economic times, net worth should be at least 10 percent higher than the previous year. In tough economic times (such as a recession), 5 percent is acceptable. Seeing the net worth growing at 15 percent or higher is great.

Looking at the income statement

Where do you look if you want to find out what a company's profit is? Check out the company's income statement. It reports, in detail, a simple accounting equation that you probably already know:

Sales – expenses = net profit (or net earnings or net income)

Look at the following figures found on the income statement:

- ✔ **Sales:** Are they increasing? If not, why not? By what percentage are sales increasing? Preferably, they should be at 10 percent higher than the year before. Sales are, after all, where the money is coming from to pay for the company's activities and subsequent profit.

- ✔ **Expenses:** Do you see any unusual items? Are total expenses reported higher than the prior year and by how much? If the item is significantly higher, why? A company with large, rising expenses will see profits suffer, which isn't good for the stock price.

- ✔ **Research and development (R&D):** How much is the company spending on R&D? Companies that rely on new product development (such as pharmaceuticals or biotech firms) should spend an adequate amount because new products mean future earnings and growth.

- ✔ **Earnings:** This figure reflects the bottom line. Are total earnings higher? How about earnings from operations (leaving out expenses such as taxes and interest)? The earnings section is the heart and soul of the income statement and of the company itself. Out of all the numbers in the financial statements, earnings have the greatest single impact on the company's stock price.

Looking at the income statement, an investor can try to answer the following questions:

- ✔ **What sales did the company make?** Companies sell products and services that generate revenue (known as *sales* or *gross sales*). Sales are also referred to as the *top line*.

- ✔ **What expenses did the company incur?** In generating sales, companies pay expenses such as payroll, utilities, advertising, administration, and so on.

- ✔ **What is the net income?** Also called earnings or net profit, net income is the *bottom line*. After paying for all expenses, what profit did the company make?

The information you glean should give you a strong idea about the company's current financial strength and whether it's successfully increasing sales, holding down expenses, and ultimately maintaining profitability. You can find out more about sales, expenses, and profits in the sections that follow.

Sales

Sales refers to the money that a company receives as customers buy its goods and/or services. It's a simple item on the income statement and a useful number to look at. Analyzing a company by looking at its sales is called *top line analysis.*

As an investor, you should take into consideration the following points about sales:

✓ **Sales should be increasing.** A healthy, growing company has growing sales. They should grow at least 10 percent from the prior year, and you should look at the most recent three years.

✓ **Core sales (sales of those products or services that the company specializes in) should be increasing.** Frequently, the sales figure has a lot of stuff lumped into it. Maybe the company sells widgets (what the heck is a widget, anyway?), but the core sales should not include other things, such as the sale of a building or other unusual items. Take a close look. Isolate the company's primary offerings and ask whether these sales are growing at a reasonable rate (such as 10 percent).

✓ **Does the company have odd items or odd ways of calculating sales?** In the late 1990s, many companies boosted their sales by aggressively offering affordable financing with easy repayment terms. Say you find out that Suspicious Sales Inc. (SSI) had annual sales of $50 million, reflecting a 25 percent increase from the year before. Looks great! But what if you find out that $20 million of that sales number comes from sales made on credit that the company extended to buyers? Some companies that use this approach later have to write off losses as uncollectible debt because the customer ultimately can't pay for the goods.

If you want to get a good clue whether a company is artificially boosting sales, check the company's *accounts receivable* (listed in the asset section of the company's balance sheet). Accounts receivable refers to money that is owed to the company for goods that customers have purchased on credit. If you find out that sales went up by $10 million (great!) but accounts receivable went up by $20 million (uh-oh), then something just isn't right. That may be a sign that the financing terms were too easy, and the company may have a problem collecting payment (especially in a recession).

Expenses

What a company spends has a direct relationship on its profitability. If spending isn't controlled or held at a sustainable level, it may spell trouble for a company.

When you look at a company's expense items, consider the following:

✔ **Compare expense items to the prior period.** Are expenses higher, lower, or about the same from the prior period? If the difference is significant, you should see commensurate benefits elsewhere. In other words, if overall expenses are 10 percent higher compared to the prior period, are sales at least 10 percent more during the same period?

✔ **Are some expenses too high?** Look at the individual expense items. Are they significantly higher than the year before? If so, why?

✔ **Have any unusual items been expensed?** Sometimes an unusual expense isn't necessarily a negative. Expenses may be higher than usual if a company writes off uncollectible accounts receivable as bad debt expense. Doing so inflates the total expenses and subsequently results in lower earnings. Pay attention to nonrecurring charges that show up on the income statement and determine whether they make sense.

Profit

Earnings or profit is the single most important item on the income statement. It's also the one that receives the most attention in the financial media. When a company makes a profit, it's usually reported as earnings per share (EPS). So if you hear that the XYZ Corporation beat last quarter's earnings by a penny, here's how to translate that news. Suppose that the company made $1 per share this quarter and 99 cents per share last quarter. If that company had 100 million shares of stock outstanding, then its profit this quarter is $100 million (the EPS times the number of shares outstanding), which is $1 million more than it made in the prior quarter ($1 million is one cent per share times 100 million shares).

Don't simply look at current earnings as an isolated figure. Always compare current earnings to earnings in past periods (usually a year). For example, if you're looking at a retailer's fourth quarter results, you can't compare that with the retailer's third quarter. Doing so is like comparing apples to oranges. What if the company usually does well during the December holidays but poorly in the fall? In that case, you don't get a fair comparison.

A strong company should show consistent earnings growth from the period (such as the year or the same quarter from the prior year) before, and you should check the period before that, too, so that you can determine whether earnings are consistently rising over time. Earnings growth is an important barometer of the company's potential growth and bodes well for the stock price.

When you look at earnings, here are some things to consider:

- **Total earnings:** This item is the most watched. Total earnings should grow year to year by at least 10 percent.

- **Operational earnings:** Break down the total earnings and look at a key subset — that portion of earnings derived from the company's core activity. Is the company continuing to make money from its primary goods and services?

- **Nonrecurring items:** Are earnings higher (or lower) than usual or than expected and why? Frequently, the difference results from items such as the sale of an asset or a large depreciation write-off.

I like to keep percentages as simple as possible. Ten percent is a good number because it's easy to calculate and it's a good benchmark. However, 5 percent isn't unacceptable if you're talking about tough times, such as a recession. Obviously, if sales, earnings, and/or net worth are hitting or passing 15 percent, that's great.

Tooling around with ratios

A ratio is a helpful numerical tool that you can use to find out the relationship between two or more figures found in the company's financial data. A ratio can add meaning to a number or put it in perspective. Ratios sound complicated, but they're easier to understand than you think.

Say that you're considering a stock investment and the company you're looking at has earnings of $1 million this year. You may think that's a nice profit, but in order for this amount to be meaningful, you have to compare it to something. What if you find out that the other companies in the industry (of similar size and scope) had earnings of $500 million? Does that change your thinking? Or what if you find out that the same company had earnings of $75 million in the prior period? Does that change your mind?

Two key ratios to be aware of include

- Price-to-earnings ratio (P/E)
- Price to sales ratio (PSR)

Every investor wants to find stocks that have a 20 percent average growth rate over the past five years and have a low P/E ratio (sounds like a dream). Use stock screening tools available for free on the Internet to do your research.

Many brokers have them at their Web sites (such as Charles Schwab at www.schwab.com and E*TRADE at www.etrade.com). Some excellent stock screening tools can also be found at Yahoo! (finance.yahoo.com), Business Week (www.businessweek.com), and Nasdaq (www.nasdaq.com). A *stock screening tool* lets you plug in numbers such as sales or earnings and ratios such as the P/E ratio or the debt to equity ratio and then click! Up come stocks that fit your criteria. This is a good starting point for serious investors. Check out Appendix B for even more on ratios.

Running into the P/E ratio

The price to earnings (P/E) ratio is very important in analyzing a potential stock investment because it's one of the most widely regarded barometers of a company's value, and it's usually reported along with the company's stock price in the financial page listing. The major significance of the P/E ratio is that it establishes a direct relationship between the bottom line of a company's operations — the earnings — and the stock price.

The *P* in P/E stands for the stock's current price. The *E* is for earnings per share (typically the most recent 12 months of earnings). The P/E ratio is also referred to as the "earnings multiple" or just "multiple."

 You calculate the P/E ratio by dividing the price of the stock by the earnings per share. If the price of a single share of stock is $10 and the earnings (on a per-share basis) are $1, then the P/E is 10. If the stock price goes to $35 per share and the earnings are unchanged, then the P/E is 35. Basically, the higher the P/E, the more you pay for the company's earnings.

Why would you buy stock in one company with a relatively high P/E ratio instead of investing in another company with a lower P/E ratio? Keep in mind that investors buy stocks based on expectations. They may bid up the price of the stock (subsequently raising the stock's P/E ratio) because they feel that the company will have increased earnings in the near future. Perhaps they feel that the company has great potential (a pending new invention or lucrative business deal) that will eventually make the company more profitable. More profitability in turn has a beneficial impact on the company's stock price. The danger with a high P/E is that if the company doesn't achieve the hopeful results, the stock price could fall.

You should look at two types of P/E ratios to get a balanced picture of the company's value:

- **Trailing P/E:** This P/E is the most frequently quoted because it deals with existing data. The trailing P/E uses the most recent 12 months of earnings in its calculation.

- **Forward P/E:** This P/E is based on projections or expectations of earnings in the coming 12-month period. Although this P/E may seem preferable because it looks into the near future, it's still considered an estimate that may or may not prove to be accurate.

The following example illustrates the importance of the P/E ratio. Say that you want to buy a business and I'm selling a business. If you come to me and say, "What do you have to offer?" I may say, "Have I got a deal for you! I operate a retail business downtown that sells spatulas. The business nets a cool $2,000 profit per year." You reluctantly say, "Uh, okay, what's the asking price for the business?" I reply, "You can have it for only $1 million! What do you say?"

If you're sane, odds are that you politely turn down that offer. Even though the business is profitable (a cool $2,000 a year), you'd be crazy to pay a million bucks for it. In other words, the business is way overvalued (too expensive for what you're getting in return for your investment dollars). The million dollars would generate a better rate of return elsewhere and probably with less risk. As for the business, the P/E ratio ($1 million divided by $2,000 = a P/E of 500) is outrageous. This is definitely a case of an overvalued company — and a lousy investment.

What if I offered the business for $12,000? Does that price make more sense? Yes. The P/E ratio is a more reasonable 6 ($12,000 divided by $2,000). In other words, the business pays for itself in about 6 years (versus 500 years in the prior example).

Looking at the P/E ratio offers a shortcut for investors asking the question, "Is this stock overvalued?" As a general rule, the lower the P/E, the safer (or more conservative) the stock is. The reverse is more noteworthy: The higher the P/E, the greater the risk.

When someone refers to a P/E as high or low, you have to ask the question, "Compared to what?" A P/E of 30 is considered very high for a large-cap electric utility but quite reasonable for a small-cap, high-technology firm. Keep in mind that phrases such as "large-cap" and "small-cap" are just a reference to the company's market value or size. "Cap" is short for capitalization (the total number of shares of stock outstanding times the share price).

The following basic points can help you evaluate P/E ratios:

- ✔ **Compare a company's P/E ratio with its industry.** Electric utility industry stocks generally have a P/E that hovers in the 9–14 range. Therefore, if you're considering an electric utility with a P/E of 45, then something is wrong with that utility.

- ✔ **Compare a company's P/E with the general market.** If you're looking at a small-cap stock on the Nasdaq that has a P/E of 100 but the average P/E for established companies on the Nasdaq is 40, find out why. You should also compare the stock's P/E ratio with the P/E ratio for major indexes such as the Dow Jones Industrial Average (DJIA), the Standard & Poor's 500 (S&P 500), and the Nasdaq Composite (for more on market indexes, see Chapter 5).

✔ Compare a company's current P/E with recent periods (such as this year versus last year). If it currently has a P/E ratio of 20 and it previously had a P/E ratio of 30, you know that either the stock price has declined or that earnings have risen. In this case, the stock is less likely to fall. That bodes well for the stock.

✔ Low P/E ratios aren't necessarily a sign of a bargain, but if you're looking at a stock for many other reasons that seem positive (solid sales, strong industry, and so on) and it also has a low P/E, that's a good sign.

✔ High P/E ratios aren't necessarily bad, but they do mean that you should investigate further. If a company is weak and the industry is shaky, heed the high P/E as a warning sign. Frequently, a high P/E ratio means that investors have bid up a stock price, anticipating future income. The problem is that if the anticipated income doesn't materialize, the stock price could fall.

✔ Watch out for a stock that doesn't have a P/E ratio. In other words, it may have a price (the P), but it doesn't have earnings (the E). No earnings means no P/E, meaning that you're better off avoiding it. Can you still make money buying a stock with no earnings? You can, but you aren't investing; you're speculating.

Stock	P/E Ratio	Stock Activity in in 1999	P/E Ratio in 2002 2000 and 2001
Cisco Systems	190	Stock price fell from $80 to $15	0
eBay	3,980	Stock price fell from $120 to $59	190
Yahoo!	896	Stock price fell from $240 to $18	0

Listening to a PSA about PSR

The price to sales ratio (PSR) is the company's stock price divided by its sales. Because the sales number is rarely expressed as a per-share figure, it's

Better safe than sorry

The stocks listed in the nearby table were among the high fliers in the late 1990s, but they came crashing back to earth within 24 months. As of January 2002, eBay's P/E fell to 190 (still too high), while Cisco and Yahoo! didn't have P/E ratios because they had losses (!) for the years 2000 and 2001. Yikes! For all three, the chances that the stocks may go lower are too great for serious investors. You're better off to wait and see whether their earnings improve.

easier to divide a company's total market value (see the section "Market value," earlier in this chapter, to find out what this term means) by its total sales for the last 12 months.

As a general rule, stock trading at a PSR of 1 or less is a reasonably priced stock worthy of your attention. For example, say that a company has sales of $1 billion and the stock has a total market value of $950 million. In that case, the PSR is 0.95. In other words, you can buy $1 of the company's sales for only 95 cents. All things being equal, that stock may be a bargain.

Analysts frequently use the PSR as an evaluation tool in the following circumstances:

- ✔ In tandem with other ratios to get a more well-rounded picture of the company and the stock.

- ✔ When you want an alternate way to value a company that doesn't have earnings.

- ✔ By analysts who want a true picture of the company's financial health, because sales are tougher for companies to manipulate than earnings, which are easier to manipulate.

- ✔ When you're considering a company offering products (versus services). PSR is more suitable for companies that sell items that are easily counted (such as products). Companies that make their money through loans, such as banks, aren't usually valued with a PSR because deriving a usable PSR for them is more difficult.

Compare the company's PSR with other companies in the same industry, along with the industry average, so that you get a better idea of the company's relative value.

Part III
Picking Winners

The 5th Wave   By Rich Tennant

"Oh Martin, you scared me half to death! Next time let me know when you're picking a new stock."

In this part . . .

Now that you have the basics down, it's time to become a pro at picking individual stocks. When you consider investing in a company, you need to know the key indications that a particular stock's price is going to rise. And because the stock market doesn't operate in a vacuum, I introduce general economic and political factors that can have a huge effect on the stock market. The chapters in this part steer you to key financial information and important company documents and show you how to interpret the information you find.

Chapter 11

Decoding Company Documents

· ·

In This Chapter

▶ Paging through an annual report

▶ Reviewing other sources of financial information

▶ Organizing your own research library

· ·

*G*ood grief. Financial documents. Some people would rather suck a hospital mop than read some dry corporate or government report. Yet, if you're serious about choosing stocks, you should be serious about your research. Fortunately, it's not as bad as you think (put away that disgusting mop). When you see that some basic research helps you build wealth, it gets easier.

In this chapter, I discuss the basic documents that you will come across (or should come across) most often in your investing life. These documents include essential information that all investors need to know, not only at the time of the initial investment decision, but also for as long as that stock remains in their portfolio.

If you plan to hold the stock for the long haul, reading the annual report and other reports covered in this chapter will be very helpful to you. If you intend to get rid of the stock soon or plan to hold it only for the short term, reading these reports diligently isn't that important.

Getting a Message from the Muckety-Muck: The Annual Report

When you're a regular stockholder, the company sends you its annual report. If you're not already a stockholder, contact the company's shareholder service department for a hard copy.

You can often view a company's annual report at its Web site. Any major search engine can help you find it. Downloading or printing the annual report should be easy.

You need to carefully analyze an annual report to find out the following:

- ✔ **You want to know how well the company is doing.** Are earnings higher, lower, or the same as the year before? How are sales doing? These numbers should be clearly presented in the financial section of the annual report.

- ✔ **You want to find out whether the company is making more money than it's spending.** How does the balance sheet look? Are assets higher or lower than the year before? Is debt growing, shrinking, or about the same as the year before? For more details on balance sheets, see Chapter 10.

- ✔ **You want to get an idea of management's strategic plan for the coming year.** How will management build on the company's success? This plan is usually covered in the beginning of the annual report — frequently in the letter from the chairman of the board.

Your task boils down to figuring out where the company has been, where it is now, and where it's going. As an investor, you don't need to read the annual report like a novel — from cover to cover. Instead, approach it like a newspaper and jump around to the relevant sections to get the answers you need to decide whether you should buy or hold on to the stock.

Analyzing the annual report's anatomy

Not every company puts its annual report together in exactly the same way — the style of presentation varies. Some annual reports have gorgeous graphics or actual coupons for the company's products, while others are in a standard black-and-white typeface with no cosmetic frills at all. But every annual report does include common basic content, such as the income statement and the balance sheet. The following sections present typical components of an average annual report. Keep in mind that every annual report may not have the sections in the same order.

Letter from the chairman of the board

The first thing you see is usually the letter from the chairman of the board. It's the "Dear Stockholder" letter that communicates views from the head muckety-muck. The chairman's letter is designed to put the best possible perspective on the company's operations during the past year. Be aware of this bias. If the company is doing well, the letter will certainly point it out. If the company is having hard times, the letter probably puts a positive spin on the company's difficulties. If the *Titanic* had an annual report, odds are that the letter would have reported, "Great news! A record number of our customers participated in our spontaneous moonlight swimming program. In addition, we confidently project no operating expenses whatsoever for the subsequent fiscal quarter." You get the point.

To get a good idea of what issues the company's management team feels are important and what goals they want to accomplish, keep the following questions in mind:

✔ What does the letter say about changing conditions in the company's business? How about in the industry?

✔ If any difficulties exist, does the letter communicate a clear and logical action plan (cutting costs, closing money-losing plants, and so on) to get the company back on a positive track?

✔ What is being highlighted and why? For example, is the company focusing on research and development for new products or on a new deal with China?

✔ Does the letter offer apologies for anything the company did? If, for example, the company fell short of sales expectations, does it offer a reason for the shortcoming?

✔ Did the company make (or will it make) new acquisitions or major developments (selling products to China or a new marketing agreement with a Fortune 500 company)?

The company's offerings

This section of an annual report can have various titles (such as "Sales and Marketing"), but it covers what the company sells. Whatever the company sells — products or services or both — understand what they are and why customers purchase them. If you don't understand what the company offers, then understanding how the company earns money, which is the driving force behind the company's stock, will be more difficult. Are the company's core or primary offerings selling well? If the earnings of McDonald's are holding steady, but earnings strictly from burgers and fries are fizzling, that's a cause for concern. If a company ceases making money from its specialty, you should become cautious. Here are some other questions to ask yourself:

✔ How does the company distribute its offerings? Through a Web site, malls, representatives, or some other means? Does it sell only to the U.S. market, or is its distribution international? The greater the distribution, the greater the sales and, ultimately, the higher the stock price.

✔ Are most of the sales to a definable marketplace? If, for example, most of the company's sales are to a war-torn or politically-unstable country, you should worry. If the company's customers aren't doing well, that has a direct impact on the company and, eventually, its stock.

✔ How are sales doing versus market standards? In other words, is the company doing better than the industry average? Is the company a market leader in what it offers? The company should be doing better than (or as well as) its peers in the industry. If the company is falling behind its competitors, that doesn't bode well for the stock in the long run.

✔ Does the report include information on the company's competitors and related matters? You should know who the company's competitors are because they have a direct effect on the company's success. If customers are choosing the competitor over your company, the slumping sales and earnings will ultimately hurt the stock's price.

Financial statements

Look over the various financial statements and find the relevant numbers. Every annual report should have (at the very least) a balance sheet and an income statement. Catching the important numbers on a financial statement isn't that difficult to do. However, it certainly helps when you pick up some basic accounting knowledge. Chapter 10 can give you more details on evaluating financial statements.

First, review the income statement (also known as the profit and loss statement, or simply P&L). The income statement gives you the company's sales, expenses, and the result (net income or net loss).

Look at the balance sheet. The balance sheet provides a snapshot of a point in time (annual reports usually provide a year-end balance sheet) that tells you what the company owns (assets), what it owes (liabilities), and the end result (net worth). For a healthy company, assets should always be greater than liabilities.

Carefully read the footnotes to the financial statements. Sometimes big changes are communicated in small print.

Summary of past financial figures

The summary of past financial figures gives you a snapshot of the company's overall long-term progress. How many years does the annual report summarize? Some reports summarize three years, while most do two years.

Management issues

The management issues section of an annual report includes a reporting of current trends and issues, such as new things happening in the industry, that affect the company. See whether you agree with management's assessment of economic and market conditions that affect the company's prospects. What significant developments in society does management perceive as affecting the company's operations? Does the report include information on current or pending lawsuits?

CPA opinion letter

Annual reports typically include comments from the company's independent accounting firm. It may be an opinion letter or a simple paragraph with the firm's views regarding the financial statements that were prepared.

The CPA opinion letter should offer an opinion about the accuracy of the financial data presented and how the statements were prepared. Check to see whether the letter includes any footnotes regarding changes in certain numbers or how they were reported. For example, a company that wants to report higher earnings may show depreciation done more conservatively versus a more aggressive method of depreciating. In any case, you should verify the numbers by looking at the company's 10K document filed with the SEC.

Company identity data

The company identity data section informs you about the company's subsidiaries (or lesser companies that it owns), brands, and addresses. It also contains standard data such as the headquarters location and names of directors and officers. Many reports also include data on the directors' and officers' positions in stock ownership at year-end.

Stock data

The stock data section may include a history of the stock price along with information such as what exchange the stock is listed on, the stock symbol, the company's dividend reinvestment plan (if any), and so on. It also includes information on stockholder services and whom to contact for further information.

Going through the proxy materials

As a shareholder (or stockholder — same thing), you're entitled to vote at the annual shareholders meeting. If you ever get the opportunity to attend one, do so. You get to meet other shareholders and ask questions of management and other company representatives. Usually, the shareholder services department provides you with complete details. At the meetings, shareholders vote on company matters, such as approving the new accounting firm or deciding whether a proposed merger with another company will go forward.

If you can't attend (which is usually true for the majority of shareholders), you can vote by proxy. *Voting by proxy* means essentially that you vote by mail. You indicate your votes on the proxy statement (or card) and authorize a representative to vote at the meeting on your behalf. The proxy statement is usually sent to all shareholders, along with the annual report, just before the meeting.

Getting a Second Opinion

A wealth of valuable information is available for your investing pursuits. The resources in this section are just a representative few — a good representation, though. The information and research they provide can be expensive if you buy or subscribe on your own, but fortunately, most of the resources mentioned are usually available in the business reference section of a well-stocked public library. To get a more balanced view of the company and its prospects, take a look at several different sources of information for the stocks you're researching.

Company documents filed with the SEC

The serious investor doesn't overlook the wealth of information that you can cull from documents filed with the Securities and Exchange Commission (SEC). Take the time and effort to review these documents because they offer great insight regarding the company's activities. Here's how to obtain the main documents that investors should be aware of:

- ✔ **Drop by the company itself.** Stockholder service departments keep these publicly available documents on hand and usually give them at no cost to interested parties.

- ✔ **Visit the SEC, either in person or online.** These documents are available for public viewing at the SEC offices. You can find out more by contacting the Securities and Exchange Commission, Publications Unit, 450 Fifth Street, N.W., Washington, DC 20549.

  At the SEC's Web site, www.sec.gov, you can check out EDGAR (Electronic Data Gathering, Analysis, and Retrieval system) to search public documents filed. It's a tremendous source of documents that date back to 1994. You can search, print, or download documents very easily. Documents can be located either by document number or keyword search.

- ✔ **Check out Public Registers Annual Report Service (www.prars.com).** This organization maintains an extensive collection of annual reports.

✔ **Review the Annual Report Service (www.annualreportservice. com).** This site maintains an extensive database of company annual reports.

✔ **Use *The Wall Street Journal* free annual report service.** If you read this newspaper's financial pages and see a company with the club symbol (like the one you see on a playing card), then you can order that company's annual report by calling 800-654-CLUB or visiting the Web site www.wsj.com.

Form 10K

Gee, how intimidating. Just the report name alone makes you scratch your head. To some people, 10K refers to running a race of 10 kilometers. But if you're reading (not running) a 10K, you may be wishing you were running one instead.

Form 10K is a report that companies must file with the SEC annually. It works like the annual report that you get from the company except that it probably provides more detailed financial information. It can be a little intimidating because it can be dry, cumbersome text. It's not exactly Shakespeare (although 10K reports would've also driven Lady Macbeth insane); then again, the data aren't laden with as much spin as the annual report the company sends to shareholders. Without going crazy, go through each section of the 10K. Take some extra time to scrutinize the section on financial data. Ask the same questions that you do when you're looking at the annual report. The following Web sites can help you make sense of 10K reports:

✔ FreeEDGAR (www.freeedgar.com)

✔ 10K Wizard (www.10Kwizard.com)

✔ Edgar Online, Inc. (www.edgar-online.com)

Form 10Q

This form is a quarterly report that gives you the same basic information as the 10K, but it details only three months' worth of activity. Because a long time can pass between 10Ks (after all, it is a year), don't wait 12 months to see how your company is progressing. Make a habit of seeing how the company is doing by comparing its recent 10Q with one that covers the same quarter last year. Is the profit higher or lower? How about sales? Debt?

Keep in mind that not every company has the same fiscal year. A company with a calendar year fiscal year (ending December 31) files a 10Q for each of the first three quarters and files a 10K for the final quarter. The company reports its fourth quarter data in the 10K, along with the statistics for the full year.

Insider reports

Two types of insiders exist: those who work within the company and those outside the company who have a significant (10 percent or more) ownership of company stock. Tracking insider activity is very profitable for investors who want to follow in the footsteps of the people who are in the know. See Chapter 19 for information about monitoring and benefiting from insider activity.

Every time an insider (such as the CEO or controller) buys or sells stock, the transaction has to be reported to the SEC. The insider actually reports the trade prior to transacting it. These reports become publicly available documents that allow you to see what the insiders are actually doing. Hearing what they say in public is one thing, but seeing what they're actually doing with their stock transactions is more important.

Value Line

The Value Line Investment Survey, one of many information products provided by Value Line Publishing, Inc., is considered a longtime favorite by many stock investing professionals. You can look it over at any library that has a good business reference department. In the *Survey,* Value Line covers the largest public companies and ranks them according to financial strength and several other key business factors. To get more information about Value Line, either head to the library or visit www.valueline.com.

Standard & Poor's

Another ubiquitous and venerable publisher is Standard & Poor's (S&P). Although it has a number of quality information products and services for both individual and institutional investors, the three you should take a look at include the following:

- ✔ **The S&P Stock Guide:** Available at many libraries, this guide comes out monthly and reports on stocks on the New York Stock Exchange, American Stock Exchange, and the largest firms listed on Nasdaq. It gives a succinct, two-page summary on each stock. It offers a snapshot of the company's current finances along with a brief history and commentary on the company's activities. This guide also rates the company based on its financial strength.

- ✔ **The S&P Industry Survey:** S&P gives detailed reports on the top industries, cramming a lot of information about a given industry in four to seven pages. This annual publication provides a nice summary of what's happened in the industry in the past 12 months, what the industry looks like today, and the prospects for the coming year. It also provides the important numbers (earnings, sales, and industry ranking) for the top 50 to 100 firms in the industry.

✔ **The S&P Bond Guide:** Yes, I know this book is about stocks. But a company's bond rating is invaluable for stock investors. S&P analyzes the strength of the bond issuer and ranks the bond for creditworthiness. If S&P looks at the company and gives it a high rating, you have added assurance that the company is financially strong. You want the company to have a bond rating of AAA, AA, or A because these ratings tell you that the company is "investment-grade." Check out S&P's Web site at www.standardandpoors.com.

Moody's Investment Service

Another stalwart publisher, Moody's offers vital research on stocks and bonds. *Moody's Handbook of Common Stocks* is usually available in the reference section of a well-stocked library. It offers stock and bond guides similar to S&P and also provides an independent bond rating service. A stock rated highly by both Moody's and S&P is a great place for investors hunting for value investments.

Brokerage reports: The good, the bad, and the ugly

Clint Eastwood, where are you? Traditionally, brokerage reports have been a good source of information for investors seeking informed opinions about stocks. And they still are, but in recent years some brokers have been penalized for biased reports. Brokers should never be the sole source of information. Otherwise, Clint may ask them whether they're lucky punks.

The good

Research departments at brokerage firms provide stock reports and make them available for their clients and investment publications. The firms' analysts and market strategists generally prepare these reports. Good research is critical, and brokerage reports can be very valuable. What better source of guidance than full-time experts backed up by million-dollar research departments? Brokerage reports have some strong points:

✔ The analysts are professionals who should understand the value of a company and its stock. They analyze and compare company data every day.

✔ They have at their disposal tremendous information and historical data that they can sift through to make informed decisions.

✔ If you have an account with the firm, you can usually access the information at no cost.

The bad

Well, brokerage reports may not be bad in every case, but at their worst, they're quite bad. Brokers make their money from commissions and investment banking fees (nothing bad here). However, they can find themselves in the awkward position of issuing brokerage reports on companies that are (or could be) customers for the brokerage firm that employs them (hmmm — could be bad). Frequently, this relationship can result in a brokerage report that paints an overly positive picture of a company that can be a bad investment (yup, that's bad).

Sometimes, good research can be compromised by conflicts of interest.

During 1998–2000, an overwhelming number of brokerage reports issued glowing praise of companies that were either mediocre or dubious. Investors bought up stocks such as tech stocks and Internet stocks. The sheer demand pushed up stock prices, which gave the appearance of genius to analysts' forecasts, yet they rose essentially as a self-fulfilling prophecy. The stocks were very overvalued and were cruisin' for a bruisin'. Analysts and investors were feeling lucky.

The ugly

Investors lost a ton of money (oooh, ugly). Money that people painstakingly accumulated over many years of work vanished in a matter of months as the bear market of 2000 hit (uglier). Retirees who had trusted the analysts saw nest eggs lose 40 to 70 percent in value (yikes, very ugly). In total, investors lost over $5 trillion during 2000–2002, much of it needlessly.

During that bear market, a record number of lawsuits and complaints were filed against brokerage firms. Wall Street and Main Street learned some tough lessons. Regarding research reports from brokerage firms, the following points can help you avoid getting a bad case of the uglies:

- Always ask yourself, "Is the provider of the report a biased source?" In other words, is the broker getting business in any way from the company they're recommending?

- Never, never, NEVER rely on just one source of information, especially if it's the same source that's selling you the stock or other investment.

- Do your research first before you rely on a brokerage report.

- Do your due diligence before you buy stocks anyway. Look at the chapters in Part 1 and Part 2 to understand your need for diversification, risk tolerance, and so on.

- Verify the information provided to you with a trip to the library or Web sites (see Appendix A). (Clint would be proud.)

Although I generally do not rely on Wall Street brokerage analysts, there are some independent investment analysts that I track. You'll find some of my favorites mentioned in Chapter 13.

Compiling Your Own Research Department

You don't need to spend an excessive amount of time or money, but you should maintain your own library of resources. You may only need one shelf (or a small amount of memory on your computer's hard drive). But why not have a few investment facts and resources at your fingertips? I maintain my own library loaded with books, magazines, newsletters, and tons of great stuff downloaded on my computer for easy search and reference. When you start your own collection, keep the following in mind:

- Keep some select newspapers. *Barron's, The Wall Street Journal,* and *Investor's Business Daily* regularly have some editions that are worth keeping. For example, *The Wall Street Journal* and *Investor's Business Daily* usually have a year-in-review issue that they do the first business week in January. *Barron's* has special issues reviewing brokers and financial Web sites.

- Subscribe to financial magazines. Publications such as *Forbes* magazine and *SmartMoney Magazine* offer great research and regularly review stocks, brokers, and resources for investors.

- Keep annual reports. Regarding the stocks that are the core holdings in your portfolio, keep all the annual reports (at the very least, the most recent three).

- Go to the library's business reference section periodically to stay updated. Hey, you pay the taxes that maintain the public library — you may as well use it to stay informed.

- The Internet (just bein' complete). The Web offers plenty of great sites to peruse, and I list some of the best in Appendix A.

 Financial reports are very important and easier to read than most people think. An investor can easily avoid a bad investment by simply noticing the data in what seems like a jumble of numbers. Figure out how to read them. For a great book to help you with reading financial reports (without needless technicality), check out *How to Read a Financial Report: Wringing Vital Signs Out of the Numbers,* 6th Edition, by John A. Tracy (Wiley).

Chapter 12

Analyzing Industries

* *

In This Chapter

▶ Understanding different categories of industries

▶ Highlighting some key industries

* *

Suppose that you have to bet your entire nest egg on a one-mile race. All you need to do is select a winning group. Your choices are the following:

Group A: A group of thoroughbred race horses

Group B: A group of overweight Elvis impersonators

Group C: A group of lethargic snails

This isn't a trick question, and you have one minute to answer. Notice that I didn't ask you to pick a single winner out of a giant mush of horses, Elvii, and snails; I only asked you to pick the winning group in the race. The obvious answer is the thoroughbred race horses (and, no, they weren't ridden by the overweight Elvis impersonators because that would take away from the eloquent point being made). In this example, even the slowest member of group A easily outdistances the fastest member of either group B or C.

Industries aren't equal, and life isn't fair. After all, if life was fair, Elvis would be alive and the impersonators wouldn't exist. Fortunately, picking stocks doesn't have to be as difficult as picking a winning racehorse. The basic point is that it's easier to pick a successful stock from a group of winners (a growing, vibrant industry). Understanding industries only enhances your stock-picking strategy.

A successful, long-term investor looks at the industry just as carefully as he looks at the individual stock. Luckily, choosing a winning industry to invest in is easier than choosing individual stocks. I know some investors who can pick a winning stock in a losing industry, and I also know investors who have chosen a losing stock in a winning industry (the former is far outnumbered by the latter). Just think how well you do when you choose a great stock in a great industry! Of course, if you repeatedly choose bad stocks in bad industries, then you may as well get out of the stock market altogether (maybe your calling is to instead be a celebrity impersonator!).

Badgering the Witness and Interrogating the Industries

Your common sense is an important tool in choosing industries with winning stocks. The following sections explore some of the most important questions to ask yourself when you're choosing an industry. Keep in mind that an industry isn't the same as a sector. Even some market pros use the two words almost interchangeably. A *sector* is basically a "mega-industry" or a group of interrelated industries. For example, pharmaceuticals and HMOs are each an industry, but both of them are part of the healthcare sector. Whereas an industry is typically a category of business that performs a precise activity (such as computer chips or trucking). Not all industries in a sector perform equally in the same market conditions.

Is the industry growing?

The question may seem too obvious, but you still need to ask it before you purchase stock. The saying "the trend is your friend" applies when choosing an industry in which to invest, as long as the trend is an upward one. If you look at three different stocks that are equal in every significant way but you find that stock A is in an industry growing 15 percent per year while the other two stocks are in industries that have either little growth or are shrinking, which stock would you choose?

Sometimes, the stock of a financially unsound or poorly run company goes up dramatically because the industry it's in is very exciting to the public. The most obvious example is Internet stocks from 1998–2000. Stocks such as Amazon.com shot up to incredible heights because investors thought the Internet was the place to be. Sooner or later, the measure of a successful company is its ability to be profitable. Serious investors look at the company's fundamentals (see Chapter 10 to find out how to do this) and the prospects for the industry's growth before settling on a particular stock.

To judge how well an industry is doing, various information sources monitor all the major industries and measure their progress. The more reliable sources include the following:

- ✔ MarketWatch (www.marketwatch.com)
- ✔ Standard & Poor's Industry Survey (www.standardpoor.com)
- ✔ Hoover's Industry Snapshots (www.hoovers.com)
- ✔ Yahoo! Industry News (www.industry.yahoo.com)
- ✔ Wall Street Journal (www.wsj.com)

The preceding sources generally give you in-depth information about the major industries. Visit their Web sites to read their current research and articles along with links to relevant sites for more details. The Wall Street Journal (published by Dow Jones & Co.), for example, publishes indexes for all the major sectors and industries so that you can get a useful snapshot of how well an industry is doing (including information about whether the stock is up or down and how it's performing year-to-date), and it updates its Web site daily.

Are the industry's products or services in demand?

Look at the products and services that an industry provides. Do they look like things that society will continue to want? Are products and services on the horizon that could replace them? Does the industry face a danger of potential obsolescence?

When evaluating future demand, look for a *sunrise industry,* which is one that is new or emerging or has promising appeal for the future. Good examples in recent years have been biotech and Internet companies. In contrast, a *sunset industry* is one that is either declining or has little potential for growth. For example, you probably shouldn't invest in the videocassette manufacturing industry as demand for DVDs increases. Owning stock in a strong, profitable company in a sunrise industry is obviously the most desirable choice.

Current research unveils the following megatrends:

- ✔ **The aging of America:** More senior citizens than ever before will be living in America. Because of this fact, financial and healthcare services will prosper.

- ✔ **Advances in high-technology:** Internet, telecom, medical, and biotechnology innovations will continue.

Ranking the industries

Standard and Poor's (S&P) Industry Survey is an excellent source of information on America's industries. Besides ranking and comparing industries and informing you about their current prospects, the survey also lists the top companies by size, sales, earnings, and other key information. The survey and other S&P publications are available in the business reference section of most libraries (or at the S&P Web site at `www.standardpoor.com`). What I like is that each industry is covered in a few pages. You get the critical information you need without reading a novel.

- ✔ **Increasing need for basic materials:** As society advances here and in the rest of the world, building blocks such as metals and other precious commodities will be in demand.

- ✔ **Security concerns:** Terrorism and other international tensions mean more attention for national defense, homeland security, and related matters.

- ✔ **Energy challenges:** Traditional and nontraditional sources of energy (such as solar, fuel cells, and so on) will demand society's attention as it faces Peak Oil.

What does the industry's growth rely on?

An industry doesn't exist in a vacuum. External factors weigh heavily on its ability to survive and thrive. Does the industry rely on an established megatrend, in which case it will probably be strong for a while, or on factors that are losing relevance? Technological and demographic changes are other factors that may contribute to an industry's growth.

Perhaps the industry offers great new medical products for senior citizens. What are the prospects for growth? The graying of America is an established megatrend. As millions of Americans climb past age 50, profitable opportunities await companies that are prepared to cater to them.

Is this industry dependent on another industry?

This twist on the prior question is a reminder that industries frequently are intertwined and can become codependent. When one industry suffers, you may find it helpful to understand which industries will subsequently suffer. The reverse can also be true — when one industry is doing well, other industries may also reap the benefits.

In either case, if the stock you choose is in an industry that's highly dependent on other industries, you should know about it. If you're considering stocks of resort companies and you see the headlines blaring "Airlines losing money as public stops flying," what do you do? This type of question forces you to think logically and consider cause and effect. Logic and common sense are powerful tools that frequently trump all the number-crunching activity performed by analysts.

Who are the leading companies in the industry?

After you've chosen the industry, what types of companies do you want to invest in? You can choose from two basic types of companies:

- ✓ **Established leaders:** These companies are considered industry leaders or have a large share of the market. Investing in these companies is the safer way to go; what better investment for novice investors than companies that have already proven themselves?

- ✓ **Innovators:** If the industry is hot and you want to be more aggressive in your approach, investigate companies that offer new products, patents, or new technologies. These companies are probably smaller but have a greater potential for growth in a proven industry.

Is the industry a target of government action?

You need to know whether the government is targeting an industry because intervention by politicians and bureaucrats (rightly or wrongly) can have an impact on an industry's economic situation. For example, would you invest in a tobacco company now that the government has issued all of its regulations and warnings?

Investors need to take heed when political "noise" starts coming out about a particular industry. An industry can be hurt either by direct government intervention or by the threat of it. Intervention can take the form of lawsuits, investigations, taxes, regulations, or sometimes an outright ban. In any case, being on the wrong end of government intervention is the greatest external threat to a company's survival.

Sometimes, government action helps an industry. Generally, beneficial action takes two forms:

- ✓ **Deregulation and/or tax decreases:** Government sometimes reduces burdens on an industry. In 1979, the federal government deregulated the airlines, an action that in turn caused a boom in travel. The airline industry subsequently experienced tremendous growth because more people flew than ever before. This increase in the number of airline passengers, in turn, spurred growth for the lodging and resort industries. Likewise, telecom deregulation in the mid-1990s helped that industry to boom.

✔ **Direct funding:** Government has the power to steer taxpayer money toward business as well. In the 1970s, when Chrysler was floundering, financing assistance helped the company get back on its feet, and Chrysler did well during the 1980s. Direct funding may be good for the business receiving funds, but the problem is that consumers (taxpayers) are forced to subsidize a failing enterprise.

Which category does the industry fall into?

Most industries can neatly be placed in one of two categories: cyclical and defensive. In a rough way, these categories generally translate into what society wants and what it needs. Society buys what it *needs* in both good and bad times. It buys what it *wants* when times are good and holds off when times are bad. A need is a "must have" while a want is a "like to have." Kapish?

Cyclical industries

Cyclical industries are industries whose fortunes rise and fall with the economy's rise and fall. In other words, if the economy is doing well and the stock market is doing well, cyclical industries tend to do well. When the economy is doing well, consumers and investors are confident and tend to spend and invest more money than usual. Real estate and automobiles are great examples of cyclical industries.

Your own situation offers you some common-sense insight into the concept of cyclical industries. Think about your behavior as a consumer, and you get a great clue into the thinking of millions of consumers. Think about the times you felt good about your career and your finances. When you (and millions of others) feel good about money and about the future, you have a greater tendency to buy more (and/or more expensive) stuff. When people feel financially strong, they're more apt to buy a new house or car or make some other large financial commitment. Also, people take on more debt because they feel

---

It takes money to spend money

The economic boom of the late 1990s was in many respects due to an explosion of spending financed by debt. Consumers and businesses felt great about the economy's expansion and spent money accordingly. Among the winning industries were automobiles, real estate, and technology. Choosing strong stocks in these categories meant tremendous profits for investors who did their homework.

confident that they can pay it back. In light of this behavior, what industries do you think would do well?

The same point also holds for business spending. When businesses think that economic times are good and foresee continuing good times, they tend to spend more money on large purchases such as new equipment or technology. They think that when they're doing well and flush with financial success, it's a good idea to reinvest that money to increase future success.

Defensive industries

Defensive industries are industries that produce goods and services that are needed no matter what's happening in the economy. Your common sense kicks in here. What do you still buy even when times are tough? Think about what millions of people buy no matter how bad the economy gets. A good example is food. People still need to eat regardless of good or bad times. Other examples of defensive industries are utilities and healthcare.

In bad economic times, defensive stocks tend to do better than cyclical stocks. However, when times are good, cyclical stocks tend to do better than defensive stocks. Defensive stocks don't do as well in good times because people don't eat twice as much or use up more electricity.

So how do defensive stocks grow? Their growth generally relies on two factors:

✔ **Population growth:** As more and more consumers are born, more people become available to buy.

✔ **New markets:** A company can grow by seeking out new groups of consumers who can buy their products and services. Coca-Cola, for example, found new markets in Asia during the 1990s. As Communist regimes fell from power and more societies embraced a free market and consumer goods, the company sold more beverages, and its stock soared.

 One way stock investors can invest in a particular industry is to take advantage of Exchange Traded Funds (ETFs), which have become very popular in recent years. If you find a winning industry but you can't find a winning stock (or don't want to bother with the necessary research), then ETFs are a great consideration.

Outlining Key Industries

Not all industries go up and down in tandem. Indeed, at any given time, some industry is successful no matter what's happening with the general economy. In fact, investors have made a lot of money simply by choosing an industry that benefits from economic trends.

For example, the economy was in bad shape during the 1970s. It was a period of *stagflation* — low growth, high unemployment, and high inflation. This decade was the worst time for the economy since the Great Depression; most industries (and therefore most stocks) were having tough times. But some industries did well; in fact, some flourished. Real estate and precious metals, for example, performed well in this environment. Because the inflation rate soared into double digits, inflationary hedges such as gold and silver did very well. During the '70s, gold skyrocketed from $35 an ounce to $850 an ounce by the end of the decade. Silver went from under $2 to over $50 in the same period. What do you think happened to stocks of gold and silver mining companies? That's right. They skyrocketed as well. Gold stocks gave investors spectacular returns.

In the 1980s, the economy became rejuvenated when taxes were cut, regulations were decreased, and inflation fell. Most industries did well. But even in a growing economy, some industries struggle. Examples of industries that struggled during that time included precious metals and energy stocks.

Now fast forward to 2005. Think about those industries that struggled and those that did well. Natural resources (energy, commodities, and so on) and real estate have done very well in recent years. In the same time frame, industries such as airlines have had a rough time. Choosing the right industries (or avoiding the wrong) has always been a major factor in successful stock picking.

For sale

I include real estate as a key industry because it's a cyclical *bellwether industry* (one that has a great effect on many other industries that may be dependent on it). It's looked at as a key component of economic health because so many other industries, including building materials, mortgages, household appliances, and contract labor services, are tied to it. When the real estate industry is booming, that bodes well for much of the economy.

Housing starts are one way to measure real estate activity. This data is an important leading indicator of health in the industry. Housing starts indicate new construction, which means more business for related industries.

Keep an eye on the real estate industry for negative news that could be bearish for the economy and the stock market. Because real estate is purchased with mortgage money, investors and analysts watch the mortgage market for trouble signs such as rising delinquencies and foreclosures. These statistics serve as a warning for general economic weakness. During 2002–2005, the real estate industry showed tremendous growth primarily driven by credit. In April 2005, housing sales hit a record high, but smart investors are exercising caution because there's growing evidence of a mania. A "mania" is typically the final part of a mature bull market. In a mania, the prices of the assets experiencing the bull market (such as stock or real estate) are skyrocketing to extreme levels, which excite more and more investors as they jump in. As more investors pile in, this causes the prices to rise even further. It gets to the point where seemingly everyone thinks that getting rich by buying this particular asset is easy and almost no one notices that the market has become unsustainable. After prices are exhausted and start to level off, investor excitement dies down and then investors try to exit by selling their holdings to realize some profit. As more and more sell off their holdings, demand decreases while supply increases. The mania disappears and the bear market has appeared.

Baby, you can drive my car

The auto industry is another business that you want to watch very carefully. When cars are selling well, you can generally interpret that as a positive indicator for the economy. People buy new cars when they're doing well. Autos are big-ticket items that are another barometer of people's economic well-being.

Conversely, trouble in the auto industry is a red flag for trouble in the general economy. If auto repossessions and car loan delinquencies are rising, that's a warning about general economic weakness. In early 2005, some weakness definitely showed up in the auto industry as GM and Ford continued to have financial troubles.

Thanking Mr. Roboto

In recent years, technology became very popular with investors. Indeed, it's a great sector, and its impact on the economy's present and future success can't be underestimated. The price of shares of technology companies can rise substantially because investors buy them based on expectations — today's untested, unproven companies may become the Microsofts and IBMs of tomorrow. In spite of the sector's potential, companies can still fail if customers don't embrace their products. Even in technology stocks, you still must apply the rules and guidelines that I discuss throughout this book about financially successful companies. Pick the best in a growing industry, and you'll succeed over the long haul. Because technology still hasn't recovered from its recent bear market, weakness in the industry means that investors need to be very picky and cautious.

Banking on it

Banking and financial services are an intrinsic part of any economy. Debt is the most telling sign of this industry for investors. If a company's debt is growing faster than the economy, you need to watch to see how it will impact its stocks and mutual funds. If debt gets out of control, it can be disastrous for the economy. As credit specialist Doug Noland points out (his column is found at www.prudentbear.com), the amount of debt and debt-related securities recently reached historic and troublesome levels. This trend means that many financial stocks are at risk if a recession hits anytime soon.

Chapter 13

Emerging Sector Opportunities

I'm thrilled to include this chapter in the 2nd edition of *Stock Investing For Dummies*. Yes, you can do your own research (and you want to, don't you?), but I may as well make you privy to what my research tells me are the unfolding megatrends that offer the greatest potential rewards for stock investors.

Only a handful of changes in your portfolio over the past four decades would have made you tremendously rich. Had you put your money into natural resources (such as gold, silver, and oil) at the beginning of the 1970s and stayed put until the end of the decade, you would have made a fortune. Then had you cashed in and switched to Japanese stocks in 1980 and held them for the rest of the decade, you would have made another fortune. Then had you switched in 1990 to U.S. stocks for the entire decade, you would have made yet another fortune. What if you had cashed in your stocks in 2000? Well, for starters, you would have avoided huge losses in the bear market. How about being bullish? What looks like a strong bull market for this decade?

By and large, this decade seems to be a repeat of the '70s. The general realm of natural resources looks to be the primary bull market for this decade. Why? First, look at what this decade has in common with the '70s:

✔ Problems with energy (rising costs, supply disruptions, and so on)

✔ Rising inflation (as the dollar loses value versus other currencies)

✔ International conflict (Iraq, Afghanistan, Iran, and so on)

✔ Sluggish domestic economy

✔ Rising prices for natural resources (grains, metals, lumber, and so on)

However, this decade has more to consider, including the following:

- ✔ Debt, debt, and more debt ($43 trillion as of July 2005 — three and a half times the U.S. GDP total of $12 trillion)

- ✔ The U.S. as a major importer (versus being an exporter in the '70s)

- ✔ China and India as major economic competitors

- ✔ Terrorism affecting the U.S. within its borders

- ✔ $372 trillion worth of derivatives (nine times larger than the world's total GDP! Much of these derivatives are very arcane and risky.)

- ✔ Social Security & Medicare liabilities (Rising costs start in 2008 as the oldest baby boomers start to retire)

This list isn't comprehensive (due to space limitations). The above points are enough to make you understand that this investing environment has changed dramatically and you need to re-focus your overall game plan to keep your money growing.

By the way, you'll see two types of opportunities in this chapter: bullish and bearish. (See Chapter 15 for more information on bullish and bearish markets.) If I can't help you find the winning stocks, then by golly I can show you what losers to stay away from.

Bullish Opportunities

Being bullish (or going "long") is the natural inclination for most investors. It's an easy concept; buy low, sell high. No rocket science there. The following sections don't identify every bullish opportunity, but they do cover the most obvious ones (at least to me).

Commodities: Feeding and housing the world

What will have a mega-impact on the world can be boiled down to two words: China and India. In the past ten years, these two countries have put their economies on the fast track. Consider the following:

- ✔ They have generally turned away from Socialism and a "command economy" and have instead turned to a free market or more capitalistic system.

✔ Industrialization, privatization, and profit incentives have ignited tremendous booms in those countries.

✔ Both countries' populations have continued to grow. China has about 1.5 billion people while India recently surpassed 1 billion.

What do these facts mean for stock investors?

Somebody's got to sell them what they need. China, for example, has a voracious appetite for natural resources such as building materials, energy, copper, grain, and so on. Companies that have provided the goods and services needed do very well. Phelps Dodge Corp., for example, produces copper and other materials and base metals necessary for industry. In early 2003, its share price was under $30. By August 2005, it was at $110 (up a sizzling 266 percent). Compare that performance against a benchmark such as the S&P 500. During the same time frame, the S&P 500 was basically flat. Another great example is Archer Daniels Midland Co. It processes and merchandises agricultural commodities and products. In early 2003, you could have bought its stock for about $10 per share. By the summer of 2005, it hit $22 (an increase of 120 percent). While many (most?) investors saw their portfolios go up a little, down a little, or "flatline," resource investors saw their stocks do very well.

Of course, China and India are only a part of the world's emerging markets, but they're certainly the most important to Americans (in terms of economic impact). They are indeed "megatrends" that will either help (or hurt) your portfolio. In the coming years, demand will likely continue to be strong, and investors will see the obvious positive implications for solid companies that meet this demand.

To find out more, check out the resources in Appendix A, such as Jim Rogers's book entitled *Hot Commodities.* You can also conduct research at sites such as www.futuresource.com, the commodities section of www.marketwatch. com, and www.bloomberg.com.

Energy

Recent headlines tell me that the costs of energy are a major challenge for the economy. For decades, U.S. society has benefited from cheap oil, but global supply and demand (among other things) has caught up with us. A barrel of oil has gone from $42 in January 2005 to about $67 by August 2005 (nearly a 60 percent increase!). A gallon of gas has seen a similar meteoric rise. A major news item has been the condition called "Peak Oil" (for more on this condition, check out the sidebar "Taking a peek at Peak Oil," later in this chapter). Energy investors must become familiar with this condition because it has (and will) weigh very heavily on the economy, because people are so dependent on oil for their modern lifestyle. The days of cheap oil are now history. Higher energy prices will affect all stocks. If you're going to pay more for energy, then you may as well benefit.

As energy prices have risen strongly over the past few years, how have stocks fared? The general stock market (as represented by the Dow Jones Industrial Average and the S&P 500 index) has done little, say from 2003 to mid-2005. How about energy stocks? Look at major stocks such as Exxon Mobil Corp. You could have invested in this company in 2003 for about $35 per share (and you'd get a nice fat dividend, too). By August 2005, the stock hit $60 (a gain of 71 percent, not including dividends).

Compare Exxon Mobil with a tech stock like Dell (a former high-flying growth stock). In that same time frame, Dell went from about $31 to $36 (a modest gain of 16 percent, and it had no dividends). Well, at least it grew.

The bottom line is that stock investors will either have to consider energy in their investment strategies or risk having energy prices steamroll over their potential gains. Investment opportunities are plentiful in companies that provide, sell, distribute, or explore energy. But you may want to consider energy alternatives as well. America and the world will be forced to turn to alternative energy sources in the coming years. As conventional oil and gas become scarce, America will look into gaining energy from sources such as Canada's oil sands and also to sources such as wind, solar, and fuel cell technologies, among others.

As you read this chapter, you may not be sure about what particular company you should invest in. If that's the case, why not consider a convenient way to invest in an entire industry or sector? A good consideration is an Exchange Traded Fund (ETF). An ETF is like buying a whole portfolio of stocks as if it was a single stock. An example is an ETF with the symbol XLE. XLE has a cross section of the largest public oil and gas companies such as Exxon Mobil, Chevron, and others. In 2003, I bought this XLE for $18 per share. By August 2005, it hit $50. To find out more about ETFs, go to the American Stock Exchange (www.amex.com) for all the details.

Gold

Over the ages, gold has come to be synonymous with wealth. In modern times it has become known as an inflation hedge and "investment insurance," especially during times of inflation and geopolitical uncertainty. After being in a 20-year bear market (from its market top of $850 in 1980 to its low of $252 in 2000), conditions are ripe in the marketplace for a gold bull market that could reach or surpass its old high. Aggressive investors should be investigating gold stocks. Why now?

Taking a peek at Peak Oil

In the late 1950s and early 1960s, geologist Marion King Hubbert conducted landmark studies related to the global supply of oil. His research indicated that the life of a particular underground reserve of oil goes through two phases. During the first phase, the oil can be easily and inexpensively extracted. However, after you get past the 50 percent mark, the remaining oil is very difficult (and hence very expensive) to extract. That 50 percent mark has come to be known as "Hubbert's Peak" and experts have come to call this condition Peak Oil.

Hubbert correctly made forecasts of when the major oil-producing countries of the world would hit this peak. So far the forecasts have been accurate. The United States hit Hubbert's Peak in the early 1970s (American dependence on foreign oil grew significantly after that). Current industry research suggests that all the major oil-producing countries will reach their peak either now or before the end of this decade. To find out more about Peak Oil, check out Web sites such as the Association for the Study of Peak Oil & Gas (www.peakoil.net).

According to many (if not most) gold market analysts, such as Bill Murphy of the Gold Anti-Trust Action Committee (www.gata.org), and sites that specialize on the gold market, such as www.LeMetropoleCafe.com, www.gold-eagle.com, and www.kitco.com, the fundamentals for gold are more bullish than ever. In recent years, demand has begun to significantly exceed supply. The shortfall has been filled from gold sales by central banks. Because of continued and growing demand both in the U.S. and abroad (most notably India and China), total worldwide annual demand is outstripping supply by anywhere from 1000–2000 tons (depending on whose estimates you believe). Juxtapose this demand with current economic conditions (such as the declining value of the dollar and other paper currencies) and geopolitical instability, and it's easy to see that gold and gold-related investments (such as gold stocks) show bullish potential.

Because gold does well in an inflationary environment, understanding inflation itself is important. Inflation isn't the price of things going up; it's the value of the currency itself going down. The reason it goes down in value is primarily due to the fact that the government can print money at will ("the money supply"). When you significantly increase the money supply, you create a bullish environment for hard assets such as gold.

Gold analysts such as Bill Murphy, Doug Casey, Jay Taylor, James Sinclair, and many others easily see the gold price hitting four figures in the not-too-distant future. In that case, gold mining stocks would perform fantastically well (not unlike their heyday in the late 1970s). For conservative investors, consider the large, established mining firms such as Newmont Mining (NEM) or Gold Corp. (GG). For the more daring, consider junior mining stocks. Do your research with the Web sites mentioned in this segment.

A common practice in the mining industry in recent years has been the practice of forward selling (also called "hedging"). Forward selling is the process in which a company sells next year's production at a locked-in price today. The benefit for the company is that it makes money even if next year's gold price stays stable or goes down. However, if gold rises next year, the company loses out on the potential profit. Since 2000, as gold went from $252 per ounce all the way to $439 in August 2005 (a 74 percent rise), most un-hedged gold companies saw their stocks double and triple in the same time frame. In comparison, hedged gold companies either went up more modestly or not at all. Some companies even went bankrupt because of hedging.

Silver

I could easily have lumped silver in with gold and just labeled the section "precious metals," but I think that silver merits special attention. Out of all the precious metals (and base metals) that I've analyzed, silver probably has the strongest potential. Why? Demand for silver is strong and growing stronger for various reasons (including investment, jewelry, industrial, and so on). Yet the above-ground supply of silver has been shrinking for more than two decades. In fact, silver has been experiencing a chronic deficit for more than a decade. The U.S. government, for example, had over 1 billion ounces inventoried as a strategic stockpile. That inventory was depleted as of early 2004.

Although some point out that silver's primary use in industry (photography) is shrinking due to the growing popularity of digital photography, silver demand has been growing significantly in healthcare, electronics, and military equipment. For these reasons, the supply and demand fundamentals are outstanding. As a matter of fact, silver is more rare than gold. As the market catches on, silver's current modest bull market can easily become a "raging bull." Here are some bullish factors facing silver in 2005 and beyond:

- ✔ 43 million oz. deficit according to XYZ industry report
- ✔ Major sources of supply are disappearing (China is now an importer)

What's the potential for stock investors? One way to look at silver today is to take a look at the last great silver bull market and see how silver stocks performed. In the late 1970s, silver soared from $2 per ounce all the way to $52 per ounce by 1980. In 1975, investors could have bought Lion Mines Co. for only 7 cents per share. As silver hit its high in 1980, Lion Mines stock hit an astounding $380 per share. That means that $184 worth of stock in 1975 could have been worth $1 million only five years later (talk about your silver lining!).

If silver and silver stocks interest you, do your homework. The most widely followed silver analysts are Ted Butler and David Morgan. The most comprehensive Web sites on silver are www.silver-investor.com and www.silverstrategies.com.

Healthcare

I'm sure that you've heard much about the "graying of America." This phrase obviously represents a firm megatrend in place. For stock investors, this megatrend is a purely demographic play and the "numbers" are with you. The number of people who are over the age of 50, and especially those considered "senior citizens," are the fastest growing segment of American society. The same megatrend is in place in all corners of the world (especially Europe). As more and more people get into this category, the idea that companies that serve this segment will also prosper becomes a no-brainer. Well-managed companies that run nursing homes and eldercare services will see their stocks rise.

Be careful about what healthcare firms you select because this sector can include stocks that are defensive and also some that are cyclical. Companies that sell expensive equipment (such as CAT scans or MRI technology) may not do that well in an economic downturn because hospitals and other healthcare facilities may not want to upgrade or replace their equipment. Therefore, healthcare companies that sell big-ticket items can be considered cyclical. On the other hand, companies that sell medicine (pharmaceuticals) can be considered defensive. People who need medicine (such as aspirin or antacids) will buy it no matter how bad the economy is. In fact, people will probably buy even more aspirin and antacids in bad economic times.

Also be wary of political trends as they affect healthcare. America may be slowly lurching toward socialized medicine. If this possibility develops, then turn your bullish expectations into bearish ones. History (and my experience) tells me that a government takeover of an industry like healthcare spells danger for investors (and patients, too).

To find out more about healthcare opportunities, check out the industry and main stocks by using the resources in Appendix A.

National Security

The horrific events of September 11, 2001, remind the world how vulnerable America is as a free and open society. It has been a brave, new world since. Americans watch their TV screens and listen to their radios to discover that terrorism's wretched tentacles reach across the globe. The most obvious way the country can respond is to increase security at home while deploying forces across the world to combat terrorists and tangle with the countries that support them. Foes of the U.S. aren't singular nations that are easily defined, fought, and defeated within a few months or a few years. Instead, they're implacable and virulent, and they're spread out over many countries.

Securing the nation becomes an unprecedented undertaking. The largest new federal bureaucracy is Homeland Security. Funding for security measures and for military needs is huge and "getting huger" for the foreseeable future. Because American industry predominantly provides the goods and services necessary in this extensive national security effort, stock investors should take notice.

Look at select stocks that serve national defense needs. A good example is General Dynamics Corporation (GD). In the fall of 2001, the stock was at $60, and it surpassed $115 by mid-2005 (a 92 percent gain four years later). Another is Alliant Techsystems, Inc. (ATK), a provider of munitions and defense systems. Its stock right after 9/11 was about $20. By mid-2005, ATK was at $76 (a gain of $56 per share or 280 percent in only four years).

As America continues to re-tool its military and as it continues to seek ways to monitor, track, and attack terrorists, that (unfortunately) bodes well for companies in the right products and services. For publications that do a great job informing investors and speculators regarding "the war economy," check out the U.S. & World Early Warning Report (www.chaostan.com).

Bearish Outlook

Stocks are versatile in that you can even make money when they go down in value. Techniques range from "using put options" to "going short" or doing a short sale of stock. (See Chapter 17 regarding "going short," and find out more about put options at www.cboe.com.) For traditional investors, the more appropriate strategy is first and foremost to "avoid or minimize losses." Making money betting that a stock will fall is closer to speculating than actual investing. So all I want is that investors see the pitfalls and act accordingly. The following sections offer cautionary alerts to keep you away from troubled areas in the economy (or find speculative opportunities to short stocks).

Warning on housing

Real estate investing has been all the rage in recent years. As I do my seminars across the country, I see the adult education programs top-heavy in real estate courses. "How to Get Rich in Real Estate." "Buy Real Estate with No Money Down." But I think "Real Estate Meets Frankenstein" is more like it.

In the old days, when asked the question about how to be successful invest-ing in real estate, the answer was always "location, location, location." In this decade, that answer has morphed into "credit, credit, credit," which — if you're not careful — is really "debt, debt, debt." You come to see that the housing bubble isn't really a problem; it's a symptom. If it is a symptom, then what is the problem? The problem with real estate in recent years has really been too much debt, very lax lending standards, and rampant speculation. By the second quarter of 2005, the data clearly shows a real estate market that's overheated, overpriced, seriously imbalanced, and plainly unsustainable.

Most mortgages issued have been either adjustable rate mortgages (ARMs), interest-only mortgages, or negative amortization mortgages. In the latter two mortgages, buyers only pay interest and put no dent into the principal. In addition, many of these mortgages are being issued to buyers who are "sub-prime," which means that their credit is less than strong, so to speak. These people have purchased a house and used "creative" financing to lower the monthly payment. When interest rates (and other costs such as real estate taxes) rise, millions of over-burdened property owners will have financial problems and this will have a negative effect on the overall economy.

On top of that, many of these mortgages are issued at 100 percent of the property's market value. When you add up these troublesome mortgages, they easily exceed $2 trillion. The value of all mortgages now exceeds 80 per-cent of the value of America's GDP. Some analysts will tell you that this isn't a problem because "the economy is strong and job growth is good." What they don't see is that during 2004–2005, the economy's GDP expanded primarily due to real estate. And real estate (and related industries) accounted for 43 percent of the jobs created since 2001. As housing & construction begin to decline due to overbuilding (more supply) and fewer buyers (lower demand), that means a shrinking real estate market and fewer jobs. As the housing market gets into trouble, this will harm the economy. As the robot on the old TV show "Lost in Space" used to say, "Warning Will Robinson! Danger! Danger!"

What should stock investors be looking at? The most obvious thing to look at is housing stocks. The stock market tends to be a leading indicator of how well (or how poorly) the economy is doing. Frequently, subsections of the stock market give you clues about a particular industry. Housing stocks (as of August 2005) have come down substantially from their highs in July 2005. Among the first things I ask myself about the direction of an industry is "How are insiders behaving in the main companies of that industry?"

During 2000–2005, as real estate was on a blazing hot streak, the home build-ing stocks were also very bullish. A good example was Toll Brothers (TOL). That stock was on a meteoric rise during the 12-month period ending in mid-2005. From July to July, it went from $20 (price adjusted for split) to $57 — a gain of 185 percent! Guess what? In July '05, most of the insiders sold their stock. By August 2005, the stock was already down more than 20 percent. Hmmm. Coincidence? I think not! Homebuilders are among the first to see what's going on in their industry. Similar events occurred at other companies in the industry. The industry has probably hit its peak and sales will soften. Saying that its torrid pace is over is probably safe. What's a stock investor to do?

First of all, be safe. Minimize exposure to this vulnerable sector. I'm not just talking about real estate directly, but also indirectly. Companies and industries that are reliant on the housing sector are also at risk, such as some financial institutions, suppliers, and so on. For those of you who are aggressive, bearish strategies (like going short or, even better, buying put options) are a good speculation. To find out more about what's going on with this historic and gigantic housing bubble, check out some great Web sites, such as www.housingbubble.blogspot.com and www.realestatebubble.net.

The great credit monster

Too much debt means that someone will get hurt. As the unprecedented explosion in debt gave a huge "boost" to the economy in the late 1990s, it now poses great dangers for the rest of this decade. This massive debt problem is obviously tied to the previous topic of real estate. However, it goes much further. Individuals, companies, and government agencies are carrying too much debt for comfort. It's not just mortgage debt; it's also consumer, business, government, and margin debt. With total debt now in the vicinity of 40–43 trillion dollars, saying that a lot of this debt won't be repaid is probably a safe bet. Individual and institutional defaults will rock the economy and the financial markets. Bankruptcy will be a huge issue (in spite of bankruptcy reforms that became law on October 17, 2005).

Debt will (does) weigh heavily on stocks either directly or indirectly. Because every type of debt is now at record levels, no one is truly immune. Say the stock you have is in a retailer that has no debt whatsoever. Are you immune? Not really, because consumer debt (credit cards, personal loans, and so on) is at an all-time high. If consumer spending declines, then the retailer's sales go down, its profits shrink, and . . . ultimately . . . its stock goes down.

Exposure to debt is quite pervasive. Check your 401(k) plan, your bond funds, and your insurance company's annuity. Why? Remember those mortgages I spoke about earlier in this chapter? Banks and mortgage companies issued trillions of dollars worth of those mortgages in recent years. But after the mortgages were issued, they were sold to other financial institutions. Huge amounts were sold to the most obvious buyers, the Federal National Mortgage Association (FNM) and the Federal Mortgage Assurance Corporation (FRE). These giant government-sponsored entities are usually referred to as "Fannie Mae" and "Freddie Mac." They hold many mortgages but they also package and resell these mortgages to third parties, such as pension plans, corporations, and insurance companies. Remember that many of these mortgages are "sub-prime" (that is to say, risky). Hmmm. There goes that alarmist robot with the flailing arms again.

What's a stock investor to do? Well, remember that first commandment to "avoid or minimize losses." Make sure that you review your portfolio and sell stocks that may get pulverized by the credit monster. Make sure that the companies themselves have no, low, or manageable debt. (Check their financial reports. See Chapter 11 for more details.) For the venturesome, seek shorting opportunities in those companies most exposed to the dangers of debt. (For more information on shorting, go to Chapter 17.)

Cyclical stocks

The environment is generally bullish for stocks and can be quite bearish for some vulnerable groups such as the "cyclical" stocks. Heavy equipment, automobiles, and technology tend to be cyclical and are very susceptible to downturns in the general economy. Conversely, cyclical stocks do very well when the economy is growing or on an upswing (hence the label).

As individuals and corporations get squeezed with more debt and less disposable income, hard choices need to be made. Ultimately, the result is that people buy fewer "big-ticket" items. That means that a company selling these items ends up selling less and earning less profit. This loss of profit, in turn, makes that company's stock go down.

Companies that experience lagging sales often turn to aggressive discounting. Recently, General Motors Corporation (GM) and Ford Motor Company (F) offered "employee discount" sales to the public. Both companies have been experiencing plunging sales and profits and ballooning debt in recent years. Subsequently, both companies have seen their stocks plummet (over 50 percent share price decline) during most of 2005.

In a struggling, recessionary economy, investing in cyclical stocks is like sunbathing on an ant hill and using jam instead of sun block. Not a pretty picture.

The Dow Jones Industrial Average hit its all-time high of 11,722 in January 2000. Five years later, it's still stuck in the range of 10,000–11,000. While some stock groups have grown very well, stocks in general have struggled. Some sectors have done much worse. Choosing the right sector is critical for your stock investing success.

Important for Bulls & Bears

I just want to reiterate some points that apply here. I don't presume that stocks go straight up or that they zig-zag upward indefinitely. Your due diligence is necessary for your success. Make sure that you're investing appropriately for your situation. If you're 35 and heading into your peak earnings years and want to "ride a home-run stock," and you understand the risks, then go ahead and speculate with that small-cap gold mining stock or the solar power technology junior stock.

But if you're more risk adverse or your situation is screaming out loud for you to be conservative, then don't speculate. Go instead with a more diversified portfolio of large-cap stocks or get the ETF for that particular sector.

For those people who want to make money by "going short" in those sectors that look bearish, again take a deep breath and remember what's appropriate. Conservative investors will simply avoid the risky areas. Aggressive investors or speculators may want to deploy profitable bearish strategies (with a portion of their investable funds). Here are some highlights for all of you.

Conservative and bullish

Once you choose a promising sector, just select large-cap companies that are financially strong, are earning a profit, have low debt, and are market leaders. This entire book shows you how to do just that. However, you may not like the idea of buying stocks directly. Consider either sector mutual funds or ETFs. That way you can choose the industry and be able to effectively buy a basket of the top stocks in that area. ETFs have been a hot item lately, and I think that they're a great consideration for most investors because they offer some advantages over mutual funds. For example, you can put stop loss orders on them or borrow against them in your stock portfolio. Check with your financial advisor to see whether ETFs are appropriate for you.

Being conservative and bullish is proper when you're in (or near) retirement, have a family to support, or live in a very large shoe with so many kids that you don't know what to do.

Aggressive and bullish

If you're aggressive and bullis you want to buy the stocks directly. For real growth potential, look at mid-caps or small-caps. Remember that you're speculating, so you understand the downside risk but are willing to tolerate the risk because the upside potential can reward you so handsomely. Few things in the investment world give you a better gain than a super-charged stock in a hot sector.

Conservative and bearish

For many (if not most) investors, making money on a falling market isn't generally a good idea. Doing so takes a lot of expertise and risk tolerance. Really, for conservative investors, the key word is "safety." Analyze your portfolio with an advisor you trust and sell the potentially troubled stocks. If you're not sure what to do on a particular stock, then (at the very least) put in stop loss orders and make them GTC (good til cancelled). (See Chapter 17 for details.) As odd as it sounds, sometimes losing less than others makes you come out ahead if you play it right.

For example, look at the bear market that hit the U.S. in the mid-1970s. In 1974–75, the stock market fell 45 percent. Stocks didn't recover until 1982. If you had a stock that was at $100, that means it would have fallen to $55 and not returned to $100 until eight years later. Whew! Sometimes just burying your money in the backyard sounds like genius. What if you had a stop loss at $90? You would have gotten out with a minimal loss and could have reinvested the money elsewhere (such as bonds or CDs) and looked much brighter than your neighbor feverishly digging for money in his backyard.

Aggressive and bearish

Being aggressive in a bearish market isn't for the faint of heart. However, this is where the quickest fortunes have been made by some of history's greatest investors. Going short can make you great money when the market is bearish but it can sink you if you're wrong. I usually don't tell my clients and students to "short a stock" because it can backfire. Yes, ways to go short with less risk are out there, but I prefer to buy put options.

Put options are a way to make money with limited risk when you essentially make a bet on an investment (such as stocks) that it will go down. Obviously, options go beyond the scope of this book, but at least let me give you some direction, because there is an appropriate options strategy for most stock portfolios. You can find great (free) tutorials on using options at Web sites such at the Chicago Board Options Exchange (www.cboe.com) and at the Options Industry Council site (www.888options.com).

Diversification

This point is self-explanatory, right? If you take a portfolio approach and spread your capital across three to five sectors, then you're making a "safer bet." And don't forget the trailing stop loss strategy (see Chapter 17). 'Nuff said.

Chapter 14

Money, Mayhem, and Votes

*P*olitics can be infuriating, disruptive, meddlesome, corrupting, and harmful. But . . . enough positive spin! I'll try to be negative too. Even if politics doesn't amuse or interest you, you can't ignore it. If you aren't careful, it can wreak great havoc on your portfolio. Politics wields great influence with the economic and social environment, which in turn affects how companies succeed or fail. This success or failure in turn either helps or hurts your stock's price. Politics (manifested in taxes, regulations, and legislation) can make or break a company or industry quicker than any other external force. Economics — how people spend, save, and invest their money in society — also does its share to drive stock prices up and down.

What people must understand (especially government policy makers) is that a new tax, law, regulation, or government action has a *macro* effect on a stock, an industry, or even an entire economic system, whereas a company has a *micro* effect on an economy. The following gives you a simple snapshot of these effects:

Politics → policy → economy → industry → the company → the stock → stock investor

Now, this chapter doesn't moralize about politics or advocate a political point of view; after all, this book is about stock investing. In general, policies can be good or bad regardless of their effect on the economy — some policies are enacted to achieve greater purposes even if they kick you in the wallet. However, in the context of this chapter, politics is covered from a cause-and-effect perspective: How does politics affect prosperity in general and stock investing in particular?

A proficient stock investor cannot — must not — look at stocks as though they exist in a vacuum. My favorite example of this rule is the idea of fish in a lake. You can have a great fish (your stock) among a whole school of fish (the stock market) in a wonderful lake (the economy). But what if the lake gets polluted (bad policy)? What happens to the fish? Politics controls the lake and can make it hospitable — or dangerous — for the participants. You get the point. The example may sound too simple, yet it isn't. So many people — political committees, corporate managers, bureaucrats, and politicians — still get it so wrong time and time again, to the detriment of the economy and stock investors.

Although the two get inexorably intertwined, I try to treat politics and economics as separate issues.

Avoiding the Bull When Elephants and Donkeys Talk Turkey

The campaigns heat up. Democrats, Republicans, and smaller parties vie for your attention and subsequent votes. Conservatives, liberals, socialists, moderates, and libertarians joust in the battlefield of ideas. But, after all is said and done, voters make their decisions. Election day brings a new slate of politicians into power, and they, in turn, joust and debate on new rules and programs in the legislative halls of power. Before and after election time, investors must keep a watchful eye.

For stock investors, politics manifests itself as a major factor in investment-making decisions in ways shown in Table 13-1.

Table 13-1	Politics and Investing
Possible Legislation	*Effect on Investing*
Taxes	Will a new tax affect a particular stock (industry or economy)? Generally, more or higher taxes ultimately have a negative impact on stock investing. Income taxes and capital gains taxes are good examples.
Laws	Will Congress (or, in some instances, state legislatures) pass a law that will have a negative impact on a stock, the industry, or the economy? Price controls — laws that set the price of a product, service, or commodity — are examples of negative laws.

Possible Legislation	Effect on Investing
Regulations	Will a new (or existing) regulation have a negative (or positive) effect on the stock of your choice? Generally, more or tougher regulations have a negative impact on stocks.
Government spending and debt	If government agencies spend too much or misallocate resources, they may create greater burdens on society, which in turn will be bearish for the economy and the stock market. (For information on investing in bear or bull markets, see Chapter 15.)
Money supply	The U.S. money supply — the dollars you use — is controlled by the Federal Reserve. It's basically a governmental agency that serves as America's central bank. How can it affect stocks? You can find more on this question in the "Showing interest in the Fed" section, later in the chapter.
Interest rates	The Federal Reserve has crucial influence here. It can raise key interest rates that in turn can have an effect on the entire economy and the stock market. I cover this effect in the "Showing interest in the Fed" section, later in this chapter.

Doomed to repeat it?

History provides abundant lessons for stock investors because you can easily see how government policies have impacted our economy in general and the stock market specifically. The greatest financial calamities in history occurred either because politicians made mistakes or because they made purposeful policies that produced unintended negative effects.

During the 1920s and 1930s, Presidents Herbert Hoover and Franklin D. Roosevelt and Congress produced disastrous policies that turned what should have been a minor recession into the Great Depression. From 1928 to 1938, federal government spending ballooned out of control, and stringent regulations were placed on the country's domestic economy and its international trade (including the Smoot-Hawley Tariff Act). These events, along with increasing income tax rates to 91 percent (yikes!), placed a drag on economic growth that lasted an entire decade.

How did successful stock investors react in those tough years? In the late 1920s, when the signs of pending trouble were clearly becoming evident, alert investors such as Bernard Baruch got out of the stock market before it crashed in 1929, when the Great Depression produced the "mother of all bear markets."

When many of the items in Table 13-1 work in tandem, they can have a magnified effect that can have tremendous consequences for your stock portfolio. Alert investors keep a constant vigil when the legislature is open for business, and they adjust their portfolios accordingly.

Understanding price controls

Stock investors should be very wary of price controls (they're a great example of regulation). A price control is a fixed price on a particular product, commodity, or service mandated by the government.

Price controls have been tried continuously throughout history, and they have continuously been removed because they ultimately do more harm than good. It's easy to see why. Imagine that you run a business that sells chairs, and a law is passed that states, "From this point onward, chairs can be sold only for $10." If all your costs stay constant at $9 or less, the regulation isn't that bad. However, price controls put two dynamics in motion. First, the artificially lower price encourages consumption — more people buy chairs. Secondly, production is discouraged. Who wants to make chairs if they can't sell them for a decent profit?

What happens to the company with a fixed sales price (in this example, $10) and rising costs? Profits shrink, and depending on how long the price controls are in effect, the company eventually experiences losses. The chair producer is eventually driven out of business. The chair-building industry shrinks, and a chair shortage is the result. Profits (and jobs) soon vanish. So what happens if you own stock in a company that builds chairs? I'll just say that if I tell you which way the stock price is going, you better be sitting down (if, of course, you have a chair).

Ascertaining the political climate

The bottom line is that you ignore political realities at your own (economic) risk. To be and stay aware, ask yourself the following questions about the stock of each company in which you invest:

- ✔ What laws will directly affect my stock investment adversely?
- ✔ Will any laws affect that company's industry?
- ✔ Will any current or prospective laws affect the company's sources of revenue?

✔ Will any current or prospective laws affect the company's expenses or supplies?

✔ Am I staying informed about political and economic issues that may possibly have a negative impact on my investment?

✔ Will such things as excessive regulations, price controls, or new taxes have a negative impact on my stock's industry?

Oil and gas service and exploration companies benefited from the U.S. need for more energy supplies. But investment opportunities didn't stop there. As oil and gas supplies became costly and problematic, alternative energy sources gained national attention. The debate was rekindled on solar power and exciting new technologies, such as fuel cells. As traditional sources of energy (sweet crude) became more expensive, alternate sources became more economical. Investors who anticipated the new interest in alternative energy sought companies that would logically benefit. A good example of this is Evergreen Solar, Inc. (ESLR). The firm's stock rose from $2.50 in September 2004 to $8 by September 2005; just a scant 12 months later. With an impressive 220 percent gain, proactive investors sang "Here Comes the Sun" without getting burned.

Politics and economics are a double-edged sword. Understand them, and you can profit; misunderstand them, and you become a financial victim.

Discovering systemic and nonsystemic effects

Politics can affect your investments in two basic ways: systemic and nonsystemic.

Nonsystemic means that the system isn't affected but a particular participant is affected. A *systemic effect* means that all the players in that system are affected. In this case, the "system" is the economy at large. Politics imposes itself (through taxes, laws, regulations, and so on) and has an undue influence on all the members of that system.

Nonsystemic

Say that you decide to buy stock in a company called Golf Carts Unlimited, Inc. (GCU). You believe that the market for golf carts has great potential and that GCU stands to grow substantially. How can politics affect GCU?

Playing monopoly

Government action against large companies for real (or alleged) abuses has happened many times. In 2004, the New York State Attorney General targeted insurer American International Group, Inc. (AIG). In a few months, AIG's stock fell from $74 to a low of $50 in April 2005. Long-time investors remember how companies such as IBM (in the 1970s) and Microsoft (during 1999 and 2000) faced monopolistic allegations. The federal government is a massive entity, and it has trillions of taxpayer dollars at its disposal. When it targets a company, regardless of the merits of the case, avoid investing in that company (until the trouble has passed). Investors should be wary when the government starts making noise about any company and potential legal actions against it.

What if politicians believe that GCU is too big and that it controls too much of the golf cart industry? Maybe they view GCU as a monopoly and want the federal government to step in to shrink GCU's reach and influence for the benefit of competition and consumers. Maybe the government believes that GCU engages in unfair or predatory business practices and that it's in violation of antitrust (or antimonopoly) laws. If the government acts against GCU, the action is a nonsystemic issue: The action is directed toward the participant (in this case, GCU) and not the golf cart industry.

What happens if you're an investor in GCU? Does your stock investment suffer as a result of government action directed against the company? Let's just say that the stock price will hook left and end up in the lake.

Systemic

Say that politicians want to target the golf industry for intervention because they maintain that golf should be free for all to participate in and that a law must be passed to make it accessible to all, especially those people who can't afford to play. So to remedy the situation, the following law is enacted: "Law #67590305598002 declares that from this day forward, all golf courses that operate must charge only one dollar for any golfer who chooses to participate."

That law sounds great to any golfer. But what are the unintended effects when such a law becomes reality? Many people agree with the sentiment of the law, but what about the cause-and-effect aspects of it? Obviously, all things being equal, golf courses will be forced to close. Staying in business is uneconomical if their costs are higher than their income. If they can't charge any more than a dollar, how can they possibly stay open? Ultimately (and ironically), no one can play golf.

What happens to investors of Golf Carts Unlimited, Inc.? If the world of golf shrinks, then demand for golf carts shrinks as well. The value of GCU's stock will certainly be "triple-bogeyed."

Examples of politics creating systemic problems are endless, but you get the point.

Poking into politics: Resources

To find out about new laws being passed or proposed, check out Congress and what's going on at its primary Web sites: the U.S. House of Representatives (www.house.gov) and the U.S. Senate (www.senate.gov). For presidential information and proposals, check the White House's Web site at www.white house.gov.

You also may want to check out THOMAS, the service performed by the Library of Congress, at http://thomas.loc.gov. THOMAS is a search engine that helps you find any piece of legislation either by bill number or keyword. This search engine is an excellent way to find out whether an industry is being targeted for increased regulation or deregulation. In the late 1980s, real estate was hit hard when the government passed new regulations and tax rules (related stocks went down). When the telecom industry was deregulated in the mid-1990s, the industry grew dramatically (related stocks went up).

You can find more resources in Appendix A. The more knowledge you pick up about how politics and government actions can help (or harm) an investment, the better you'll be at growing (and protecting) your wealth.

Easing into Economics

Economics sounds like a deadly dull pursuit. Actually, the wrong book on the topic or the wrong instructor can make the topic so boring that you feel like you're crawling backward through Death Valley. Economics really does matter, but do you have to really understand phrases such as "inelasticity coefficient" and the "Index of Leading Economic Indicators"? No, not really. But do you need to be familiar with phrases such as "supply and demand" and "price controls don't work" to operate in today's modern stock market? The answer is a resounding yes. Of course, you can invest without knowing much about economics. However, your chances for success are tremendously enhanced when you have a basic understanding of how economics works. Actually, economics explained in the proper way is fascinating. Knowing how the world ticks can be fun and profitable.

Understanding economic impact

When people comment about the economy, they make it sound like a giant, amorphous thing in the same way they talk about the stock market and the weather. To put it into perspective, the economy is you and me and millions of others — producers, consumers, entrepreneurs, and workers all trading money for goods and services. The economy is millions of people and organizations voluntarily transacting with each other day in and day out. People and organizations buy, spend, save, and invest billions every hour of every day.

Looking at the economy is like seeing a huge picture and deciding where on the canvas are the greatest points of interest — investment opportunities. When you look at the economy, you look at the major numbers and trends and judge whether a particular company is well suited to profit from trends and opportunities. You simply rely on your common sense and apply it with the statistics that track the economy in general. If millions of consumers are buying product X and the market and demand for X are growing, then it stands to reason that the best company offering product X will prosper as well. The reverse can be true as well: If more and more people avoid, or just don't spend their money on, a particular product or industry, then the fortunes of those companies will decline as well.

Economic reports are important because sometimes just one report or statistic released is enough to move the stock market. The economic statistics and reports that are the most meaningful to you are the ones that have a direct bearing on your stock or industry. If you invest in real estate or construction stocks, reports that cover housing starts and interest rates are critical to you. If you invest in retail stocks, then information on consumer confidence and debt is important to you.

In the following table, I give some examples of key industries and a statistic that's a relevant indicator:

Industry	Statistic	Comments
Real estate	Housing starts	This indicator tracks permits given for new housing to be built. Rising housing starts are desirable.
Auto	Auto sales	The industry's annual sales figure is a closely watched indicator. Rising sales are desirable.
Retail	Retail sales	The overall sales are watched, and you want them to be rising (especially in the fourth quarter of the year).

Note: Industry trade publications and general financial publications, such as *The Wall Street Journal* and *Investor's Business Daily,* regularly report this data. You can also find it (along with a tremendous database of economic data and statistics) at www.freelunch.com.

What are some important things in economic data that you want to be aware of? Keep reading. The following sections make this information clear.

Grossing you out with GDP

Gross domestic product (GDP), which measures the nation's total output of goods and services for the quarter, is considered the broadest measure of economic activity. Although it's measured in dollars (the U.S. GDP surpassed $12 trillion by July 2005), it's usually quoted as a percentage. You typically hear a news report that says something like, "The economy grew by 2.5 percent last quarter." Because the GDP is an important overall barometer for the economy, it should be a positive number. The report on GDP is released quarterly by the Commerce Department (www.doc.gov).

You should regularly monitor the GDP along with economic data that relates directly to your stock portfolio. The following list gives some general guidelines for evaluating GDP:

- **Over 3 percent:** This number indicates strong growth and bodes well for stocks. At 5 percent or higher, the economy is sizzling!

- **1 to 3 percent:** This figure indicates moderate growth and can occur either as the economy is rebounding from a recession or as it's slowing down from a previously strong period.

- **0 percent or negative (as low as –3 percent):** This number isn't good and indicates that the economy is either not growing or is actually shrinking a bit. A negative GDP is considered *recessionary* (meaning that the economy's growth is receding).

- **Under –3 percent:** A GDP this low indicates a very difficult period for the economy. A GDP under –3 percent, especially for two or more quarters, indicates a serious recession or possibly a depression.

Looking at a single quarter isn't that useful. Track GDP over many quarters to see which way the general economy is trending. When you look at GDP for a particular quarter of a year, ask yourself whether it's better (or worse) than the quarter before. If it's better (or worse), then ask yourself to what extent it has changed. Is it dramatically better (or worse) than the quarter before? Is the economy showing steady growth, or is it slowing? If several quarters show solid growth, the overall economy is generally bullish.

Traditionally, if two or more consecutive quarters show negative growth (economic output is shrinking), the economy is considered to be in a recession. A recession can be a painful necessity; it usually occurs when the economy can't absorb the total amount of goods being produced due to too much excess production. A bear market in stocks usually accompanies a recession.

GDP is just a rough estimate at best. It can't possibly calculate all the factors that go into economic growth. For example, crime has a negative effect on economic growth, but it's not reflected in GDP. Still, most economists agree that GDP provides a ballpark snapshot of the overall economy's progress.

Showing interest in the Fed

The Federal Reserve System (often called simply the Fed) is the nation's independent central bank. It plays a pivotal role in the U.S. economy and — because the United States is the most powerful economy — in the global economy as well.

For more information about the Fed's money supply and interest rate policies, go to its Web site at www.federalreserve.gov. Also, the American Institute for Economic Research (www.aier.org) offers useful, readable research on the relationships between money growth, interest rates, and the stock market.

The Fed is one of the most closely watched institutions in the world because it has such an impact on financial markets as well as the growth of the U.S. economy. Although it performs a number of functions, the Fed's most fundamental roles are

- **Controlling the money supply:** Because the Fed controls the actual quantity of dollars that goes into circulation, it has the responsibility of fighting or controlling inflation. People think that inflation is the cost of goods and services going up, when actually *inflation* refers to the value of money going down because of too much money in the marketplace (the currency being "inflated"). In other words, too many dollars are chasing too few goods and services.

  The Fed tries to manage the very difficult task of having just the right amount of money in the economy. Having too much money can create inflation, meaning that consumers see the purchasing power of their dollars shrink. Too little money means that not enough money is circulating in the economy. (In these financial conditions, some people use the terminology "tight money," and others say that "the economy lacks liquidity.") Inflation, if not held in check, can have very negative consequences. After all, how would you feel if the money in your pocket was rapidly shrinking in value? (The odds are that you'd feel like a parent with too many teenagers in the house!)

Inflation is reported as the consumer price index (CPI). The *CPI* (also known as the cost-of-living index) is calculated by the Bureau of Labor Statistics (www.dol.gov) and measures changes in the price of a typical basket of consumer goods that reflect what the average consumer buys on a regular basis. The CPI is considered a warning of pending inflation.

✔ **Influencing interest rates:** Financial markets, such as the stock market and the bond market, closely monitor the Fed's influence on interest rates. Because the Fed can raise or lower some key interest rates at will, its actions become a powerful lever that can raise or lower many rates that literally millions of individuals and businesses pay primarily on their short-term debt.

You need to watch interest rates for several reasons:

- Interest rates affect corporate earnings. If companies pay more interest, that additional cost directly affects their profits. If profits shrink, then that puts downward pressure on stock prices. Conversely, if the Fed cuts interest rates, companies will typically see a positive impact on profits.

- Interest rates influence income investors. (See Chapter 9 for more on income investing.) Investors looking for a higher return on their investments will make decisions to pull their money out of stocks and into other vehicles such as bonds or bank accounts. When interest rates continue to climb, more and more investors sell their stocks, sending stock prices down.

- Interest rates figure prominently in fighting inflation. Generally, interest rates have been a key weapon in the past 20 years in fighting inflation. Because inflation means that the value of a dollar shrinks, the Fed uses higher interest rates to offset this devaluation. In the late 1970s, when inflation hovered near double-digit rates, interest rates went through the roof (surpassing 15 percent). Conversely, lower interest rates coupled with an expanding money supply can ignite higher inflation.

Debting your sweet bippy

Debt can be very burdensome and have a negative impact on economic growth. As an investor, you need to know how much debt is in the economy and whether the debt is growing or shrinking. Whether the debt is consumer (credit cards, mortgages, and so on) or corporate (short-term borrowing, bonds, and so on), it will harm the economy if not kept under control.

A major reason for the economy's (and stock market's) downturn in 2000–2002 was massive debt. In fact, during the 1990s, virtually every major category of debt hit record levels. The only ways to remove debt are to pay it off or go bankrupt. Because so many individuals and businesses became overextended in debt during that time period, bankruptcies hit record levels as well.

Stock investors must monitor debt levels for bear market potential (especially in this decade!). Too much debt slows the economy, which in turn can adversely affect the stock market. Overly indebted individuals don't have money to spend or invest. Overly indebted companies may face employee layoffs, cuts in spending, declining profits, and other negative actions. Watch also for corporate problems. If you have stock in a company that has too much debt or that sells to customers who are overburdened with debt, then that company will suffer. The Fed and other sources, including such publications as *The Wall Street Journal,* report consumer and corporate debt levels.

Raising confident consumers

As you often hear on television, consumer spending accounts for two-thirds of the economy. Therefore, the consumer's behavior is something that investors watch carefully. You can break down consumer activity into two categories:

- ✓ **Consumer income:** If consumer income meets or exceeds the CPI rate (see "Showing interest in the Fed," earlier in this chapter), that bodes well for the economy.

- ✓ **Consumer confidence:** This index is measured by prominent surveys that essentially track how consumers feel about the economy in general and their personal situations in particular. The University of Michigan and the Conference Board (which presents its survey in the Consumer Confidence Index) do the most widely-followed surveys. If consumers feel good about the economy and their immediate futures, that bodes well for consumer spending.

Lumping together the data with economic indexes

Because so much economic data is available, many investors prefer to look at indexes that put the data in a nutshell. Indexes try to summarize many economic indicators and put them into a neat, digestible format.

Economic indicators are grouped into categories that try to give a rough idea about the economy's upward and downward cycle. These cyclical indicators are put in three categories that try to time the various phases of the economy's movement:

- ✓ **Leading:** The leading indicators try to be predictive of the economy's path. Stock investors are particularly interested in leading economic indicators because stock investors usually don't invest because of past or present conditions — investors buy stocks because of expectations for the future.

✔ **Coincident:** The coincident indicators essentially tell you where the economy is right now. (For stock investors, most coincident indicators are like the indicator on your car's dashboard blinking "hot" when you see steam rising from your hood.) The most valuable coincident indicator is the GDP. (See the section "Grossing you out with GDP," earlier in this chapter.)

✔ **Lagging:** This type of indicator tells you what just passed in the economy's path (which can be significant because some lagging indicators do precede leading indicators). The unemployment rate is a good example of a lagging indicator.

Of the three categories, the most widely followed is the Index of Leading Economic Indicators (LEI). A good example of an indicator that's included in the LEI is the statistic on new construction. If more new construction is being started, that's a positive harbinger of economic growth. The Conference Board (`www.conferenceboard.org`) compiles the LEI monthly.

Inquiring about economics: Resources

Keep in mind that, because of the scope of the topic and the finite number of pages in this book, this chapter can't do justice to the burgeoning world of economics. I encourage you to continue learning about economics by doing some easy and interesting research with the resources listed here and in Appendix A.

Turn to the following sources for economic data:

✔ Conference Board, `www.conferenceboard.org`

✔ Department of Commerce, `www.doc.gov`

✔ The Federal Reserve, `www.federalreserve.gov`

✔ Free Lunch, `www.freelunch.com`

Here are some sources to help you understand economics:

✔ American Institute for Economic Research, `www.aier.org`

✔ Dismal.com, `www.dismal.com`

✔ FinancialSense.com, `www.financialsense.com`

✔ Foundation for Economic Education, `www.fee.org`

✔ The Mises Institute, `www.mises.org`

TIP

Predicting the economic weather

Excellent sources are available that make the arcane world of economics more readable and understandable. One is the American Institute for Economic Research (AIER), a nonprofit organization that offers excellent information for beginners on economics and markets. AIER offers a booklet called *Forecasting Business Trends* that gives investors some clear yet detailed explanations and insights on the business cycle. To find out more, write to American Institute for Economic Research, P.O. Box 1000, Great Barrington, MA 01230, or visit its Web site at www.aier.org. Another source with excellent essays and easy-to-read analysis is the Ludwig von Mises Institute at www.mises.

org. By the way, as you navigate the world of economics, you'll come across various "schools of thought." The most well-known is the Keynesian school and the most problematic is the Marx school (by the way, Groucho knows more than Karl). In my opinion and experience, the best is the Austrian school of economics (Mises is considered the "dean" of this school). Austrian economists have been the most accurate in interpreting and forecasting economic events. Among the events they warned about were the Great Depression, the collapse of communism, and the dangers of America's current mammoth debt bubble.

Part IV

Investment Strategies and Tactics

The 5th Wave   By Rich Tennant

"I read about investing in a company called UniHandle Ohio, but I'm uneasy about a stock that's listed on the NASDAQ as UhOh."

In this part . . .

Successful stock investing is more than choosing a particular stock. It's also understanding the environment in which the market operates. Just as goldfish can thrive in good water (or die in bad water), the stock market reacts to the general economic climate. Successful investors go beyond merely picking good stocks and watching the financial news. They implement techniques and strategies that help them either minimize losses or maximize gains (hopefully both). The chapters in this part introduce some of the most effective investing techniques to help you profit from stocks in a bull or a bear market and describe some smart ways to hold on to more of your profits when tax time rolls around.

Chapter 15

Taking the Bull (Or Bear) by the Horns

. . . .

In This Chapter

▶ Looking at the bull market

▶ Recognizing the bear market

▶ Deciding what to do in an uncertain market

. . . .

*U*nderstanding the general markets and their major directional trend may even be more important to your wealth-building success than choosing the right stock. Recent years — and a century of stock market history — bear (no pun intended) witness to this point.

Bull and bear markets have a tremendous effect on your stock choices. Generally, bull markets tend to precede economic uptrends (also called economic rebound, economic recovery, or economic growth), while bear markets tend to precede economic downtrends (also called recession, depression, or economic contraction).

The stock market's movement is based on the fact that stock prices go up (or down) based on people's buying or selling behavior. If more people are buying stock (versus selling), then stock prices rise. If more people are selling stocks, then stock prices fall. Why do people buy or sell a stock? It can be explained in one word: expectations. People generally buy (or sell) stock in expectation of economic events. If they feel that times are getting bad and the economic stats back them up (in the form of rising unemployment, shrinking corporate profits, cutbacks in consumer spending, and so on), then they become more cautious, which can have a couple of results:

✔ They sell stock that they currently own.

✔ They don't buy stock because they feel that stocks won't do well.

Of course, when the economy is doing well, the reverse is true.

Bulling Up

In the beginning, a bull market doesn't look like a bull market at all. It looks like anything but. Maybe that's why so few catch on early. Bull markets are marked by great optimism as the economy roars forward and stocks go skyward. Everyone knows what a bull market should look like, and everyone can recognize it when it's become a mature trend. The saying "I don't know what it is, but I'll know it when I see it" is one that applies to a bull market. But if you can foresee it coming, you may be able to make a fortune by getting in just before the crowd sees it.

Just keep in mind that you personally want to behave like a contrarian. A *contrarian* is an investor who decides which securities to buy and sell by going against the crowd. To paraphrase the legendary billionaire J. Paul Getty, buy when people are selling and sell when people are buying. This is the essence of successful investing.

This contrarian attitude reminds me of the time I bought some gold and silver mining stocks in 2001 and made a 1000% gain when I sold them only a few years later. That group of stocks was very unpopular when I purchased it, but it benefited from the unfolding bull market in precious metals.

Because bull markets usually start in the depths of a bear market, do some research regarding bear markets; read the section "Identifying the beast," later in this chapter.

Recognizing the beast

In this book I concentrate on the modern era, starting in the early part of the twentieth century, but bull markets in stocks have shown themselves many times throughout the past few hundred years — plenty of time to have established some recognizable traits, such as the following:

✔ **Bull markets tend to start at the depths of pessimism — the same way that dawn starts at the edge of darkness.** People have probably just been beaten up by a bear market. The phrase "I'm into stock investing" is about as welcome in polite conversation as "I have a contagious disease." If investors are avoiding stocks like the plague (or selling stocks they already have), share prices drop to the point that much of the risk is wrung out of them. Value-oriented investors then can pick up some solid companies at great prices. (See Chapter 10 for information on recognizing a good stock value.)

✔ **The major media mirror this pessimism and amplify it.** Usually, the mainstream media have greater value as a *counterindicator* because by the time the major publications find out about the economic trend and report it, the major trend has already played itself out and is probably ready to change course.

For example, *Time* magazine featured Amazon.com CEO Jeff Bezos as its Man of the Year in 2000, but immediately thereafter, Amazon.com's stock price continued a long and painful descent, ultimately dropping over 90 percent from its high in late 1999. Another example is the famous issue of *Business Week* with the pessimistic cover story titled "The Death of Equities" that came out at the tail end of the bear market of the 1970s. What timing — an issue warning investors about the dangers of stock investing just before the greatest bull market in history started.

✔ **Economic statistics stabilize.** After the economy has hit rock bottom, the economic statistics start to improve. The most-watched set of economic indicators is called the Index of Leading Economic Indicators (which I describe in Chapters 6 and 14). Investors want to make sure that the economy is getting back on its feet before it starts its next move upward. In 1982, the economy was just starting to recover from the 1981 recession. The economic expansion (and accompanying bull market) became the longest in history.

✔ **Economic conditions for individuals and companies are stable and strong.** You know that's true if profits are stable or growing for companies in general and if consumers are seeing strong and increasing income growth. The logic holds up well: More money being made means more money to eventually spend and invest.

✔ **Industries producing large-ticket items hit rock bottom and begin their climb.** After consumers and companies have been pummeled by a tough economy, they're not apt to make major financial commitments to items such as new cars, houses, equipment, and so on. Industries that produce these large, expensive items will see sales fall to a low and slowly start to rebound as the economy picks up. In a growing economy, consumers and companies experience greater confidence (both psychologically and financially).

✔ **Demographics appear favorable.** Take a look at the census and government statistics on trends for population growth, as well as the growth in the number of business enterprises. The 1980s and 1990s, for example, saw the rise of the baby boomers, those born during the post-World War II period of 1946 to 1964. Baby boomers wielded much financial clout, much of it in the stock market. Their investment money played a major role in propelling the stock market to new highs.

> ✔ **General peace and stability prevail.** A major war or international conflict may have just ended. Beyond death and destruction, war is also bad for the economy and presents uncertainty and anxiety for stock investors.

Avoiding the horns of a bull market

Believe it or not, a mature bull market poses problems for investors and stock market experts. In a mature bull market, just about any stock — good, bad, or indifferent — tends to go up. You could be a blind monkey throwing darts and pick a rising stock. When everything goes up and everybody seems to be making a winning pick, human nature kicks in. Both beginning and serious investors believe that their good fortune can be chalked up to superior stock-picking prowess and not simple luck or circumstance. Overconfidence is rampant at the top of the market and it becomes a prelude for disaster.

When investors become convinced that they have the newfound ability to consistently choose winning stocks, they grow more daring in their investment approach; they make riskier choices, using less discipline and relying on less diligence and research. Then . . . whammo! They get socked by the market. Overconfidence lures the unsuspecting investor to more dangerous territory, invariably resulting in a very expensive lesson. Overconfidence and money don't mix.

Let me tell you about a common phenomenon of human behavior that I refer to as the Wile E. Coyote effect. Do you remember Wile E. Coyote from those great Road Runner cartoons? Of course you do! You know the plot: Mr. Coyote is chasing the Road Runner and seems to be gaining on him. He's confidently ready to pounce on the seemingly unsuspecting bird, but the Road Runner makes a quick turn and watches as Mr. Coyote continues running over the cliff, ultimately plummeting down the ravine.

A mature bull market (also known as the "mania" stage) does that to investors. Scores of true stories tell of investors lured to a game of easy riches (the dot-com fiasco, for example) only to watch their investments get pulverized. This phenomenon happened not only to beginners but also to experienced investors and many stock investing experts who were familiar faces on your television screen. Crowd psychology, whether driven by fear or greed, is fascinating. It's like watching a hang-gliding tournament in a hurricane.

Toro! Approaching a bull market

Being fully invested in stocks at the beginning of a bull market makes for spectacular success. But doing so takes some courage. Then again, who says you have to get the whole enchilada? You can begin looking and get your first stock now and slowly build your portfolio as the bull market emerges.

Choose the type of stocks as well as the mix to fit into your unique situation and needs. So, when the bull market is in its infancy, start investing by using the following approach:

- **Be a bargain hunter.** Frequently, at the tail end of a bear market, stock prices have been sufficiently battered after going through an extended period of low demand and/or disproportionately more selling of the shares by nervous investors. Let the shopping begin! At the bottom of the bear market, you have a good chance of acquiring stock at share prices that are near (or in some cases below) the book value of the companies they represent. You'll also have less risk when you acquire the shares of a company that is generating positive growth in sales and earnings. Chapter 10 can help you better understand concepts such as book value.

- **Look for strong fundamentals.** Is the company you're choosing exhibiting solid sales and earnings? Are sales and earnings rising compared to the prior year? How about from the same quarter last year? Conduct top line and bottom line analyses (which I discuss in Chapter 10). Do the company's products and services make sense to you? In other words, is it selling stuff that the public is starting to demand more of?

- **Consider the stock's class.** Remember that some stocks are more aggressive choices than others. This choice reflects your risk tolerance as well. Figure out whether you want to invest in a small-cap stock with phenomenal growth prospects (and commensurate risk) or a large-cap stock that's a tried-and-true market leader.

   All things being equal, small-cap stocks exhibit the best growth performance in an emerging bull market. Small-cap stocks are more appropriate for investors who have a higher risk tolerance. Of course, most stocks do well in an emerging bull market (actually, that's what makes it a bull market!), so even risk-adverse investors who put their money into larger companies will gain. (For more information on growth stocks such as small-caps, see Chapter 8.)

- **Choose appropriate industries.** Look at industries that are poised to rebound as the economy picks up and individuals and organizations begin to spend again. In a rising market, cyclical stocks such as those in the automobile, housing, industrial equipment, and technology industries resume growth. When the economy is doing well, individuals and organizations begin to spend more on items that will meet their needs in an expanding economy. Companies upgrade their technology. Families get a new car or move to a bigger house. Construction firms need more and better equipment as residential and commercial building increases.

- **Take stock of your portfolio.** As you start to add stocks to your portfolio, first analyze your situation to make sure that you have diversification not only in different stocks and/or stock mutual funds but also in non-stock investments, such as savings bonds and bank accounts. You don't have to have 100 percent of your investment in stocks just because the market is bullish. Instead, you should consider putting as much as 100 percent of the growth component of your investment money in stocks.

Say that you're investing for the long term. You're not that concerned with risk, and you want maximum growth from your investments. After setting aside money in an emergency fund, you decide that you want to devote your remaining funds of $50,000 to growth stocks. In this case, 100 percent of that sum becomes the *growth component* of your investment portfolio. If you decide to play it safer and split it 50/50 between bonds and stocks, then $25,000 (or 50 percent of your portfolio) is your growth component. The bonds are then your *income component.*

✔ **Evaluate your personal goals.** No matter how good the market and the foreseeable prospects for growth are, stock investing is a personal matter that should serve your unique needs. For example, how old are you, and how many years away is your retirement? All things being equal, a 35-year-old should have predominately growth stocks, while a 65-year-old requires a more proven, stable performance with large-cap market leaders. The information in Chapter 2 can help you identify appropriate investment goals.

Some investors in a bull market may have very little money in stocks. Why? Maybe they have already reached their financial goals, so wealth preservation is more appropriate than growth. Perhaps they have a million-dollar portfolio and are 70 years old and no longer working. In that case, having, say, 80 percent of their investments in stable, income-producing investments and 20 percent in proven (yet modestly) growing stocks may make more sense for them.

Bearing Down

Alas, stocks go down as well as up. Some ferocious bear markets have hit stocks on several occasions since the Great Depression. The bear markets of 1973–1975 and 2000–2002 rank as the toughest in modern times. A few brief, relatively minor ones occurred in the late 1980s and early 1990s. You don't need to worry about the occasional dips (referred to as *corrections*); however, be wary about *secular* (long-term) bear markets, which can last years. Discipline and a watchful eye can keep you and your money out of trouble.

Identifying the beast

Bear markets can be foreseen and they have been most often seen starting during apparently bullish, jubilant times. Bear markets come immediately on the heels of market tops (when stock buying reaches "mania" levels). Anecdotal evidence about market tops makes shrewd investors become cautious. It's alleged that John D. Rockefeller (or was it Joe Kennedy?) got totally out of the stock market just before the 1929 crash when his shoeshine boy gave him a hot stock tip. Whether that story is true isn't the issue. It's believable because you know similar moments have indeed happened in recent times. In 2000, ads featured hunky baseball players and sexy tennis stars who were giving stock market advice. In 2005, centerfold models and taxi drivers told the public about getting rich in real estate! Long-time professional observers have come to realize that once everybody and their uncle (and their aunt and their parrot) starts telling you about easy riches in a market, it's time to get out!

Emerging bear markets have some telltale signs, including the following:

- ✔ **Optimism abounds.** Everyone from Main Street to Wall Street feels great. Financial reports declare that the business cycle has been conquered and a new economy or new paradigm has arrived. Good times are here for the foreseeable future! You start to see books with titles such as *The Dow at 100,000* and *Easy Riches in the Stock Market* hit the bestseller lists. The *business cycle* refers to the economy's roller-coaster-like behavior when it expands (growth) and contracts (recession).

  Sometimes, the financial experts believe that an economy is doing so well that it can continue to grow indefinitely. Examples of misguided exuberance abound in stock market history. In 1929, Irving Fisher, the best-known financial expert and stock millionaire of his day, made the ill-fated declaration "Stocks have reached a permanent plateau" as he predicted the bull market would continue for the foreseeable future. A few weeks later, the infamous stock market crash occurred. Everyone who had listened to Fisher got clobbered in the greatest bear market of the twentieth century. Even Irving Fisher himself filed for bankruptcy. Gee, not even Irving Fisher should've listened to Irving Fisher. In stark contrast, Ludwig von Mises warned about the oncoming depression throughout the late 1920s and was ignored. Who needs a party-pooper, right? In 1999, I heard one economist on TV boldly state that the economy would continue growing forever and that "recessions are a thing of the past." Yikes! Today, I'm sure that economist is probably in a new job saying, "Would you like some fries with that?"

- ✔ **Debt levels hit new highs.** When optimism is high, people buy things. In 1999, debt levels hit a record high in almost every category; corporate, consumer, mortgage, and margin debt ballooned during the late 1990s. The financial press mostly ignored this massive debt, yet it was one of the major reasons for the subsequent bear market and recession. When people or companies accrue too much debt, it can be removed in only one of two ways: through repayment or by bankruptcy. The year 2005 became the eighth year in a row that more than 1 million people filed for bankruptcy in the United States. The pace of 1+ million bankruptcies per year has continued into 2005.

- ✔ **Excessive speculation, credit, and money supply expand.** Whenever a country's money supply grows beyond the economy's needs, massive problems can result. When the money supply expands, more money is circulated into the banking system. (Go to `www.federalreserve.gov` to find out more about the money supply.) The banks then lend or invest this excess money. The oversupply of money flows into investment projects, such as initial public offerings and bond offerings. When too much money is available for too few worthy projects, invariably a lot of money is invested unwisely. This situation causes massive imbalances in the economic system, ultimately resulting in economic downturns that can take years to rectify.

History proves the truth of this economic situation. It happened to the U.S. economy in the late 1920s and to Japan in the late 1980s. Fortunately, statistics on credit and the money supply are easy to come by and readily available on the Internet. (See Appendix A for resources.)

✔ **Government intervention increases.** Government has the power to do much good, but when it uses its power improperly, it can do a great deal of harm. Every economy throughout history that collapsed ultimately did so because of excessive government intervention. In progressive, free-market economies, this intervention usually occurs in the form of taxes, laws, and regulations. Keep a watchful eye on the president and Congress to monitor government intervention. Are they proposing policies that add burdens to the private economy? Are they advocating stringent new laws and regulations? I explain more about government's influence on the stock market and the general economy in Chapters 13 and 14.

✔ **National and/or international conflict arises.** Nothing can have a more negative impact on the economy than war or political or civil unrest. (I guess war is a good example of "excessive government intervention.") Keep your eye on the news. Ask yourself what effect a particular conflict may have on the economy and the stock market. Sometimes the conflict isn't a violent one; sometimes it takes the form of a trade war when competing countries aggressively implement tariffs and boycotts that could devastate companies or even industries in one or both of the countries.

History in the making

One of the worst bear markets since the Great Depression started in 1973. The stock market was pummeled as the Dow Jones Industrial Average (DJIA) fell 45 percent during an 18-month period ending in 1975. However, the DJIA did not recover to its 1973 high until (you guessed it) 1982. The period from 1973 to 1982 had the hallmarks of tough times — high inflation, high unemployment, war (the Middle East conflict in 1973 and expansive Soviet aggression in Africa and Afghanistan), the energy crisis, and high taxes. The 1970s were a tough decade for most stocks. The 1980s and '90s were great decades for stock investors. Alas, 2000–2002 were very rough years for stocks as investors cumulatively lost over $5 trillion.

Looking for Titanic tickets

In early 2000, I was infuriated when the dapper pundits on TV told viewers to hang tight and hold on for the long haul. Stocks then took a beating, prompting the pundits to say, "It's a buying opportunity. Add to your portfolio." Then what happened? The bear market took stocks down again.

Losing trillions during 2000–2002 could've been avoidable if investors had been more disciplined and if the pundits had been more careful in their pronouncements. When the economy is heading into treacherous waters, stocks get the worst of it, yet experts continue to advise people to buy stocks because they're good for the long term. Hold on! Liking stocks doesn't mean that you should always be in them. I mean, just because you like boating doesn't mean that you should take advantage of a free ticket on the *Titanic*.

Heading into the woods: Approaching a bear market

Sticking to a buy-and-hold strategy (where you buy stock and hold onto it for better or worse) at the onset of a bear market is financial suicide. People have a tough time selling, and financial advisors have an even tougher time telling them to cut their losses because that's tantamount to saying, "Sorry, I was wrong." Admitting failure is hard for most people to do.

Understand that investing should be a logical, practical, and unemotional pursuit. You can't be married to stocks — until death do you part — especially because bear markets can divorce you from your money.

In an emerging bear market, keep the following points in mind to maximize your gains (or just to minimize your losses):

- ✔ **Review your situation.** Before you consider any move in or out of the market, review your overall financial situation to make sure that your money and financial condition are as secure as possible. Make sure that you have an emergency fund of three to six months' worth of gross living expenses. Keep your debt at a comfortably low level. Review your career, insurance, and so on. Schedule a financial checkup with your financial planner.

- ✔ **Remember that cash is king.** When the bear market is coming and economic storm clouds are rolling in, keep the bulk of your money in safe, interest-bearing vehicles such as bank investments, U.S. treasury securities, and/or money market funds. Doing so keeps your money safe. When stocks are falling by 10 to 20 percent or more, you're better off earning a low-percentage interest in a secure, stable investment. In addition, you can do some research while your money is earning interest. Start shopping for undervalued stocks with strong fundamentals.

✔ **Stick to necessities.** In an economic downturn, defensive stocks generally outperform the market. *Defensive stocks* are stocks of companies that sell goods and services that people need no matter how good or bad the economy is doing. Good examples are food and beverage, energy, utilities, and certain healthcare stocks.

✔ **Use trailing stops.** Trailing stops is just the active use of stop loss orders on a given stock. (If a stock is at $40, you have the stop loss at $36, if the stock moves to $46, then change the stop loss from $36 to $41, and so on. Chapter 17 provides a fuller explanation). In the case of a bear market, you set your stop losses closer to the stock's market price ("tighten the trail"). Say, for example, that you once bought a stock for $50 per share and it's now at $110. Presume that you usually kept a trailing stop at 10 percent below the current market price. If the bear market is becoming more evident to you, then change that 10 percent to 5 percent. Before, that trailing stop on the $110 stock was $99 ($110 less 10 percent, or $11), but now it's at $104.50 ($110 less 5 percent, or $5.50). The trailing stop strategy is one of my favorite ways to protect my stock's gains.

Straddling Bear and Bull: Uncertain Markets

Uncertain markets are . . . well . . . uncertain. Markets aren't always up or down. The end of a bear market doesn't automatically mean the beginning of a bull market and vice versa. Sometimes markets move sideways or very little either way until investors and participants in the economy figure out what's what.

Pinpointing uncertainty is tough

Clashing points of view in the media tell you that even the experts aren't sure which way the market and the economy will go in the coming months. In uncertain markets, compelling evidence and loads of opinions will evenly line up on both the pro and con sides of the economic debate. Bullish and bearish advisors and commentators may both seem persuasive, so you may be left scratching your head, wondering what to do. In this case, your patience and diligence will pay off.

Deciding whether you want to approach an uncertain market

The approach to take in uncertain markets is almost simplistic. If you think that a bull market is starting, you want to have 100 percent of your growth portfolio invested in stocks, and if a bear market is starting, you want the percentage to be 0. Therefore, in an uncertain market, 50 percent in stocks and 50 percent in other investments is just right. Of course, these three scenarios need to be balanced by many nonstock factors, such as your individual financial situation, age, debt level, career concerns, and so on. However, all things being equal, those allocations aren't far off the mark.

Treat uncertain markets as bear markets until your research starts to give you a clear idea of the market's direction. No matter how adventurous you are, the first rule of stock investing is to minimize or avoid losses. If no one can agree on the direction of the market, then you stand a 50 percent chance of being wrong should you take the bullish stance. However, if you take a bearish stance and the market becomes decidedly bullish, no real harm is done except that you may miss a stock investing opportunity during a brief period of time. Just keep in mind that stock investing is indeed a long-term pursuit. Jumping into a bullish market is easy, but recovering from losses may not be.

Chapter 16

Choosing a Strategy That's Just Right for You

. . . .

. . . .

Stocks are a means to an end. What end are you seeking? You should look at stocks as tools for wealth building. Sometimes they're great tools, and sometimes they're awful. It depends on your approach. Some stocks are appropriate for a conservative approach, while others are more suitable for an aggressive approach. Sometimes stocks aren't a good idea at all. Golly! A stock investing book that suggests that stocks aren't always the answer! That's like a teenager saying, "Dad, I respectfully decline your generous offer of money for my weekend trip, and I'd be glad to mow the lawn."

Laying Out Your Plans

A senior citizen in one of my investment seminars in 2000 wanted to be more aggressive with his portfolio; his broker was more than happy to cater to his desire for growth stocks. Of course, stocks got clobbered in the volatile bear market of 2000–2002, and yes, he did lose lots of money. However, I soon discovered that even after the losses, he still had a substantial stock portfolio valued at over $1 million. He had more than enough to ensure a comfortable retirement. He had sought aggressive growth even though it was really unnecessary for his situation. If anything, the aggressive strategy could have put his portfolio (and hence his retirement) in jeopardy.

Growth is desirable even in your twilight years because inflation can eat away at a fixed-income portfolio. But different rates of growth exist, and the type you choose should be commensurate with your unique situation and financial needs. Notice that I say "needs," not "wants." These perspectives are entirely different. You may *want* to invest in aggressive stocks regardless of their suitability (after all, it's your money), but your financial situation may dictate that you *need* to take another approach. Just understand the difference.

Stocks can play a role in all sorts of investment strategies, but in this chapter, I discuss only a few well-known approaches. Keep in mind that a stock investing strategy can change based on the major changes in your life and the lifestyle that you lead, such as the ones I present in the following sections.

Living the bachelor life: Young single with no dependents

If you're young (age 20–40) and single, with no children or other dependents, being more aggressive with your stock selection is fine (as long as you don't use your rent money for investments). The reasoning is that if you do make riskier choices and they backfire, individuals dependent on you won't get hurt. In addition, if you're in this category, you can usually bounce back a lot easier over the long term even if you have financial challenges or if a bear market hits your stocks. Chapter 15 can tell you more about bear and bull markets.

Consider a mix of small-cap, mid-cap, and large-cap (see Chapter 1 for an explanation of each of these stocks) growth stocks in growth industries. Invest some of your money in five to seven stocks and the remainder in growth-stock mutual funds. You can revise your investment allocations along the way as the general economy changes and/or your personal situation (like when you finally say "I do" to the love of your life) changes.

Going together like a horse and carriage: Married with children

Married couples with children must follow a more conservative investing strategy, regardless of whether one spouse works or both spouses work. Children change the picture drastically (believe me, I have them and the baggy eyes to prove it). You need more stable growth in your portfolio (and unbreakable furniture in your home).

Safety first: Examining savings bonds

For the rest of this decade (I'm writing this book real-time 2005), fixed-interest bonds and other debt instruments (such as corporate bonds) generally aren't the right place to be because debt and interest rates are problematic for investors. A nice oasis in the valley of death known as America's debt load (currently $38+ trillion, which dwarfs our national GDP of about $12 trillion!) is U.S. Treasury issued savings bonds. Two types are out there — EE and I bonds. Savings bonds are bonds that are issued by the U.S. Treasury that can be purchased for as little as $25. The interest rates of both types change every six months as needed to reflect changing interest rates. If rates go up, The U.S. Treasury automatically updates the interest rates on your savings bonds every six months so you aren't locked in to low rates when market rates are rising. Savings bonds are ultrasafe, convenient, and inexpensive to buy, and they're free from state and local taxes. Find out more at the U.S. Treasury Web site www.savingsbonds.gov.

Consider a mix of large-cap growth stocks and dividend-paying defensive stocks. (See Chapter 9 for more on defensive stocks.) Invest some of your money in five to seven stocks and the remainder in growth and income mutual funds. Of course, you can tweak your allocations along the way according to changes in the general economic conditions or to your personal situation. Consider setting aside money for college in a growth-oriented mutual fund and in other vehicles such as savings bonds (as early as possible). For more information on financing college, check out *529 and Other College Savings Plans For Dummies* (Wiley).

Getting ready for retirement: Over 40 and either single or married

Whether you're over 40 and single, or you're over 40 and married (whether one or both of you work), you should start to slowly convert your portfolio from aggressive growth to conservative growth. Shift more of your money out of individual stocks and into less-volatile investments, such as balanced funds, investment-grade bonds, and bank certificates of deposit.

Devote some time and effort (with a financial planner if necessary) to calculating what your potential financial needs will be at retirement time. This step is critical in helping you decide what age to target for financial independence. (What's that? I can stop working?! Yee-Ha!)

Consider five to seven large-cap stocks that are predominantly dividend-paying defensive stocks in stable and needed industries (such as utilities, food and beverage, and so on). Put the remainder of your investment money in balanced mutual funds and short-term investment-grade bond funds. Have a large portion of your money in savings bonds and bank investments. Remember that you can revise your allocations in the future as necessary.

Kicking back in the hammock: Already retired

If you're retired, you're probably in your 60s or older. Safe, reliable income and wealth preservation form the crux of your investment strategy. Some growth-oriented investments are okay as long as they're conservative and don't jeopardize your need for income. At one time, financial planners told their retired clients to replace growth-oriented investments with safe income-oriented investments. However, times have changed as senior citizens live longer than ever before.

Issues such as longevity and inflation (steadily increasing costs of living) mean that today's (and tomorrow's) retirees need growth in their portfolios. To be safe, make sure that 5–20 percent of retirement portfolios have some growth-oriented securities such as stocks to make sure that you continue meeting your financial needs as the years pass. You should perform an annual review to see whether the stock allocation needs to be adjusted.

Consider a mix of large-cap stocks dominated by dividend-paying defensive stocks in stable industries. Spread your money over three to six stocks and the remainder in balanced mutual funds and short-term investment-grade bond funds. Have a large portion of your money in savings bonds and bank investments. You need to monitor and tweak your investment portfolio along the way to account for changes in either the general economic environment or your lifestyle needs.

Allocating Your Assets

Asset allocation is really an attempt to properly implement the concept of diversification — the key to safety and stability. *Diversification* is the inclusion in your portfolio of different (and frequently offsetting) investments to shield your wealth from most types of current risk while planning for future growth. To achieve proper diversification, you need to analyze your entire portfolio to look for glaring weaknesses or vulnerable areas. I don't discuss your total investment plan here, only the stock portion.

Investors frequently believe that having different stocks in different industries constitutes proper diversification. Well . . . not quite. Stocks in closely related industries tend to be affected (in differing degrees) by the same economic events, government policies, and so on. It's best to invest in stocks across different sectors. As I mention in Chapter 12, a sector is essentially a group of related industries. Water, gas, and electric services are industries, but together they (plus a few other industries) make up the utilities sector. For more on analyzing industries in order to pick winning stocks, see Chapter 12.

So far in this chapter, I talk about some basics for investing, depending on your lifestyle, but how do you know how much you need to invest in order to meet your financial goals? In the following sections, I present some typical amounts most typical investors can (and should) devote to stock investing.

Investors with less than $10,000

If you have $10,000 or less to allocate to stocks, you may want to consider a mutual fund rather than individual stocks because that sum of money may not be enough to properly diversify. But if you're going to invest a sum that small, consider allocating it equally into two to four stocks in two different sectors that look strong for the foreseeable future. For small investors, consider sectors that are defensive in nature (such as food and utilities).

Because $10,000 or less is a small sum in the world of stock investing, you may have to purchase in odd lots. (*Odd lots* usually mean 99 shares or less. A block of 100 shares is considered a *round lot.* Two hundred shares would be considered two round lots.) Say that you're buying four stocks and all of them are priced at $50 per share. An investment of $10,000 doesn't buy you 100 shares of each. You may have to consider investing $2,500 in each stock, which means that you end up buying only 50 shares of each stock (not including commissions). Whether you buy an odd lot or a round lot, find out whether the company has a dividend reinvestment plan (DRP), and use the dividend money you earn to buy more shares of stock. (I discuss DRPs more fully in Chapter 18.)

Try to avoid the temptation of getting into initial public offerings (IPOs), penny stocks, and other speculative issues. Participation in them may cost little (stock prices are often under $10 per share and can be under $1), but the risk exposure is too high for inexperienced investors. (See Chapter 8 for more on IPOs.)

Investors with $10,000–$50,000

If you have between $10,000 and $50,000 to invest, you have more breathing space for diversification. Consider buying four to six stocks in two or three different sectors. If you're the cautious type, defensive stocks will do. For growth investors, seek the industries in those sectors that have proven growth. This approach gets you off to a good start, and the section "Knowing When to Sell," later in this chapter, can help you maintain your portfolio with changing strategy (if necessary).

Does diversification mean that you shouldn't in any circumstance have all your stocks in one sector? It depends on you. For example, if you've worked all your life in a particular field and you're knowledgeable and comfortable with the sector, having a greater exposure is okay, because your greater personal expertise offsets the risk. If you worked in retail for 20 years and know the industry inside and out, you probably know more about the good, the bad, and the ugly of the retail sector than most Wall Street analysts. Use your insight for more profitability. You still shouldn't invest all your money in that single sector, however, because diversification is still vital.

Investors with $50,000 or more

If you have $50,000 or more to invest, have no more than five to ten stocks in two or three different sectors. It's difficult to thoroughly track more than two or three sectors and do it successfully — best to keep it simple. For example, Warren Buffett, considered the greatest stock market investor of all time, never invested in Web site businesses because he didn't understand them. He invests only in businesses that he understands. If that strategy works for billionaire investors, then, by golly, it can't be that bad for smaller investors.

I suggest investing in no more than seven stocks, because there is such a thing as overdiversification. The more stocks you have, the tougher it is to keep track of them. Owning more stocks means that you need to do more research, read more annual reports and news articles, and follow the business news of more companies. Even in the best of times, you need to regularly monitor your stocks because successful investing requires diligent effort.

Consider whether to hire a personal money manager (a person that manages investment portfolios for a fee). If you have $50,000 or $100,000 or more, doing so may make sense. Get a referral from a financial planner and carefully weigh the benefits against the costs. Here are some points to consider:

> ✔ **Make sure that the money manager has a philosophy and an approach that you agree with.**
>
> Ask the money manager to give you a copy of her written investment philosophy. How does she feel about small-cap stocks versus large-caps? Income versus growth?
>
> ✔ **Find out whether you're comfortable with how the money manager selects stocks.**
>
> Is she a value investor or a growth investor? Is she aggressive or conservative? Does she analyze a stock because of its fundamentals (sales, earnings, book value, and so on), or does she use stock price charts?
>
> ✔ **Ask the money manager to explain her strategy.**
>
> A good way to evaluate the success (or failure) of the strategy is to ask the money manager for her past recommendations. Did she pick more winners than losers?

Knowing When to Sell

The act of buying stock is relatively easy. However, the act of selling stock can be an agonizing decision for investors. But it's agonizing only in two instances: when you have made money with your stock and when you have lost it. That about covers it. It sounds like a bad joke, but it's not that far from the truth.

The idea of selling stock when it has appreciated (the stock price has increased in value) comes with the following concerns:

> ✔ **Tax implications:** This concern is a good reason to consider selling. See Chapter 20 for information about how selling stocks under given circumstances can affect your taxes.
>
> ✔ **Emotional baggage:** "That stock was in our family for years." Believe it or not, investors cite this personal reason (or one of a dozen other personal reasons) for agonizing over the sale of an appreciated stock.

The following is a list of issues that investors want to be aware of when they're selling a stock that has lost money:

> ✔ **Tax benefits:** This issue is a good reason to consider selling a stock. See Chapter 20 for more on timing your stock sales to minimize your tax burden.

✔ **Pride:** "If I sell, I'll have to admit I was wrong" (followed by silent sobbing). So what? The best investors in history have made bad investments (some that have been quite embarrassing, in fact). Losing a little pride is cheaper than losing your money.

✔ **Doubt:** "If I sell my stock now, it may rebound later." Frequently, when an investor buys a stock at $50 and it goes to $40, the investor believes that if he sells, the stock will make an immediate rebound and go to $60, and then he'll be kicking himself. That may happen, but usually the stock price goes lower.

✔ **Separation anxiety:** "But I've had this stock so long that it's become a part of me." People hang on to a losing stock for all sorts of illogical reasons. Being married to a person is great; being married to a stock is ludicrous. If a stock isn't helping your goals, then it's hurting your goals.

People have plenty more reasons to agonize over the sale of a bad stock. But you can learn to handle the stock sale in a disciplined manner.

You have only two reasons to consider selling a stock regardless of whether the stock price has gone up or down:

✔ **You need the money.** Obviously, if you need the money for a bona fide reason — such as paying off debt, wiping out a tax bill, or buying a home — then you need the money. This reason is easy to see. After all, regardless of investment or tax considerations, stocks are there to serve you. I hope that you do some financial planning so that you don't need to sell your stocks for these types of expenses, but you can't avoid unexpected expenditures.

✔ **The stock ceased to perform as you desired.** If the stock isn't serving your wealth-building goals or fulfilling your investment objectives, it's time to get rid of it and move on to the next stock. Just as soon as you get a stiff upper lip and resolve to unload this losing stock, a little voice saying, "If I sell my stock now, it may rebound later," starts to haunt you. So you hang on to the stock, but then — bam! — before you know it, you lose more money.

Selling a stock shouldn't require a psychologist. This place is where discipline steps in. This belief is why I'm a big proponent of trailing stops. (See Chapter 17 for more on stop orders.) Trailing stops take the agony out of selling the stock. All else being equal, you shouldn't sell a winning stock. If it's doing well, why sell it? Keep it as long as possible. But if it stops being a winning stock, sell it. If you don't know how or when to sell it, then apply a stop-loss order at 5 or 10 percent below the market value and let the market action take its course.

Chapter 17

Understanding Brokerage Orders and Trading Techniques

*I*nvestment success isn't just about picking rising stocks; it's also about how you go about doing it. Frequently, investors think that good stock picking means doing your homework and then making that buy (or sell). However, you can take it a step further to maximize profits (or minimize losses). As a stock investor, you can take advantage of techniques and services available through your standard brokerage account. (See Chapter 7 for more on brokerage accounts.) This chapter presents some of the best ways you can use these powerful techniques — useful whether you're buying or selling stock. In fact, if you retain nothing more from this chapter than the concept of *trailing stops* (see the section "Trailing stops"), you'll have gotten your money's worth. (Really!)

Just before the stock market bubble popped, I warned my students and readers that a bear market was on the way. All the data warned me about it, and undoubtedly, it seemed like a time for caution. (See Chapter 15 for information about bull and bear markets.) Investors didn't have to necessarily believe me, but they could have (at the very least) used trailing stops and other techniques to ensure greater investing success. Investors that used stop loss orders avoided the carnage of trillions of dollars in stock losses. In this chapter, I show you how to use these techniques to maximize your investing profit.

Checking Out Brokerage Orders

Orders you place with your stockbroker neatly fit into two categories:

- ✔ Time-related orders
- ✔ Condition-related orders

Get familiar with both orders, because they're easy to implement and invaluable tools for wealth building and (more importantly) wealth saving!

 Using a combination of orders helps you fine-tune your strategy so that you can maintain greater control over your investments. Speak with your broker about the different types of orders you can use to maximize the gains (or minimize the losses) from your stock investing activities. You also can read the broker's policies on stock orders at the brokerage Web site.

Time-related orders

Time-related orders mean just that; the order has a time limit. Typically, investors use these orders in conjunction with conditional orders. The two most common time-related orders are day orders and good-till-canceled (or GTC) orders.

Day order

A *day order* is an order to buy a stock that expires at the end of that particular trading day. If you tell your broker, "Buy BYOB, Inc., at $37.50 and make it a day order," you mean that you want to purchase the stock at $37.50. But if the stock doesn't hit that price, your order expires at the end of the trading day unfilled. Why would you place such an order? Maybe BYOB is trading at $39, but you don't want to buy it at that price because you don't believe the stock is worth it. Consequently, you have no problem not getting the stock that day.

When would you use day orders? It depends on your preferences and personal circumstances. I rarely use day orders because few events cause me to say, "Gee, I'll just try to buy or sell between now and the end of today's trading action." However, you may feel that you don't want a specified order to linger beyond today's market action. Perhaps you want to test a price. ("I want to get rid of stock A at $39 to make a quick profit, but it's currently trading at $37.50. However, I may change my mind tomorrow.") A day order is the perfect strategy to use in this case.

If you make any trade and don't specify time with the order, most (if not all) brokers automatically treat it as a day order.

Good-till-canceled (GTC)

A good-till-canceled (GTC) order is the most commonly requested order by investors. Although GTC orders are time-related, they're always tied to a condition, such as when the stock achieves a certain price. The GTC order means just what it says: The order stays in effect until it's transacted or until the investor cancels it. Although the order implies that it can run indefinitely, most brokers have a limit of 30 or 60 days (or more). By that time, either the broker cancels the order or contacts you to see whether you want to extend it. Ask your broker about his particular policy.

A GTC order is usually coupled with conditional or condition-related orders. For example, say that you want to buy ASAP Corp. stock but you don't want to buy it at the current price of $48 per share. You've done your homework on the stock, including looking at the stock's price-to-earnings ratio, price-to-book ratio, and so on (see Appendix B for more on ratios), and you say, "Hey, this stock isn't worth $48 a share. I'd only buy it at $36 per share." You think the stock would make a good addition to your portfolio but not at the current market price. (It's overpriced or overvalued according to your analysis.) How should you proceed? Your best bet is to ask your broker to do a "GTC order at $36." This request means that your broker will buy the shares if and when they hit the $36 mark (or until you cancel the order). Just make sure that your account has the funds available to complete the transaction.

GTC orders are very useful, so you should become familiar with your broker's policy on them. While you're at it, ask whether any fees apply. Many brokers don't charge for GTC orders because, if they happen to result in a buy (or sell) order, they generate a normal commission just as any stock transaction does. Other brokers may charge a small fee.

To be successful with GTC orders, you need to know

✔ **When you want to buy:** In recent years, people have had a tendency to rush into buying a stock without giving some thought to what they could do to get more for their money. Some investors don't realize that the stock market can be a place for bargain-hunting consumers. If you're ready to buy a quality pair of socks for $16 in a department store but the sales clerk says that those same socks are going on sale tomorrow for only $8, what would you do — assuming that you're a cost-conscious consumer? Unless you're barefoot, you're probably better off waiting. The same point holds true with stocks.

Say that you want to buy SOX, Inc., at $26 but it's currently trading at $30. You think that $30 is too expensive, but you're happy to buy the stock at $26 or lower. However, you have no idea whether the stock will move to your desired price today, tomorrow, next week, or even next month (maybe never). In this case, a GTC order is appropriate.

✔ **When you want to sell:** What if you bought some socks at a department store, and you discovered that they have holes (darn it!)? Wouldn't you want to get rid of them? Of course you would. If a stock's price starts to unravel, you want to be able to get rid of it as well.

Perhaps you already own SOX (at $25, for instance) but are concerned that market conditions may drive the price lower. You're not certain which way the stock will move in the coming days and weeks. In this case, a GTC order to sell the stock at a specified price is a suitable strategy. Because the stock price is $25, you may want to place a GTC order to sell it if it falls to $22.50, to prevent further losses. Again, in this example, GTC is the time frame, and it accompanies a condition (sell when the stock hits $22.50).

Condition-related orders

A condition-related order means that the order is executed only when a certain condition is met. Conditional orders enhance your ability to buy stocks at a lower price, to sell at a better price, or to minimize potential losses. When stock markets become bearish or uncertain, conditional orders are highly recommended. A good example of a conditional order is a *limit order*. A limit order may say, "Buy Mojeski Corp. at $45." But if Mojeski Corp. isn't at $45 (this price is the condition), then the order isn't executed.

Market orders

When you buy stock, the simplest type of order is a *market order* — an order to buy or sell a stock at the market's current best available price. It doesn't get any more basic than that.

Here's an example: Kowalski, Inc., is available at the market price of $10. When you call up your broker and instruct him to buy 100 shares "at the market," the broker will implement the order for your account, and you pay $1,000 plus commission.

I say "current best available price" because the stock's price is constantly moving, and catching the best price can be a function of the broker's ability to process the stock purchase. For very active stocks, the price change can happen within seconds. It's not unheard of to have three brokers simultaneously place orders for the same stocks and get three different prices because of differences in the broker's capability. (Some computers are faster than others.)

The advantage of a market order is that the transaction is processed immediately, and you get your stock without worrying about whether it hits a particular price. For example, if you buy Kowalski, Inc., with a market order, you know that by the end of that phone call (or Web site visit), you're assured of getting the stock. The disadvantage of a market order is that you can't control the price that you pay for the stock. Whether you're buying or selling your shares, you may not realize the exact price you expect (especially if you're buying a volatile stock).

Market orders get finalized in the chronological order in which they're placed. Your price may change because the orders ahead of you in line caused the stock price to rise or fall based on the latest news.

Stop orders (also known as stop-loss orders)

A *stop order* (or *stop-loss order* if you own the stock) is a condition-related order that instructs the broker to sell a particular stock only when the stock reaches a particular price. It acts like a trigger, and the stop order converts to a market order to sell the stock immediately.

The stop-loss order isn't designed to take advantage of small, short-term moves in the stock's price. It's meant to help you protect the bulk of your money when the market turns against your stock investment in a sudden manner.

Say that your Kowalski, Inc., stock rises to $20 per share and you seek to protect your investment against a possible future market decline. A stop-loss order at $18 triggers your broker to sell the stock immediately if it falls to the $18 mark. In this example, if the stock suddenly drops to $17, it still triggers the stop-loss order, but the finalized sale price is $17. In a volatile market, you may not be able to sell at your precise stop-loss price. However, because the order automatically gets converted into a market order, the sale will be done, and you prevent further declines in the stock.

The main benefit of a stop-loss order is that it prevents a major decline in a stock that you own. It's a form of discipline that's important in investing in order to minimize potential losses. Investors can find it agonizing to sell a stock that has fallen. If they don't sell, however, the stock often continues to plummet as investors continue to hold on while hoping for a rebound in the price.

Most investors set a stop-loss amount at about 10 percent below the market value of a stock. This percentage gives the stock some room to fluctuate, which most stocks tend to do on a day-to-day basis.

Practice discipline

I have a stack of several years' worth of investment newsletters in which investment experts made all sorts of calls regarding the prospects of a company, industry, or the economy in general. Some made forecasts that were spectacularly on target, but you should see the ones that were spectacularly wrong — ouch! However, even some of the winners suffered because of a lack of discipline. Those spectacular gains disappeared like football fans at a chess match.

One of the biggest recommendations by newsletter experts in 2000 was Cisco Systems (CSCO). In March 2000, it was at $85 and its market value (stock price times total shares outstanding) was a whopping $600 billion. Some stock gurus even said that it would become the first trillion-dollar stock. Other gurus said that CSCO's earnings would grow 30–40 percent per year, indefinitely. Right about now you know that

some of these gurus are in a new profession asking their clients, "Would you like those loafers in black or brown?"

From March 2000 to October 2003, CSCO painfully descended from $85 to just under $9 per share — a spectacular 90 percent collapse. By June 2005, it had recovered to about $19 per share. It didn't recover its old glory. Had investors placed a stop-loss order at about 10 percent below its then high ($85 less 10 percent or about $77), they would have kept their wealth basically intact and would subsequently have had enough cash to buy four or five times more stock when it hit bottom.

Investing can be an emotional roller coaster. Keep your sanity and your profits by being disciplined. Use your stop-loss orders and fasten those seat belts.

Trailing stops

Trailing stops are an important technique in wealth preservation for seasoned stock investors and can be one of your key strategies in using stop-loss orders. A *trailing stop* is a stop-loss order that the investor actively manages by moving it up along with the stock's market price. The stop-loss order "trails" the stock price upward. As the stop-loss goes upward, it protects more and more of the stock's value from declining.

A real-life example may be the best way to help you understand trailing stops. Say that in 1999 you bought Lucent Technologies (LU) at $25 per share. As soon as you finished buying it, you immediately told your broker to put a stop-loss order at $22 and make it a good-till-canceled (GTC) order. Think of what you did. In effect, you placed an ongoing (GTC) safety net under your stock. The stock can go as high as the sky, but if it should fall, the stock's price triggers a market order at $22. Your stock is automatically sold, minimizing your loss.

If Lucent goes to $50 per share in a few months, you can call your broker and cancel the former stop-loss order at $22 and replace it with a new (higher) stop-loss order. You simply say, "Please put a new stop-loss order at $45 and make it a GTC order." This higher stop-loss price protects not only your original investment of $20 but also a big chunk of your profit as well. As time goes by, and the stock price climbs, you can continue to raise the stop-loss price and add a GTC provision. Now you know why it's called a trailing stop: It trails the stock price upward like a giant tail. All along the way, it protects more and more of your growing investment without limiting its upward movement.

William O'Neill, publisher and founder of *Investor's Business Daily,* advocates setting a trailing stop of 8 percent below your purchase price. That's his preference. Some investors who invest in very volatile stocks may put in trailing stops of 20 or 25 percent. Is a stop-loss order desirable or advisable in every situation? No. It depends on your level of experience, your investment goals, and the market environment. Still, stop-loss orders are appropriate in most cases, especially if the market seems uncertain (or you do!).

A trailing stop is a stop-loss order that you actively manage. The stop-loss order is good-till-canceled (GTC), and it constantly trails the stock's price as it moves up. To successfully implement trailing stops, keep the following points in mind:

- ✔ **Remember that brokers usually don't place trailing stops for you automatically.** In fact, they won't (or shouldn't) place any type of order without your consent. Deciding on the type of order to place is your responsibility. You can raise, lower, or cancel a trailing stop order at will, but you need to monitor your investment when substantial moves do occur to respond to the movement appropriately.

- ✔ **Change the stop-loss order when the stock price moves significantly.** Hopefully, you won't call your broker every time the stock moves 50 cents. Change the stop-loss order when the stock price moves around 10 percent. When you initially purchase the stock (say at $90 per share), request the broker to place the stop-loss order at $81. When the stock moves to $100, cancel the $81 stop-loss order and replace it at $90. When the stock's price moves to $110, change the stop-loss order to $99, and so on.

- ✔ **Understand your broker's policy on GTC orders.** If your broker usually has a GTC order expire after 30 or 60 days, you should be aware of it. You don't want to risk a sudden drop in your stock's price without the stop-loss order protection. If your broker's time limit is 60 days, note it so that you can renew the order for additional time.

- ✔ **Monitor your stock.** A trailing stop isn't a "set it and forget it" technique. Monitoring your investment is critical. Of course, if investment falls, the stop-loss order you have prevents further loss. Should the stock price rise substantially, remember to adjust your trailing stop accordingly. Keep raising the safety net as the stock continues to rise. Part of monitoring the stock is knowing the beta, which you can read more about in the next section.

Using beta measurement

To be a successful investor, you need to understand the volatility of the particular stock you invest in. In stock market parlance, this volatility is also called the beta of a stock. *Beta* is a quantitative measure of the volatility of a given stock (mutual funds and portfolios, too) relative to the overall market, usually the S&P 500 index. (For more information on the S&P 500, see Chapter 5.) Beta specifically measures the performance movement of the stock as the S&P moves 1 percent up or down. A beta measurement above 1 is more volatile than the overall market, while a beta below 1 is less volatile. Some stocks are relatively stable in the price movements; others jump around.

Because beta measures how volatile or unstable the stock's price is, it tends to be uttered in the same breath as "risk" — more volatility indicates more risk. Similarly, less volatility tends to mean less risk.

Table 17-1 shows some sample betas of well-known companies (as of July 2005).

Table 17-1	Looking at Well-Known Betas	
Company	*Beta*	*Comments*
Exxon Mobil (XOM)	.464	Less volatile than the market. If the S&P moves 10%, XOM only moves 4.64%.
Cypress Semiconductor (CY)	3.287	Three times more volatile than the market.
Public Service Enterprise Group (PEG)	.369	Statistically considered much less volatile than the market.

You can find a company's beta at Web sites that usually provide a lot of financial information about the company, such as Nasdaq's Web site (www. nasdaq.com) or Yahoo!Finance (finance.yahoo.com).

The beta is useful to know because it gives you a general idea of the stock's trading range. If a stock is currently priced at $50 and it typically trades in the $48–$52 range, then a trailing stop at $49 doesn't make sense. Your stock would probably be sold the same day you initiated the stop-loss order. If your stock is a volatile growth stock that could swing up and down by 10 percent, you should more logically set your stop-loss at 15 percent below that day's price.

The stock of a large-cap company in a mature industry tends to have a low beta — one close to the overall market. Small and mid-cap stocks in new or emerging industries tend to have greater volatility in their day-to-day price fluctuations; hence, they tend to have a high beta. (You can find out more about large, small, and mid-cap stocks in Chapter 1.)

Limit orders

A *limit order* is a very precise condition-related order, implying that a limit exists either on the buy or the sell side of the transaction. You want to buy (or sell) only at a specified price or better. Period. Limit orders work better for you if you're buying the stock, but they may not be good for you if you're selling the stock. Here's how it works in both instances:

✓ **When you're buying:** Just because you like a particular company and you want its stock doesn't mean that you're willing to pay the current market price. Maybe you want to buy Kowalski, Inc., but the current market price of $20 per share isn't acceptable to you. You prefer to buy it at $16 because you think that price reflects its true market value. What do you do? You tell your broker, "Buy Kowalski with a limit order at $16." You have to specify whether it's a day order (good for the day) or a GTC order, which I discuss in its own section earlier in this chapter.

What happens if the stock experiences great volatility? What if it drops to $16.01 and then suddenly drops to $15.95 on the next move? Actually, nothing, you may be dismayed to hear. Because your order was limited to $16, it can be transacted only at $16, no more or less. The only way for this particular trade to occur is if the stock rises back to $16. However, if the price keeps dropping, then your limit order isn't transacted and may expire or be canceled.

When you're buying a stock, many brokers interpret the limit order as "buy at this specific price or better." Presumably, if your limit order is to buy the stock at $10, you'll be just as happy if your broker buys that stock for you at $9.95. This way, if you don't get exactly $10, because the stock's price was volatile, you'll still get the stock at a lower price. Speak to your particular broker to be clear on the meaning of the limit order.

✓ **When you're selling:** Limit orders are activated only when a stock hits a specific price. If you buy Kowalski, Inc., at $20 and you worry about a decline in the share price, you may decide to put in a limit order at $18. If you watch the news and hear that Kowalski's price is dropping, you may sigh and say, "I sure am glad that I put in that limit order at $18!" However, in a volatile market, the share price may leapfrog over your specified price. It could go from $18.01 to $17.99 and then continue its descent. Because the stock price never hit $18 on the mark, it isn't sold. You may be sitting at home satisfied (mistakenly) that you played it smart, while your stock plummets to $15 or $10 or worse! Having a stop-loss order in place is best.

Buying on Margin

Margin means buying securities, such as stocks, by using funds you borrow from your broker. Buying stock on margin is similar to buying a house with a mortgage. If you buy a house at a purchase price of $100,000 and put 10 percent down, your equity (the part you own) is $10,000, and you borrow the remaining $90,000 with a mortgage. If the value of the house rises to $120,000 and you sell (for the sake of simplicity, I don't include closing costs in this example), you make a profit of 200 percent. How is that? The $20,000 gain on the property represents a gain of 20 percent on the purchase price of $100,000, but because your real investment is $10,000 (the down payment), your gain works out to 200 percent (a gain of $20,000 on your initial investment of $10,000).

Buying on margin is an example of using leverage to maximize your gain when prices rise. *Leverage* is simply using borrowed money when you make an asset purchase in order to increase your potential profit. This type of leverage is great in a favorable (bull) market, but it works against you in an unfavorable (bear) market. Say that a $100,000 house you purchase with a $90,000 mortgage falls in value to $80,000 (and property values can decrease during economic hard times). Your outstanding debt of $90,000 exceeds the value of the property. Because you owe more than you own, you're left with a negative net worth. Leverage is a double-edged sword.

Examining marginal outcomes

Suppose that you think that the stock for the company Mergatroid, Inc., currently at $40 per share, will go up in value. You want to buy 100 shares, but you have only $2,000. What can you do? If you're intent on buying 100 shares (versus simply buying the 50 shares that you have cash for), you can borrow the additional $2,000 from your broker on margin. If you do that, what are the potential outcomes?

If the stock price goes up

This outcome is the best for you. If Mergatroid goes to $50 per share, your investment is worth $5,000, and your outstanding margin loan is $2,000. If you sell, the total proceeds will pay off the loan and leave you with $3,000. Because your initial investment was $2,000, your profit is a solid 50 percent because ultimately your $2,000 principal amount generated a $1,000 profit. (For the sake of this example, I leave out any charges, such as commissions and interest paid on the margin loan.) However, if you pay the entire $4,000 upfront without the margin loan, then your $4,000 investment generates a profit of $1,000, or 25 percent. Using margin, you double the return on your money.

Leverage, when used properly, is very profitable. However, it's still debt, so understand that you must pay it off eventually, regardless of the stock's performance.

If the stock price fails to rise

If the stock goes nowhere, you still have to pay interest on that margin loan. If the stock pays dividends, this money can defray some of the cost of the margin loan. In other words, dividends can help you pay off what you borrow from the broker.

Having the stock neither rise nor fall may seem like a neutral situation, but you pay interest on your margin loan with each passing day. For this reason, margin trading can be a good consideration for conservative investors if the stock pays a high dividend. Many times, a high dividend from $5,000 worth of stock can exceed the margin interest you have to pay from the $2,500 (50 percent) you borrow from the broker to buy that stock.

If the stock price goes down, buying on margin can work against you. What if Mergatroid goes to $38 per share? The market value of 100 shares is then $3,800, but your equity shrinks to only $1,800 because you have to pay your $2,000 margin loan. You're not exactly looking at a disaster at this point, but you'd better be careful, because the margin loan exceeds 50 percent of your stock investment. If it goes any lower, you may get the dreaded *margin call,* when the broker actually contacts you to ask you to restore the ratio between the margin loan and the value of the securities. See the following section for information about appropriate debt to equity ratios.

Maintaining your balance

When you purchase stock on margin, you must maintain a balanced ratio of margin debt to equity of at least 50 percent. If the debt portion exceeds this limit, then you're required to restore that ratio by depositing either more stock or more cash into your brokerage account. The additional stock you deposit can be stock that's transferred from another account.

If, for example, Mergatroid goes to $28 per share, the margin loan portion exceeds 50 percent of the equity value in that stock — in this case, because the market value of your stock is $2,800 but the margin loan is still at $2,000, the margin loan is a worrisome 71 percent of the market value ($2,000 divided by $2,800 = 71 percent). Expect to get a call from your broker to put more securities or cash into the account to restore the 50 percent balance.

If you can't come up with more stock, other securities, or cash, then the next step is to sell stock from the account and use the proceeds to pay off the margin loan. For you, it means realizing a capital loss — you lost money on your investment.

The Federal Reserve Board governs margin requirements for brokers with Regulation T. Discuss this rule with your broker to understand fully your (and the broker's) risks and obligations. Regulation T dictates margin requirements set by brokers to their customers. For most listed stocks, it's 50 percent.

Margin, as you can see, can escalate your profits on the up side but magnify your losses on the down side. If your stock plummets drastically, you can end up with a margin loan that exceeds the market value of the stock you used the loan to purchase. In the emerging bear market of 2000–2002, stock losses hurt many people, and a large number of these losses were made worse because people didn't manage the responsibilities involved with margin trading.

If you buy stock on margin, use a disciplined approach. Be extra careful when using leverage, such as a margin loan, because it can backfire. Keep the following points in mind:

- ✔ **Have ample reserves of cash or marginable securities in your account.** Try to keep the margin ratio at 40 percent or less to minimize the chance of a margin call.

- ✔ **If you're a beginner, consider using margin to buy stock in large companies that have a relatively stable price and pay a good dividend.** Some people buy income stocks that have dividend yields that exceed the margin interest rate, meaning that the stock ends up paying for its own margin loan. Just remember those stop orders.

- ✔ **Constantly monitor your stocks.** If the market turns against you, the result will be especially painful if you use margin.

- ✔ **Have a payback plan for your margin debt.** Margin loans against your investments mean that you're paying interest. Your ultimate goal is to make money, and paying interest eats into your profits.

Going Short and Coming Out Ahead

The vast majority of stock investors are familiar with buying stock, holding on to it for a while, and hoping its value goes up. This kind of thinking is called *going long,* and investors who go long are considered to be *long on stocks.* Going long essentially means that you're bullish and seeking your profits from rising prices. However, astute investors also profit in the market when stock prices fall. *Going short* (also called *shorting a stock, selling short,* or *doing a short sale*) on a stock is a common technique for profiting from a stock price decline. Investors have made big profits during bear markets by going short. A short sale is a bet that a particular stock is going down.

To go short, you have to be deemed (by your broker) creditworthy — your account needs to be approved for short selling. When you're approved for margin trading, you're probably set to sell short, too. Speak to your broker (or check for this information on the broker's Web site) about limitations in your account regarding going short.

Because going short on stocks has greater risks than going long, I strongly advise beginning investors to avoid shorting stocks until they become more seasoned.

Most people easily understand making money by going long. It boils down to "buy low and sell high." Piece of cake. Going short means making money by selling high and then buying low. Huh? Thinking in reverse isn't a piece of cake. Although thinking of this stock adage in reverse may be challenging, the mechanics of going short are really simple. Consider an example that uses a fictitious company called DOA, Inc. As a stock, DOA ($50 per share) is looking pretty sickly. It has lots of debt and plummeting sales and earnings, and the news is out that DOA's industry will face hard times for the foreseeable future. This situation describes a stock that's an ideal candidate for shorting. The future may be bleak for DOA, but promising for savvy investors.

You must understand brokerage rules before you conduct short selling. The broker must approve you for it (see Chapter 7 for information on working with brokers), and you must meet the minimum collateral requirement, which is typically $2,000 or 50 percent of the shorted stock's market value. If the stock generates dividends, those dividends are paid to the owner of the stock, not to the person who is borrowing it to go short. (See the next section, "Setting up a short sale," to see how this technique works.) Check with your broker for complete details and review the resources in Appendix A.

Setting up a short sale

This section explains how to go short. Say that you believe that DOA is the right stock to short — you're pretty sure its price is going to fall. With DOA at $50, you instruct your broker to "go short 100 shares on DOA." (It doesn't have to be 100 shares. I'm just using that as an example.) Now, here's what happens next:

1. **Your broker borrows 100 shares of DOA stock, either from his own inventory or from another client or broker.**

   That's right. The stock can be borrowed from a client, no permission necessary. The broker guarantees the transaction, and the client/owner of the stock never has to be informed about it, because he never loses legal and beneficial right to the stock. You borrow 100 shares, and you'll return 100 shares when it's time to complete the transaction.

2. **Your broker then sells the stock and puts the money in your account.**

    Your account is credited with $5,000 (100 shares × $50) in cash — the money gained from selling the borrowed stock. This cash acts like a loan on which you're going to have to pay interest.

3. **You buy the stock back and return it to its rightful owner.**

    When it's time to close the transaction (either you want to close it, or the owner of the shares wants to sell them, so you have to give them back), you must return the number of shares you borrowed (in this case, it was 100 shares). If you buy back the 100 shares at $40 per share (remember that you shorted this particular stock because you were sure its price was going to fall) and these 100 shares are returned to their owner, you make a $1,000 profit. (To keep the example tidy, I don't include brokerage commissions.)

Oops! Going short when prices grow taller

I bet you guessed that the wonderful profitability of selling short has a flip side. Presume that you were wrong about DOA and that the stock price rises from the ashes as it goes from $50 to $87. Now what? You still have to return the 100 shares you borrowed. With the stock's price at $87, that means that you have to buy the stock for $8,700 (100 shares at the new, higher price of $87). Ouch! How do you pay for it? Well, you have that original $5,000 in your account from when you initially went short on the stock. But where do you get the other $3,700 ($8,700 less the original $5,000)? You guessed it — your pocket! You have to cough up the difference. If the stock continues to rise, that's a lot of coughing.

How much money do you lose if the stock goes to $100 or more? A heck of a lot. As a matter of fact, there's no limit to how much you can lose. That's why going short can be riskier than going long. With going long, the most you can lose is 100 percent of your money. However, with going short, you can lose more than 100 percent of the money you invest. Yikes!

Because the potential for loss is unlimited when you short a stock, I suggest that you use a stop order (also called a *buy-stop order*) to minimize the damage. Better yet, make it a good-till-canceled order, which I discuss earlier in this chapter. You can set the stop order at a given price, and if the stock hits that price, you buy the stock back so that you can return it to its owner before the price rises even higher. You still lose money, but you limit your losses.

Watching out for ticks

Short sellers should be aware of the *uptick rule,* which states that you can enter into a short sale only when the stock has just completed an uptick. "Tick" in this case means the actual incremental price movement of the stock you're shorting. For a $10 stock that was just $9.95 a moment ago, the 5-cent difference represents an uptick. If the $10 stock was just $10.10 a moment before, the 10-cent difference is a downtick. The amount of the tick doesn't matter. So, if you short a stock at the price of $40, the immediate prior price must have been $39.99 or lower. The reason for this rule (a Federal Reserve regulation) is that short selling can aggravate declining stock prices in a rapidly falling market. In practice, going short on a stock whose price is already declining can make the stock price fall even farther. Excessive short selling can make the stock more volatile than it would be otherwise.

Feeling the squeeze

If you go short on a stock, remember that, sooner or later, you have to buy that stock back so that you can return it to its owner. What happens when a lot of people are short on a particular stock and its price starts to rise? All those short sellers are scrambling to buy the stock back so that they can close their transactions before they lose too much money. This mass buying quickens the pace of the stock's ascent and puts a squeeze (called a *short squeeze*) on the investors who had been shorting the stock.

Earlier in the chapter, I explain that your broker can borrow stock from another client so that you can go short on it. What happens when that client wants to sell the stock in her account — the stock that you borrowed and so is no longer in her account? When that happens, your broker asks you to return the borrowed stock. That's when you feel the squeeze — you have to buy the stock back at the current price.

Going short can be a great maneuver in a declining (bear) market, but it can be brutal if the stock price goes up. If you're a beginner, stay away from short selling until you have enough experience (and money) to risk it.

Chapter 18

Getting a Handle on DPPs, DRPs, and DCA . . . PDQ

. . . .

In This Chapter

▶ Buying stock directly from a company

▶ Looking at dividend reinvestment plans

▶ Using dollar cost averaging

. . . .

Who says that you must buy 100 shares of a stock to invest? Do you really have to go through a broker to buy stock, or can you buy direct? What if you only want to put your toe in the water and buy just one share for starters? Can you do that without paying through the nose for transaction costs, such as commissions? The answer to these questions is that you can buy stocks directly (without a broker) and save money in the process. That's what this chapter is about. In this chapter, I show you how direct purchase programs (DPPs) and dividend reinvestment plans (DRPs) make a lot of sense for long-term stock investors, and how you can do them on your own — no broker necessary. I also show you how to use the method of dollar cost averaging (DCA) to acquire stock, a technique that works especially well with DRPs.

The types of programs are well-suited for those people who like to invest small sums of money and plan on doing so on a consistent basis in the same stock (or stocks) over a long period of time.

Being Direct with DPPs

If you're going to buy a stock anyway, why not buy it directly from the company and bypass the broker (and commissions) altogether? Several hundred companies now offer *direct purchase programs* (DPPs), also called DIPs (or direct investment programs), which give investors an opportunity to buy stock directly from these companies.

DPPs give investors the opportunity to get involved with little upfront money (usually enough to cover the purchase of one share) and usually no commissions. Why do companies give investors this opportunity? For their sake, they want to encourage more attention and participation from investors. For your purposes, however, a DPP gives you what you may need most: a low-cost entry into that particular company's DRP (which you can read more about in the section "Dipping into DRPs," later in this chapter).

Investing in a DPP

If you have your sights set on a particular company and have only a few bucks to start out with, a DPP is probably the best way to make your initial investment. The following steps can guide you toward your first stock purchase using a DPP:

1. **Decide what stock you want to invest in. (This whole book is about that topic.)**

   Say that you did your homework and you decide to invest in Yumpin Yimminy Corp. (YYC). Contact the company directly and request to speak to someone in the shareholder services department. You can get YYC's contact information through the stock exchange YYC trades on. For example, if YYC is traded on the New York Stock Exchange, you can call the NYSE or visit its Web site (www.nyse.com) and ask for the contact information for YYC. So, you can contact NYSE to reach YYC for its DPP ASAP. OK?

2. **Find out whether YYC has a DPP (before it's DOA! OK?).**

   Call YYC's shareholder services department and ask whether it has a DPP. If it does, great; if it doesn't, ask whether it plans to start one. At the very least, it may have a DRP.

3. **Look into enrolling.**

   The company will send you an application along with a prospectus — the program document that serves as a brochure and, hopefully, answers your basic questions.

   The processing is typically handled by an organization that the company designates (the plan administrator). From this point forward, you're in the dividend reinvestment plan. (See the section "Dipping into DRPs," later in this chapter.)

Finding DPP alternatives

Although several hundred companies offer DPPs, the majority of companies don't. What do you do if you want to invest in a company directly and it doesn't have a DPP? The following sections present some alternatives.

Buy the first share through a broker to qualify for DRPs

Yes, buying your first share through a broker will cost you a commission; however, after you make the stock purchase, you can contact that company's shareholder services department and ask about its DRP. (See the section "Dipping into DRPs," later in this chapter.) After you're an existing stockholder, qualifying for the DRP is a piece of cake.

To qualify for the DRP, you must be on the books of record with the transfer agent. A *book of record* is simply the database that the company uses to track every single outstanding share of stock and the owner of the stock. The *transfer agent* is the person responsible for maintaining the database. Whenever stock is bought or sold, the transfer agent must implement the change and update the records on stock ownership. In many cases, you must have the broker issue a stock certificate in your name once you own the stock. This is the most common way to get your name on the books of record, hence qualifying you for the DRP.

Sometimes, simply buying the stock isn't enough to get your name on the book of record, because brokers often keep the stock in your account under a *street name*. Having a street name means that although you technically own the stock, your broker may keep it registered under a different name for ease of transaction. Having the stock in a street name really doesn't mean much to you until you want to qualify for the company's DPP or DRP. Remember to address this point with your broker.

Get started in a DRP directly through a broker

These days, more brokers are able to offer the features of the DRP (like compounding interest) right in the brokerage account itself, making it more convenient than having to go to the trouble of setting up a DRP with the company. This service is most likely a response to the growing number of long-term investors who have fled traditional brokerage accounts for the benefits of direct investing that DPPs and DRPs offer. The main drawback of a broker-run DRP is that usually it doesn't allow you to make optional cash purchases (a big negative!). See the section "Building wealth with optional cash payments (OCPs)," later in this chapter, for more on this topic.

Purchase via alternate buying services

Organizations have set up services to help small investors buy stock in small quantities. The primary drawback to these middlemen is that you will probably pay more in transaction costs than if you approach the companies directly. Check out the most prominent services, which include the following:

✔ Money Paper at `www.directinvesting.com`

✔ National Association of Investors Corporation at `www.better investing.org`

✔ Sharebuilder at `www.sharebuilder.com`

Recognizing that every pro has a con

As beneficial as DPPs are, they do have some minor drawbacks. (Doesn't everything?) Keep the following points in mind when considering DPPs as part of your stock portfolio:

✔ Although more and more companies are starting to offer DPPs, still relatively few companies have them.

✔ Some DPPs require a high initial amount to invest (as much as $250 or more) or a commitment of monthly investments. In any case, ask the plan administrator about the investing requirements.

✔ A growing number of DPPs have some type of service charge. Usually this charge (if your DPP has a charge) is very modest and lower than typical brokerage commissions. Ask about all the incidents, such as getting into the plan, getting out, and so on, that may trigger a service charge.

Don't invest in a company just because it has a DPP or DRP. DPPs and DRPs are simply a means for getting into a particular stock with very little money. They shouldn't be a substitute for doing diligent research and analysis on a particular stock.

Dipping into DRPs

Sometimes dividend reinvestment plans (DRPs) are called "DRIPs," which makes me scratch my head. *Reinvestment* is one word not two, so where does that *I* come from? But I digress. Whether you call them DRIPs or DRPs, they're great for small investors and for investors who are truly long-term investors in a particular stock. A *DRP* is a program that a company may offer to allow investors to accumulate more shares of its stock without paying commissions.

A DRP has two primary advantages:

- **Compounding:** The dividends get reinvested and give you the opportunity to buy more stock.

- **Optional cash purchases:** Most DRPs give participants the ability to invest through the plan to purchase more stock, usually with no commissions.

To be in a dividend reinvestment plan, here are the requirements:

- You must already be a stockholder for that particular stock.

- You must already have a dividend reinvestment plan set up.

- The stock must be paying dividends. (You had to guess this one!)

Getting a clue about compounding

Dividends are reinvested, offering a form of compounding for the small investor. Dividends buy more of the shares, in turn generating more dividends. Usually the dividends generated don't buy entire shares, so what they do purchase are fractional shares.

Say, for example, that you own 20 shares of Fraction Corp. at $10 per share for a total value of $200. Fraction Corp.'s annual dividend is $1, meaning that a quarterly dividend of 25 cents is issued every three months. What happens if this stock is in the DRP? The 20 shares generate a $5 dividend payout in the first quarter, and this amount is applied to the stock purchase as soon as the amount is credited to the DRP account. If you presume for this example that the stock price hasn't changed, the total shares in the DRP are 20.50 shares valued at $205 (20.50 shares × $10 share price). The dividend payout wasn't enough to buy an entire share, so it bought a fractional share and credited that to the account.

Say that, in the preceding example, three months have passed and that no other shares have been acquired since your prior dividend payout. Fraction Corp. issues another quarterly dividend for 25 cents per share. Now what?

- The original 20 shares of Fraction Corp. generate a $5 dividend payout.

- The .50, or half share, in the account generates a 12.5 cent dividend (half the dividend of a full share because it's only .50 of a share).

- The total dividend payout is $5.125 (rounded to $5.13), and the new total of shares in the account is 21.125 shares (the former 20.50 shares plus .625 shares purchased by the dividend payout). Full shares generate full dividends, and fractional shares generate fractional dividends.

To illustrate my point, the preceding example uses a price that doesn't fluctuate. Stock in a DRP acts like any other stock; the share price changes constantly. Every time the DRP makes a stock purchase, whether it's monthly or quarterly, the purchase price will likely change each time.

Building wealth with optional cash payments (OCPs)

Most DRPs give the participant the opportunity to make optional cash payments (OCPs). DRPs usually establish a minimum and a maximum payment. The minimum is typically very modest, such as $25 or $50. A few plans even have no minimum. This feature makes it very affordable to regularly invest modest amounts and build up a sizeable portfolio of stock in a shorter period of time, unencumbered by commissions.

DRPs also have a maximum investment limitation, such as specifying that "DRP participants cannot invest any more than $10,000 per year." For most investors, the maximum isn't a showstopper. However, consult with the administrator of the plan because all plans are a little different.

OCPs are probably the most advantageous aspect of a DRP. If you can invest $25 to $50 per month consistently, year after year, at no (or little) cost, you may find that doing so is a superb way to build wealth.

Checking out the cost advantages

In spite of the fact that more and more DRPs are charging service fees, DRPs are still an economical way to invest, especially for small investors. The big savings come from not paying commissions. Although many DPPs and DRPs do have charges, they tend to be relatively small (but keep track of them, because the costs can add up).

Some DRPs actually offer a discount of between 2 percent and 5 percent (a few are higher) when buying stock through the plan. Still others offer special programs and discounts on the company's products and services. Some companies offer the service of debiting your checking account or paycheck to invest in the DRP. One company offered its shareholders significant discounts to its restaurant subsidiary. In any case, ask the plan administrator because any plus is . . . well . . . a plus.

Weighing the pros with the cons

When you're in a DRP, you reap all the benefits of stock investing (along with the risks and responsibilities). You get an annual report, and you qualify for stock splits, dividend increases, and so on.

Before you start to salivate over all the goodies that come with DRPs, be clear-eyed about some of the negative aspects to them as well. Negative aspects include the following:

✔ You need to get that first share. But you knew that.

✔ Even small fees cut into your profits.

✔ Many DRPs may not have some types of services, such as Individual Retirement Accounts (IRAs). (Chapter 20 offers more information on IRAs.)

✔ DRPs are designed for long-term investing. Although getting in and out of the plan is easy, the transactions may take weeks to process because stock purchases and sales are typically done all at once on a certain day during the month (or quarter).

✔ Read the prospectus. You may not consider this a negative point, but for some people, reading a prospectus is not unlike giving blood by using leeches. Even if that is your opinion, you need to read the prospectus to avoid any surprises, such as hidden fees or unreasonable terms.

✔ Understand the tax issues. There, ya see? I knew that I'd ruin it for you. The point is that you should understand the tax consequences. Chapter 20 goes into greater detail. Just know that dividends, whether or not they occur in a DRP, are usually taxable (unless the DRP is in an IRA, which is a different matter).

✔ Perhaps the biggest headache of DRPs is the need to keep good records. Keep all your statements together and use a good spreadsheet program or accounting program if you plan on doing a lot of DRP investing. These records will become especially important at tax time, when you have to report any subsequent gains or losses from stock sales. Because capital gains taxes can be complicated as you sort out short term versus long term, DRP calculations can be a nightmare without good record keeping.

DRPs offer a great way to accumulate a large stock holding over an extended period of time. However, think about what you can do with this stock. Say that you accumulate 110 shares of stock, valued at $50 per share, in your DRP. You can, for example, take out $5,000 worth of stock (100 shares at $50 per share) and place those 100 shares in your brokerage account. The remaining 10 shares can stay in your account to keep the DRP and continue with dividend reinvestment to keep your wealth growing. Why remove those shares?

All things being equal, you are better off keeping the stock in the DRP, but what if you have $2,500 in credit card debt and don't have extra cash to pay off that debt? Brokerage accounts still have plenty of advantages, such as, in this example, the use of margin (a topic I discuss in detail in Chapter 17). If your situation merits it, you can borrow up to 50 percent of the $5,000, or $2,500, as a margin loan and use it, for example, to pay off $2,500 worth of credit card debt. Because you're replacing unsecured debt (credit card debt that may be charging 15 percent, 18 percent, or more) with secured debt, you can save a lot of money (borrowing against stock in a brokerage account is cheaper than credit card debt). Another benefit is that the margin loan with your broker doesn't require monthly payments as do the credit card balances. Additionally, ask your tax consultant about potential tax benefits. Investment interest expense is deductible, while consumer credit card debt is not.

The One-Two Punch: Dollar Cost Averaging and DRPs

Whoa! Have I veered away from DRPs into a brand-new topic? Actually, no. Dollar cost averaging (DCA) is a splendid technique for buying stock and lowering your cost for doing so. The example illustrated in Table 18-1 will show that it is not uncommon for investors to see a total cost that reflects a discount to the market value. DCA works especially well with DRPs.

DCA is a simple method for acquiring stock. It rests on the idea that you invest a fixed amount of money at regular intervals (monthly, usually) over a long period of time in that particular stock. Because a fixed amount (say, $50 per month) is going into a fluctuating investment, you end up buying less of that investment when it goes up in price and more of it when it goes down in price. As Table 18-1 illustrates, your average cost per share is usually lower than if you buy all the shares at once.

DCA is best presented with an example. Presume that you decide to get into the DRP of the company Acme Elevator, Inc. (AE). On your first day in the DRP, AE's stock is at $25, and the plan allows you to invest a minimum of $25 through its optional cash purchase program. You decide to invest $25 per month and assess how well (hopefully) you're doing six months from now. Table 18-1 shows how this technique works.

Table 18-1		Dollar Cost Averaging (AE)		
Months	**Investment Amount**	**Purchase Price**	**Shares Bought**	**Accumulated Shares**
1	25	25	1	1
2	25	20	1.25	2.25
3	25	17.5	1.43	3.68
4	25	15	1.67	5.35
5	25	17.5	1.43	6.78
6	25	20	1.25	8.03
Totals	150	N/A	8.02	8.03

To assess the wisdom of your decision to invest in the DRP, ask yourself some questions:

✔ **How much did you invest over the entire six months?**

Your total investment is $150. So far, so good.

✔ **What is the first share price for AE, and what is the last share price?**

The first share price is $25, but the last share price is $20.

✔ **What is the market value of your investment at the end of six months?**

You can easily calculate the value of your investment. Just multiply the number of shares you now own (8.03 shares) by the most recent share price ($20). The total value of your investment is $160.60.

✔ **What is the average share price you bought at?**

The average share price is also easy to calculate. Take the total amount of your purchases ($150) and divide it by the number of shares that you acquired (8.03 shares). Your average cost per share price becomes $18.68.

✔ **Is that your final answer?** (Do your best Regis Philbin voice.)

Yes, these are my final answers (look Ma, no lifelines!), but you should take note of the following:

- Even though the last share price ($20) is lower than the original share price ($25), your total investment's market value is still higher than your purchase amount ($160.60 compared to $150)! How could that be?! Dollar cost averaging is the culprit here. Your disciplined approach (using DCA) was able to overcome the fluctuations in the stock price to help you gain more shares at the lower prices of $17.50 and $15.

- Your average cost per share is only $18.68. The DCA method helped you buy more shares at a lower cost, which ultimately helped you make money when the stock price made a modest rebound.

- DCA works in helping you invest with small sums, all the while helping you smooth out the volatility in stock prices. This helps you make more money in your wealth-building program over the long haul. Can you visualize that retirement hammock yet?

The bottom line for long-term stock investors is that DCA is a solid investing technique and DRPs are a great stock investment vehicle for building wealth.

Dollar cost averaging is a fantastic technique in a bull market and an "OK" technique in a flat or sideways market, but it is really not a good consideration during bear markets because the stock you are buying is going down in price and the market value could very easily be lower than your total investment. If you plan on holding onto the stock long term, then simply cease your dollar cost averaging approach until times improve for the stock (and its industry and the economy). Learn more about bear markets in Chapter 15.

Chapter 19

Looking at What the Insiders Do: Corporate Hijinks

- -

- -

*I*magine that you're boarding a cruise ship, ready to enjoy a hard-earned vacation. As you merrily walk up the plank, you notice that the ship's captain and crew are charging out of the vessel, flailing their arms, and screaming at the top of their lungs — some are even jumping into the water below. Quiz: Would you get on that ship? You get double credit if you can also explain why (or why not). What does this scenario have to do with stock investing? Plenty. The behavior of the people running the boat gives you important clues about the near-term prospects for the boat. Similarly, the actions of company insiders can provide important clues into the near-term prospects for their company.

Company *insiders* are individuals who are key managers or investors in the company. Insiders may be the president of the company, the treasurer, or another managing officer. An insider can be someone who owns a large stake in the company or someone on the board of directors. In any case, insiders usually have a bird's-eye view of what's going on with the company. They have a good idea of how well (or how poorly) the company is doing.

Keep tabs on what insiders are doing, because their buy/sell transactions do have a strong correlation to the near-term movement of their company's stock. However, don't buy or sell stock only because you heard that some insider did it. Use the information on insider trading to confirm your own good sense in buying or selling stock. Insider trading sometimes can be a great precursor to a significant move that you can profit from if you know what to look for. Many shrewd investors have made their profits (or avoided losses) by tracking the activity of the insiders.

Tracking Insider Trading

Fortunately, we live in an age of disclosure. Insiders who buy or sell stock must file reports that document their trading activity with the Securities and Exchange Commission (SEC), which makes the documents available to the public. You can view these documents either at the SEC office or at the Web site of the SEC, which maintains the EDGAR (Electronic Data Gathering, Analysis, and Retrieval) database (`www.sec.gov/edgar.shtml`). Just click on the "Search for company filings" button. Some of the most useful documents you can view there include the following:

- ✔ **Form 3:** This form is the initial statement that insiders provide. Insiders must file Form 3 within ten days of obtaining insider status. An insider files this report even if he hasn't made a purchase yet; the report establishes the insider's status.

- ✔ **Form 4:** Form 4 is the document that shows the insider's activity. For example, Form 4 would include a change in the insider's position as stockholder — how many shares the person bought and sold or other relevant changes. Any activity in a particular month must be reported on Form 4 by the 10th of the following month. If, for example, an insider sells stock during January, the SEC must get the report by February 10.

- ✔ **Form 5:** This annual report covers transactions that are small and not required on Form 4. Transactions may include minor, internal transfers of stock, or other transactions.

- ✔ **Form 144:** This form serves as the public declaration by an insider of the intention to sell restricted stock. This is stock that the insider received from the company as compensation, was awarded, or bought as a term of employment. Insiders must hold restricted stock for at least one year before they can sell it. After an insider decides to sell, he files Form 144 and then must sell within 90 days or else must submit a new Form 144. The insider must file the form on or before the stock's sale date. When the sale is finalized, the insider is then required to file Form 4.

Companies are required to make public the documents that track their trading activity. The SEC's Web site offers limited access to these documents, but for greater access, check out one of the many companies that report insider trading data, such as `www.marketwatch.com` and `www.bloomberg.com`.

Sarbanes-Oxley Act

Very often, a market that reaches a mania stage sees abuse reach extreme conditions as well. Abuse by insiders is a good example. In the stock market mania of 1997–2000, this abuse wasn't just limited to insider buying and selling of stock; it also covered the related abuse of accounting fraud. Because insiders are primarily the top management, they deceived investors about the financial conditions of the company and subsequently were able to increase the perceived value of the company's stock. The stock could then be sold at a price that was higher than market value. Congress took notice of these activities and, in 2002, passed the Sarbanes-Oxley Act (SOX). Congress designed this act to protect investors from fraudulent accounting activities by corporations. SOX established a public accounting oversight board and also tightened the rules on corporate financial reporting.

The SEC has enacted the short-swing profit rule to protect the investing public. This rule prevents insiders from quickly buying the stock that they just sold at a profit. The insider must wait at least six months before buying it again. The SEC created this rule to prevent insiders from using their privileged knowledge to make an unfair profit, while the investing public can't react fast enough. The rule is also true if an insider sells stock. An insider can't sell it at a higher price within a six-month period.

Looking at Insider Transactions

The classic phrase "Actions speak louder than words" was probably coined for insider trading. Insiders are in the know, and keeping a watchful eye on their transactions — both buying and selling their company's stock — can provide you with very useful investing information. Analyzing insider buying versus insider selling can be as different as day and night. Insider buying is simple, while insider selling can be complicated. In the following sections, I present both sides of insider trading.

Learning from insider buying

Insider buying is usually an unambiguous signal about how an insider feels about his company. After all, the primary reason that all investors buy stock is that they expect it to do well. If one insider is buying stock, that's generally not a monumental event. But if several or more insiders are buying, those purchases should certainly catch your attention.

Insider buying is generally a positive omen and beneficial for the stock's price. Also, when insiders buy stock, less stock is available to the public. If the investing public meets this decreased supply with increased demand, then the stock price rises. Keep these factors in mind when analyzing insider buying:

✔ **Identify who's buying the stock.** The CEO is buying 5,000 shares. Is that reason enough for you to jump in? Maybe. After all, the CEO certainly knows how well the company is doing. But what if that CEO is just starting her new position? What if before this purchase she had no stock in the company at all? Maybe the stock is part of her employment package.

The fact that a new company executive is making her first stock purchase isn't as strong a signal urging you to buy as the fact that a long-time CEO is doubling her holdings. Also, if large numbers of insiders are buying, that sends a stronger signal than if a single insider is buying.

✔ **See how much is being bought.** In the example in the previous section, the CEO bought 5,000 shares, which is a lot of stock no matter how you count it. But is it enough for you to base an investment decision on? Maybe, but a closer look may reveal more. If she already owned 1 million shares at the time of the purchase, then buying 5,000 additional shares wouldn't be such an exciting indicator of a pending stock rise. In this case, 5,000 shares is a small incremental move and doesn't offer much to get excited about.

However, what if this particular insider has owned only 5,000 shares for the past three years and is now buying 1 million shares? Now that should arouse your interest! Usually, a massive purchase tells you that particular insider has strong feelings about the company's prospects and that she's making a huge increase in her share of stock ownership. Still, a purchase of 1 million shares by the CEO isn't as strong a signal as ten insiders buying 100,000 shares each. Again, if only one person is buying, that may or may not be a strong indication of an impending rise. However, if lots of people are buying, consider it a fantastic indication.

An insider purchase of any kind is a positive sign. But it's always more significant when a greater number of insiders are making purchases. "The more the merrier!" is a good rule for judging insider buying. All these individuals have their own, unique perspectives on the company and its prospects for the foreseeable future. Mass buying indicates mass optimism for the company's future. If the treasurer, the president, the vice-president of sales, and several other key players are putting their wealth on the line and investing it in a company that they know intimately, that's a good sign for your stock investment as well.

✔ **Notice the timing of the purchase.** The timing of insider stock purchases is important as well. If I tell you that five insiders bought stock at various points last year, you may say, "Hmm." But if I tell you that all five people bought substantial chunks of stock at the same time and right before earnings season, that should make you say, "HMMMMM!"

Picking up tips from insider selling

Insider buying either bodes well for the stock or is a neutral event at worst. Insider stock buying is rarely a negative event. But how about insider selling? When an insider sells his stock, the event can either be neutral or negative. Insider selling is usually a little tougher to figure out because insiders may have many different motivations to sell stock that have nothing to do with the company's future prospects. (See the next paragraph for a list of some common reasons.) Just because the president of the company is selling 5,000 shares from his personal portfolio, that doesn't necessarily mean you should sell, too.

Insiders may sell their stock for a couple reasons: They may think that the company won't be doing well in the near future — a negative sign for you — or they may simply need the money for a variety of personal reasons that have nothing to do with the company's potential. Some typical reasons why insiders may sell stock include the following:

✔ **To diversify their holdings.** If an insider's portfolio is heavily weighted with one company's stock, a financial advisor may suggest that he balance his portfolio by selling some of that company's stock and purchasing other securities.

✔ **To finance personal emergencies.** Sometimes an insider needs money for medical, legal, or family reasons.

✔ **To buy a home or make another major purchase.** An insider may need the money to make a down payment or perhaps to buy something outright without having to take out a loan.

How do you find out about the details regarding insider stock selling? Although insiders must report their pertinent stock sales and purchases to the SEC, the information isn't always revealing. As a general rule, consider the following questions when analyzing insider selling:

✔ **How many insiders are selling?** If only one insider is selling, that single transaction doesn't give you enough information to act on. However, if many insiders are selling, you should see a red flag. Check out any news or information that is currently available. Web sites such as www.marketwatch.com, www.sec.gov, and finance.yahoo.com can help you get that information (along with other sources in Appendix A).

✔ **Are the sales showing a pattern or unusual activity?** If one insider sold some stock last month, that sale alone isn't that significant an event. However, if ten insiders have each made multiple sales in the past few months, those sales are cause for concern. See whether any new developments at the company are potentially negative. If massive insider selling has recently occurred and you don't know why, consider putting a stop-loss order on your stock immediately. I cover stop-loss orders more fully in Chapter 17.

✔ **How much stock is being sold?** If a CEO sells 5,000 shares of stock but still retains 100,000 shares, that's not a big deal. But if the CEO sells all or most of his holdings, that's a possible negative. Check to see whether other company executives have also sold stock.

✔ **Do outside events or analyst reports seem coincidental with the sale of the stock?** Sometimes, an influential analyst may issue a report warning about a company's prospects. If the company's management pooh-poohs the report but most of them are bailing out anyway (selling their stock), you may want to do the same. Frequently, when insiders know that damaging information is forthcoming, they sell the stock before it takes a dip.

Similarly, if the company's management issues positive public statements or reports that are contradictory to their own behavior (they're selling their stock holdings), the SEC may investigate to see whether the company is doing anything that may require a penalty. The SEC regularly tracks insider sales.

Considering Corporate Stock Buybacks

When you read the financial pages or watch the financial shows on television, you sometimes hear that a company is buying its own stock. The announcement may be something like, "SuperBucks Corp. has announced that it will spend $2 billion dollars to buy back its own stock." Why would a company do that, and what does that mean to you if you own the stock or are considering buying it?

W hen companies buy back their own stock, they're generally indicating that they believe their stock is undervalued and that it has the potential to rise. If a company shows strong fundamentals (for example, good financial condition and increasing sales and earnings) and it's buying more of its own stock, it's worth investigating — it may make a great addition to your portfolio.

Just because a company announces a stock buyback doesn't always mean that one will happen. The announcement itself is meant to stir interest in the stock and cause the price to rise. The stock buyback may be only an opportunity for insiders to sell stock, or it may be needed for executive compensation — recruiting and retaining competent management is a positive use of money.

If you see that a company is buying back its stock while most of the insiders are selling their personal shares, that's not a good sign. It may not necessarily be a bad sign, but it's not a positive sign. Play it safe and invest elsewhere.

The following sections present some common reasons a company may buy back its shares from investors as well as some ideas on the negative effects of stock buybacks.

Boosting earnings per share

By simply buying back its own shares from stockholders, a company can increase its earnings per share (see Chapter 10 and Appendix B for more on earnings per share) without actually earning extra money. Sound like a magician's trick? Well, it is, kind of. A corporate stock buyback is a financial sleight of hand that investors should be aware of. Here's how it works: Noware Earnings, Inc., (NEI) has 10 million shares outstanding, and it's expected to net earnings of $10 million for the fourth quarter. NEI's earnings per share (EPS) would be $1 per share. So far so good. But what happens if NEI buys 2 million of its own shares? Total shares outstanding shrink to 8 million. The new EPS becomes $1.25 — the stock buyback artificially boosts the earnings per share by 25 percent!

The important point to remember about stock buybacks is that actual company earnings don't change — no fundamental changes occur in company management or operations — so the increase in EPS can be misleading. But the marketplace can be obsessive about earnings, and because earnings are the lifeblood of any company, an earnings boost, even if it's cosmetic, can also boost the stock price.

If you watch a company's price-to-earnings ratio (see Chapter 10), you know that increased earnings usually mean an eventual increase in the stock price. Additionally, a stock buyback affects supply and demand. With less available stock in the market, demand necessarily sends the stock price upward.

Whenever a company makes a major purchase, such as buying back its own stock, think about how the company is paying for it and whether it seems like a good use of the company's purchasing power. In general, companies buy their stock for the same reasons any investor buys stock — they believe that the stock is a good investment and will appreciate in time. Companies generally pay for a stock buyback in one of two basic ways: funds from operations or borrowed money. Both methods have a downside. For more details, see the section "Exploring the downside of buybacks," later in this chapter.

Beating back a takeover bid

Suppose that you read in the financial pages that Company X is doing a hostile takeover of Company Z. A hostile takeover doesn't mean that Company X sent storm troopers armed with mace to Company Z's headquarters to trounce its management. All a *hostile takeover* means is that X wants to buy enough shares of Z's stock to effectively control Z (and Z is unhappy about being owned or controlled by X). Because buying and selling stock are done in a public market or exchange, companies can buy each other's stock. Sometimes the target company prefers not to be acquired, in which case it may buy back shares of its own stock to give it a measure of protection against unwanted moves by interested companies.

In some cases, the company attempting the takeover already owns some of the target company's stock. In this case, the targeted company may offer to buy those shares back from the aggressor at a premium to thwart the takeover bid. This type of offer is often referred to as *greenmail*.

Takeover concerns generally prompt interest in the investing public, driving the stock price upward and benefiting current stockholders.

Exploring the downside of buybacks

As beneficial as stock buybacks can be, they have to be paid for, and this expense has consequences. If a company pays for the stock with funds from operations, it may have a negative effect on the company's ability to finance current and prospective operations. When a company uses funds from operations for the stock buyback, less money is available for other activities, such as upgrading technology or research and development. In general, any misuse of money, such as using debt to buy back stock, affects a company's ability to grow its sales and earnings — two measures that need to maintain upward mobility in order to keep stock prices rising.

A company faces even greater dangers when it uses debt to finance a stock buyback. If the company uses borrowed funds, it has less borrowing power for other uses (such as upgrading technology or making other improvements). In addition, the company has to pay back the borrowed funds with interest, thus lowering earnings figures.

Say that NEI (a fictional company introduced in the "Boosting earnings per share" section, earlier in this chapter) typically pays an annual dividend of 25 cents per share of stock and wants to buy back shares with borrowed money with a 9 percent interest rate. If NEI buys back 2 million shares, it won't have to pay out $500,000 in dividends. That's money saved. However, NEI is going to have to pay interest on the $20 million it borrowed to buy back the shares over that same time frame to the tune of $1,800,000 (9 percent of $20,000,000). The net result from this rudimentary example is that NEI sees an outflow of $1,300,000 (the difference between the interest paid out and the dividends savings). Using debt to finance a stock buyback needs to make economic sense — it needs to strengthen the company's financial position. Perhaps NEI could have used the stock buyback money toward a better purpose, such as modernizing equipment or paying for a new marketing campaign. Because debt interest ultimately decreases earnings, companies must be careful when using debt to buy back their stock.

Stock Splits: Nothing to Go Bananas Over

Frequently, management teams decide to do a stock split. A *stock split* is the exchange of existing shares of stock for new shares from the same company. Stock splits don't increase or decrease the capitalization of the company. They just change the number of shares available in the market and the per-share price.

In a typical stock split, a company may announce that it will do a 2-for-1 stock split. For example, a company may have 10 million shares outstanding, with a market price of $40 each. In a 2-for-1 split, the company then has 20 million shares (the share total doubles), but the market price is adjusted to $20 (the share price is halved). Companies do other splits, such as a 3-for-2 or 4-for-1, but 2-for-1 is the most common split.

Why do companies split their stock? Usually, management believes that the stock's price is too high, thus possibly discouraging investors from purchasing it. The stock split is a strategy to stir interest in the stock, and this increased interest frequently results in a rise in the stock's price.

Qualifying for a stock split is similar to qualifying to receive a dividend — you must be listed as a stockholder as of the date of record. (For information on the date of record, see Chapter 6.)

A stock split is technically a neutral event because the ultimate market value of the company's stock doesn't change as a result of the split. The following sections present the two most basic types of splits: ordinary and reverse stock splits.

Ordinary stock splits

Ordinary stock splits — when the number of stock shares increase — are the ones we usually hear about. (For example, a 2-for-1 stock split doubles the number of shares.) If you own 100 shares of Dublin, Inc., stock (at $60 per share), and the company announces a stock split, what happens? If you own the stock in certificate form, you receive in the mail a stock certificate for 100 shares of Dublin, Inc. Now, before you cheer over how your money just doubled, check the stock's new price. Each share is adjusted to a $30 value.

Not all stock is in certificate form. Stocks held in a brokerage account are recorded in book entry form. Most stock, in fact, is in book entry form. A company only issues stock certificates when necessary or when the investor requests it. If you keep the stock in your brokerage account, check with your broker for the new share total to make sure that you're credited with the new number of shares after the stock split.

A stock split is primarily a neutral event, so why does a company bother to do it? The most common reason is that management believes that the stock is too expensive, so it wants to lower the stock price to make the stock more affordable and therefore more attractive to new investors. Studies have shown that stock splits frequently precede a rise in the stock price. Although stock splits are considered a non-event in and of themselves, many stock experts see them as bullish signals because of the interest they generate among the investing public.

Reverse stock splits

A *reverse stock split* usually occurs when a company's management wants to raise the price of its stock. Just as ordinary splits can occur when management believes that the price is too expensive, a reverse stock split means that the company feels that the stock's price is too cheap. If a stock's price looks too low, that may discourage interest by individual or institutional investors (such as mutual funds). Management wants to drum up more interest in the stock for the benefit of shareholders (some of whom are probably insiders).

The company may also do a reverse split to decrease costs. When you have to send an annual report and other correspondence regularly to all the stockholders, the mailings can get a little pricey, especially when you have lots of investors who have only a few shares each. A reverse split helps to consolidate the shares to lower overall management costs.

A reverse split can best be explained with an example. TuCheep, Inc., (TCI) is selling at $2 per share on the Nasdaq. At that rock-bottom price, the investing public may ignore it. So TCI announces a 10-for-1 reverse stock split. Now what? If an existing stockholder had 100 shares at $2 (the old shares), the stockholder now owns 10 shares at $20.

Technically, a reverse split is considered a neutral event. However, just as investors may infer positive expectations from an ordinary stock split, they may have negative expectations from a reverse split, because a reverse split tends to occur for negative reasons.

If, in the event of a stock split, you have an odd number of shares, the company doesn't produce a "fractional share." Instead, you get a check for the cash equivalent. For example, if you have 51 shares and the company announces a 2-for-1 reverse split, the odds are that they'll give you 25 shares and a cash payout for the odd share (or fractional share).

Keep good records regarding your stock splits in case you need to calculate capital gains for tax purposes. (See Chapter 20 for tax information.)

Chapter 20

Tax Benefits and Obligations

· ·

· ·

After conquering the world of making money with stocks, now you have another hurdle — keeping your money. Some people may tell you that taxes are brutal, complicated, and counterproductive. Other people may tell you that they're a form of legalized thievery, while still others may say that they're a necessary evil. And then there are pessimists. In any case, this chapter shows you how to keep more of the fruits of your hard-earned labor.

Keep in mind that this chapter isn't meant to be comprehensive. For a fuller treatment of personal taxes, refer to the latest edition of *Taxes For Dummies* (Wiley). However, in this chapter, I cover the most relevant points for stock investors. As a stock investor, you need to know the tax treatment for dividends and capital gains and losses, along with common tax deductions for investors and some simple tax-reduction strategies.

You must take tax planning seriously because taxes can be the single biggest expense during your lifetime. The average taxpayer pays more in taxes than in food, clothing, and shelter combined!

Paying through the Nose

This section tells you what you need to know about the tax implications you'll face when you start investing in stocks. It's good to know the basics in advance since it will matter to your investing strategy. If you're the type of investor who likes to cash in on a profitable stock quickly, then realize that you will probably pay more in taxes than if you are more patient. Sometimes the difference can be just a matter of days. What if you are about to sell a stock that you've held for 11 months and 28 days? Well waiting just a few more days means less taxes which means more money in your pocket.

Understanding ordinary income and capital gains

Profit you make from your stock investments can be taxed in one of two ways, depending on the type of profit:

✔ **Ordinary income:** If the profit you make from stock investments is taxed, your profit is taxed at the same rate as wages — at your full, regular tax rate. If your tax bracket is 28 percent, then that's the rate your ordinary income investment profits will be taxed at. Two types of investment profits get taxed as ordinary income:

- **Dividends:** When you receive dividends from your stock (either in cash or stock), these dividends get taxed as ordinary income. This is also true if those dividends are in a dividend reinvestment plan. (See Chapter 18 if you want to know more about dividend reinvestment plans, or DRPs.) If, however, those dividends occur in a tax-sheltered plan, such as an IRA or 401(k) plan, then they're exempt from taxes for as long as they're in the plan. Retirement plans are covered in the section "Taking Advantage of Tax-Advantaged Retirement Investing," later in this chapter. In January, investors receive a 1099-DIV statement from the issuer of the dividends that includes information on the amount of dividends earned the previous year. Check with your tax advisor because the latest tax laws offer tax advantages for dividends.

- **Short-term capital gains:** If you sell stock for a gain and you've owned the stock for just one year or less, the gain is considered ordinary income. If you buy a stock on August 1 and sell it on July 31 of the following year, that's less than one year. To calculate the time, you use the trade date (or date of execution). This date is the date that you executed the order instead of the settlement date. (For more on important dates, see Chapter 6.) However, if these gains occur in a tax-sheltered plan, such as a 401(k) or an IRA, no tax is triggered.

✔ **Long-term capital gains:** Long-term capital gains are usually much better for you as far as taxes are concerned. The tax laws reward patient investors. After you have held the stock for at least a year and a day (what a difference a day makes!), your tax rate will be reduced. Get more information on capital gains in IRS Publication 550 "Investment Income and Expenses".

Because the tax on capital gains is the most relevant tax for stock investors, don't forget to read the section "Minimizing the tax on your capital gains," later in this chapter.

Debt and taxes: Another angle

If you truly need cash, but you don't want to sell your stock because it's doing well and you want to avoid paying capital gains tax, consider borrowing against it. If the stock is a listed stock (listed on the New York Stock Exchange, for example) and is sitting in a brokerage account, you can borrow up to 50 percent of the value of marginable securities at favorable rates. (Listed stocks are marginable securities.) The money you borrow is considered a margin loan, and the interest you pay is low (compared to credit cards or personal loans) because it's considered a secured loan (your stock acts as collateral). On those rare occasions when I use margin, I usually make sure I use stocks that generate a high dividend. That way, the stocks help to pay off the margin loan.

Managing the tax burden from your investment profits is something that you can control. Gains are taxable only if a sale actually takes place. (In other words, only if the gain is "realized.") If your stock in GazillionBucks, Inc., goes from $5 per share to $87, that $82 appreciation isn't subject to taxation unless you actually sell the stock. Until you sell, that gain is "unrealized." Time your stock sales carefully — hold on to them at least a year — to minimize the amount of taxes you have to pay on them.

When you buy stock, record the date of purchase and the *cost basis* (the purchase price of the stock plus any ancillary charges, such as commissions). This information is very important come tax time should you decide to sell your stock. The date of purchase helps to establish the *holding period* (how long you've owned the stocks) that determines whether your gains are to be considered short-term or long-term.

Say that you buy 100 shares of GazillionBucks, Inc., at $5 and pay a commission of $18. Your cost basis is $518 (100 shares times $5 plus $18 commission). If you sell the stock at $87 per share and pay a $24 commission, the total sale amount is $8,676 (100 shares times $87 less $24 commission). If this sale occurred less than a year after the purchase, it's a short-term gain. In the 28 percent tax bracket, the short-term gain of $8,158 is also taxed at 28 percent. (Short-term gains are taxed as ordinary income.) Read the following section to see the tax implications if your gain is a long-term gain.

Any gain (or loss) from a short sale is considered short-term regardless of how long the position is held open. For more information on selling short, check out Chapter 17.

Minimizing the tax on your capital gains

Long-term capital gains are taxed at a more favorable rate than ordinary income. To qualify for long-term capital gains treatment, you must hold the investment for over one year (in other words, for at least one year and one day).

Recall the example in the previous section with GazillionBucks, Inc. As a short-term transaction at the 28 percent tax rate, the tax would have been $2,429 ($8,676 × 28 percent). After you revive, you say, "Gasp! What a chunk of dough. I better hold off a while longer." You hold on to the stock for at least a year to achieve the status of long-term capital gains. How does that change the tax? For anyone who is in the 28 percent tax bracket or higher, the long-term capital gains rate of 20 percent would apply. In this case, the tax would be $1,735 ($8,676 × 20 percent), resulting in a tax savings to you of $694 ($2,429 less $1,735). Okay, it's not a fortune, but it is a substantial difference from the original tax.

Because every taxpayer is different, check with your personal tax advisor. In addition, get the publications referenced in this chapter by either visiting the IRS Web site at www.irs.gov or call their publications department at 800-TAX-FORM.

Don't sell a stock just because it qualifies for long-term capital gains treatment, even if the sale would ease your tax burden. If the stock is doing well and meeting your investing criteria, then hold on to it.

Capital gains taxes *can* be lower than the tax on ordinary income, but they're not higher. If, for example, you're in the 15 percent tax bracket for ordinary income and you have a long-term capital gain that would normally bump you up to the 28 percent tax bracket, the gain is taxed at your lower rate of 15 percent instead of a higher capital gains rate. Check with your tax advisor on a regular basis because this can change due to new tax laws.

Coping with capital losses

Ever think that having the value of your stocks fall could be a good thing? Perhaps the only real positive regarding losses in your portfolio is that they can reduce your taxes. A *capital loss* means that you lose money on your investments. This amount is generally deductible on your tax return, and you can claim a loss on either long-term or short-term stock holdings. This loss can go against your other income and lower your overall tax.

Gains and losses scenarios

Of course, any investor can come up with hundreds of possible scenarios. For example, you may wonder what happens if you sell part of your holdings now as a short-term capital loss and the remainder later as a long-term capital gain. You must look at each sale of stock (or potential sale) methodically to calculate the gain or loss you would realize from it. Figuring out your gain or loss isn't that complicated. Here are some general rules to help you wade through the morass:

✔ If you add up all your gains and losses and *the net result is a short-term gain,* it's taxed at your highest tax bracket (as ordinary income).

✔ If you add up all your gains and losses and *the net result is a long-term gain,* it's taxed at 20 percent if you're in the 28 percent tax bracket or higher. If you're in the 15 percent tax bracket or lower, the tax rate on long-term capital gains is 10 percent.

✔ If you add up all your gains and losses and *the net result is a loss,* it's deductible as follows: If your loss is $3,000 or less, it's fully deductible against other income. If you're married filing separately, then your deduction limit is $1,500.

✔ If you add up all your gains and losses and *the net result is a loss that exceeds $3,000,* then you can only deduct up to $3,000 in that year, and the remainder goes forward to future years.

Say that you bought Worth Zilch Co. stock for a total purchase price of $3,500 and sold it later at a sale price of $800. Your capital loss would be$2,700. This loss is tax deductible.

The one string attached to deducting investment losses on your tax return is that the most you can report in a single year is $3,000. On the bright side, though, any excess loss isn't really lost — you can carry it forward to the next year. If you had net investment losses of $4,500 in 2006, then you can deduct $3,000 in 2006 and carry the remaining $1,500 loss over to 2007 and deduct it on your 2007 tax returns.

Before you can deduct losses, the IRS states that the capital losses from your investments must first be used to offset any capital gains. If you realize long-term capital gains of $7,000 in stock A and $6,000 of realized long-term capital losses in stock B, then you have a net long-term capital gain of $1,000 ($7,000 gain less the offset of $6,000 loss). Whenever possible, see whether losses in your portfolio can be realized to offset any capital gains to reduce any potential tax.

Here's your optimum strategy: Where possible, keep losses on a short-term basis and push your gains into long-term capital gains status. If a transaction can't be tax free, then at the very least try to defer the tax to keep your money working for you.

Sharing Your Gains with the IRS

Of course, you don't want to pay more taxes than you have to, but as the old cliché goes, "Don't let the tax tail wag the investment dog." You should buy or sell a stock because it makes economic sense first, and consider the tax implications as secondary issues. After all, taxes consume a relatively small portion of your gain. As long as you experience a *net gain* (gain after all transaction costs, including taxes, brokerage fees, and other related fees), consider yourself a successful investor — even if you have to give away some of your gain to taxes.

Hold on to stocks over the long term to keep transaction costs and taxes down. Remember that you don't pay tax on a stock profit until you sell the stock.

Try to make tax planning second nature in your day-to-day activities. No, you don't have to consume yourself with a blizzard of paperwork and tax projections. I simply mean that when you make a stock transaction, keep the receipt and maintain good records. When you make a large purchase or sale, pause for a moment and ask yourself whether you'll have to face any tax consequences. (Refer to the section "Paying through the Nose," earlier in this chapter, to review various tax scenarios.) Speak to a tax consultant beforehand to discuss the ramifications.

Filling out forms

Most investors report their investment-related activities on their individual tax returns (Form 1040). The reports that you will likely receive from brokers and other investment sources include the following:

- **Brokerage and bank statements:** Monthly statements that you receive
- **Trade confirmations:** Documents to confirm that you bought or sold stock
- **1099-DIV:** Reporting dividends paid to you
- **1099-INT:** Reporting interest paid to you
- **1099-B:** Reporting gross proceeds submitted to you from the sale of investments, such as stocks and mutual funds

You may receive other, more obscure forms that aren't listed here, but you should retain all documents related to your stock investments.

The IRS schedules and forms that most stock investors need to be aware of and/or attach to their Form 1040 include the following:

- ✔ **Schedule B:** For reporting interest and dividends
- ✔ **Schedule D:** To report capital gains and losses
- ✔ **Form 4952:** Investment Interest Expense Deduction
- ✔ **Publication 17:** Guide to Form 1040

You can get these publications directly from the IRS at 800-TAX-FORM, or you can download them from the Web site `www.irs.gov`.

If you plan to do your own taxes, consider using the latest tax software products, which have become inexpensive and are easy to use. These programs usually have a question-and-answer feature to help you do your taxes step-by-step, and they include all the necessary forms. Consider getting either TurboTax (`www.turbotax.com`) or H&R Block's TaxCut (`www.taxcut.com`) at your local software vendor or the companies' Web sites.

Playing by the rules

Some people get the smart idea of "Hey! Why not sell my losing stock by December 31 to grab the short-term loss and just buy back the stock on January 2 so that I can have my cake and eat it, too?" Not so fast. The IRS puts the kibosh on maneuvers such as that with something called the "wash-sale rule." This rule states that if you sell a stock for a loss and buy it back within 30 days, the loss isn't valid because you didn't make any substantial investment change. The wash-sale rule applies only to losses. The way around the rule is simple: Wait at least 31 days before you buy that identical stock back again.

Some people try to get around the wash-sale rule by doubling up on their stock position with the intention of selling half. Therefore, the IRS makes the 30-day rule cover both sides of the sale date. That way an investor can't buy the identical stock within 30 days just before the sale and then realize a short-term loss for tax purposes.

Discovering the Softer Side of the IRS: Tax Deductions for Investors

In the course of managing your portfolio of stocks and other investments, you will probably incur expenses that will be tax deductible. The tax laws allow you to write off certain investment-related expenses (as itemized expenses on Schedule A — an attachment to IRS Form 1040). Keep records of your deductions and retain a checklist to remind you of what deductions you normally take for future tax years. IRS Publication 550 ("Investment Income and Expenses") gives you more details. The following sections explain common tax deductions for investors.

Investment interest

If you have paid any interest to a stockbroker, such as margin interest or any interest to acquire a taxable financial investment, that's considered investment interest and is usually fully deductible as an itemized expense. Keep in mind that not all interest is deductible. Consumer interest or interest paid for any consumer or personal purpose isn't deductible.

Miscellaneous expenses

Most investment-related deductions are reported as miscellaneous expenses. Here are some common deductions:

- Accounting or bookkeeping fees for keeping records of investment income.
- Any expense related to tax service or education.
- Computer expense. You can take a depreciation deduction for your computer if you use it 50 percent of the time or more for managing your investments.
- Investment management or investment advisor's fees. (Fees paid for advice on tax-exempt investments aren't deductible.)
- Legal fees involving stockholder issues.
- Safe-deposit box rental fee or home safe to hold your securities, unless used to hold personal effects or tax-exempt securities.

> ✔ Service charges for collecting interest and dividends.
>
> ✔ Subscription fees for investment advisory services.
>
> ✔ Travel costs to check investments or to confer with advisors regarding income-related investments.

You can deduct only that portion of your miscellaneous expenses that exceeds 2 percent of your adjusted gross income.

Givin' it away

What happens if you donate stock to your favorite (IRS-approved) charity? Because it's a noncash charitable contribution, you can deduct the market value of the stock.

Say that last year you bought stock for $2,000 and it's worth $4,000 this year. If you donate it this year, you can write off the market value at the time of the contribution. In this case, you have a $4,000 deduction. Use IRS Form 8283, which is an attachment to Schedule A, to report noncash contributions exceeding $500.

To get more guidance from the IRS on this matter, get its free Publication #526, "Charitable Contributions," by calling 800-TAX-FORM.

Knowing what you can't deduct

Just to be complete, here are some items that you may have thought you could deduct but, alas, you can't:

> ✔ Financial planning or investment seminars
>
> ✔ Any costs connected with attending stockholder meetings
>
> ✔ Home office expenses for managing your investments

Are you having fun yet? You're probably saying "Why read the rest of the chapter? Can't I just wait for the movie?" Yeah, I know, taxes can be intimidating. So, write your representative in Congress and complain. After all, it's your money!

Taking Advantage of Tax-Advantaged Retirement Investing

If you're going to invest for the long term (such as your retirement), then you may as well maximize your usage of tax-sheltered retirement plans. Many different types of plans are available, but I touch on only the most popular ones. Although retirement plans may not seem relevant for investors who buy and sell stocks directly (as opposed to a mutual fund), some plans, called self-directed retirement accounts, allow you to invest directly.

IRAs

Individual Retirement Accounts (IRAs) are accounts that you can open with a financial institution, such as a bank or a mutual fund company. An IRA is available to almost anyone who has earned income, and it allows you to set aside and invest money to help fund your future retirement. Opening an IRA is easy, and virtually any bank or mutual fund can guide you through the process. Two basic types of IRAs are traditional and Roth.

Traditional Individual Retirement Account (IRA)

The traditional Individual Retirement Account (also called the deductible IRA) was first popularized in the early 1980s. The basic point of the traditional IRA is that you can put in a tax-deductible contribution of up to $4,000 per year for tax years 2005–2007. It reaches $5,000 in 2008. In addition, individuals who are at least age 50 can make additional "catch-up" investments of $500 in 2005. The amount rises to an additional $1,000 in years 2006–2008.

The money can then grow in the IRA account unfettered by current taxes because the money isn't taxed until you take it out. Because IRAs are designed for retirement purposes, you can start taking money out of your IRA in the year you turn 59½. (Hmmm. That must really disappoint those who want their money in the year they turn 58¾.) The withdrawals at that point are taxed as ordinary income. Fortunately, you'll probably be in a lower tax bracket then, so the tax shouldn't be as burdensome.

If you take out money from an IRA too early, the amount is included in your taxable income, and you may be zapped with a 10 percent penalty. You can avoid the penalty if you have a good reason. (The IRS provides a list of reasons that qualify the premature withdrawal of money as being exempt from the penalty. Get IRS Publication 590 "Individual Retirement Arrangements" at their Web site, www.irs.gov.)

To put money into an IRA, you must earn income equal to or greater than the amount you're contributing. *Earned income* is money made either as an employee or a self-employed person. Although traditional IRAs can be great for investors, the toughest part about them is qualifying. The reason is that there are income limitations and other qualifiers that make the traditional IRA less deductible based on how high your income is. See IRS Publication 590 for more details.

 Wait a minute! You may be thinking that IRAs usually are done with mutual funds or bank investments. How does the stock investor take advantage of an IRA? Stock investors can open a self-directed IRA with a brokerage firm. This means that you can buy and sell stocks in the account with no taxes on dividends or capital gains. The account is tax deferred, so you don't have to worry about taxes until you start making withdrawals. Also, many dividend reinvestment plans (DRPs) have IRAs as well. See Chapter 18 for more about DRPs.

Roth IRA

The Roth IRA is a great retirement plan that I wish had existed a long time ago. Here are some ways to distinguish the Roth IRA from the traditional IRA:

- ✔ The Roth IRA provides no tax deduction for contributions.
- ✔ It can grow tax free and be withdrawn tax free when you, again, turn 59½.
- ✔ It doesn't have any early distribution penalties.

The maximum contribution per year for Roth IRAs is the same as for traditional IRAs. You can open a self-directed account with a broker as well. See IRS Publication 590 for details on qualifying.

401(k) plans

Company-sponsored 401(k) plans (named after the section in the tax code that allows them) are widely used and are very popular. In a 401(k) plan, companies set aside money from their paychecks that the employees can use to invest for retirement. Generally, you can invest as much as $14,000 in 2005 and $15,000 in 2006 of your pretax earned income and have it grow tax deferred. Usually, the money is in a mutual fund through a mutual fund company or an insurance firm. Although most 401(k) plans don't give you the opportunity to be self-directed, I mention them in this book for good reason.

Because your money is in a mutual fund that may invest in stocks, take an active role in finding out the mutual funds in which you're allowed to invest. Most plans allow you several types of stock mutual funds. Use your growing knowledge about stocks to make more informed choices about your 401(k) plan options.

Keep in mind that a mutual fund is only as good as what it invests in. Ask the plan administrator some questions about the funds and the types of stocks it invests in. Are the stocks defensive or cyclical? (For more information on defensive and cyclical stocks, see Chapter 12.) Are they large-cap or small-cap? If you don't make an informed choice about the investments in your plan, someone else will (such as the plan administrator). They probably won't have the same ideas about your money as you do.

Part V
The Part of Tens

The 5th Wave   By Rich Tennant

Looks like the market's about to take a downturn.

In this part . . .

This wouldn't be a *For Dummies* book if I didn't include a Part of Tens. Here you find quick reference lists to many of the most basic stock investing concepts and practices. Check the information in this part when you don't have time to read the denser parts of the book or when you just need a quick refresher on what to do before, after, and even during your stock investing pursuits.

Chapter 21

Ten Warning Signs of a Stock's Decline

*H*ave you ever watched a movie and noticed that one of the characters coughs excessively throughout the entire film? To me, that's a dead giveaway that the character is a goner. Or maybe you've seen a movie in which a bit character annoys a crime boss, so right away you know that it's time for him to "sleep with the fishes." Stocks aren't that different. If you're alert, you can recognize some definite signs that your investment may be ready to kick the bucket.

Let the tips in this chapter serve as a "symptoms checklist" on your stock investment. This chapter will help you catch your stock as it starts to "cough," so that you can get out before it "sleeps with the fishes." (I just can't help you with mixed metaphors.)

Earnings Slow Down or Head South

Profit is the lifeblood of a company. Of course, the opposite is true as well. The lack of profit is a sign of a company's poor financial health. Watch the earnings. Are they increasing or not? If they aren't, find out why. If the general economy is experiencing a recession, stagnant earnings are still better than robust losses — everything is relative. Earnings slowdowns for a company may very well be a temporary phenomenon. If a company's earnings are holding up better than its competitors and/or the market in general, you don't need to be alarmed.

Nonetheless, a company's earnings are its most important measure of success. Keep an eye on the company's P/E ratio. It could change negatively (go up) because of one of two basic scenarios:

- ✔ The stock price goes up as earnings barely budge.
- ✔ The stock price doesn't move, yet earnings drop.

Both of these scenarios result in a rising P/E ratio that ultimately has a negative effect on the stock price.

A P/E ratio that is lower than industry competitors' P/E ratios makes a company's stock a favorable investment.

Don't buy the argument "Although the company has losses, its sales are exploding." This argument is a variation of "The company may be losing money, but it'll make it up on volume." For example, say that Sweet Patootee, Inc., (SPI) had sales of $1 billion in 2005 and that sales expect to be $1.5 billion in 2006, projecting an increase at SPI by 50 percent. But what if SPI's earnings were $200 million in 2005 and the company was actually expecting a loss for 2006? The company wouldn't succeed, because sales without earnings isn't enough — the company needs to make a profit. Remember that if you put your money in the stock of a company that has losses, you're not investing, you're speculating.

Sales Slow Down

Before you invest in a company, make sure that sales are strong and rising. If sales start to decline, that downward motion ultimately affects earnings. (See the previous section, "Earnings Slow Down or Head South.") Although the earnings of a company may go safely up and down, sales should consistently rise. If they cease to rise, a variety of reasons may be to blame. First, it may be temporary because the economy in general is having tough times. However, it may be more serious. Perhaps the company is having marketing problems, or a competitor is eating away at its market share. Maybe a new technology is replacing its products and services. In any case, falling sales raise a red flag you shouldn't ignore.

By the way, when I talk sales, I'm talking about the sales of what the company usually offers (its products or services). Sometimes a company may sell something other than what it normally offers (such as equipment, real estate, or a subdivision of its business) and this sale may make the total sales number temporarily blip upward. Watch for this because it can fool you regarding the company's financial strength. Maybe the unusual sale is due to financial or cash flow problems that the company is experiencing. The bottom line is to simply check it out.

Exuberant Analysts Despite Logic

Too often, analysts give glowing praise to stocks that any logical person with some modest financial acumen would avoid like the plague. Why is this? In many instances, there is, alas, a dark motive (or something not so dark such as . . . ugh . . . stupidity). In any case, remember that analysts are employed by companies that earn hefty investment banking fees from the very companies that these analysts tout. In that situation, issuing a less-than-complete or truthful report can be easy.

Conflict of interest was cited as a primary factor in an SEC survey taken in 2000 showing that brokers overwhelmingly give glowing recommendations on stocks ("strong buy," "buy," and "market outperform"). The SEC noticed only an outright "sell" recommendation in less than 1 percent of all the recommendations that it reviewed, even though 2000 witnessed crashing stock prices in most of the popular stocks that were analyzed. Analysts, no matter how objective they may sound, are still employees of companies that make money from the same companies that the analysts analyze.

In fact, you should be wary of analysts' views, especially the analysts who make positive recommendations even when the company in question has worrisome features, such as no income and tremendous debt. It seems like a paradox: Sell a stock when all the pros say to buy it? How can that be? Remember, the merits of any stock should speak for themselves. When a company is losing money, all the great recommendations in the world can't reverse its fortunes. Also, keep in mind that if everybody is buying a particular stock — the current analysts' favorite — who's left to buy it? When it turns out to be a dud, you aren't able to sell it because all the other suckers already own it (thanks to analysts' recommendations). And, if they already own it, they're probably already aware of the company's flaws. What happens then? You got it: More and more people end up selling it. When more people are selling rather than buying a stock, its price declines.

Insider Selling

Heavy insider selling is to a stock what garlic, sunrises, and crosses are to vampires: an almost certain sign of doom! If you notice that increasing numbers of insiders (such as the president of the company, the treasurer, and the vice-president of finance, for instance) are selling their stock holdings, you can consider it a red flag. In recent years, massive insider selling has become a telltale sign of a company's imminent fall from grace. After all, who better to know the company's prospects for success (or lack of) than the company's high-level management? What management does (selling stock, for example) speaks louder than what management says. (Do you hear that loud and persistent coughing again?) For more information on insider trading, see Chapter 19.

Dividend Cuts

For investors who own income stock, dividends are the primary consideration. But, income stock or not, dividend cuts are a negative sign. Of course, if a company is having modest financial difficulty, perhaps a dividend cut is a good thing for the overall health of the company. However, usually analysts see a dividend cut as a sign that a company is having trouble with its earnings or cash flow. In either case, a dividend cut is a warning sign that trouble may be brewing for the firm as it becomes . . . uh . . . less firm.

If the company you own stock in announces a dividend cut, find out why. The cut may be simply a temporary measure to help the company out of some minor financial difficulty, or it may be a sign of deeper trouble. Check the company's fundamentals and then decide. (Refer to Chapter 11 to find out how to read and interpret company financial documents.)

Increased Negative Coverage

You may easily recognize unfavorable reports of a company's stock as a sign to unload that stock. Or you may be a contrarian and see bad press as an opportunity to scoop up some shares of a company victimized by negative reporting. In any case, take the negative reports as a signal to further investigate the merits of holding on to the stock or as a sign for selling it so that you can make room in your portfolio for a more promising stock choice.

Industry Problems

Sometimes being a strong company doesn't matter if that company's industry is having problems; if the industry is in trouble, the company's decline probably isn't that far behind. Tighten up those trailing stops. (See Chapter 17 to find out how.) Also, try to be aware of industries that are intimately related to your industry. Very often, problems in one industry can affect or spread to a related industry. If auto sales are plummeting (for example), then that may have a negative effect on prospects for auto parts or auto services companies.

Political Problems

Political considerations are always a factor in investing. Be it taxes, regulations, or other government actions, politics can easily break a company and send its stock plummeting. If your company's stock is sensitive to political developments, be aware of potential political pitfalls for your stock (or industry) of choice. Reading *The Wall Street Journal* and regularly viewing major financial Web sites can help you stay informed. (I give you lists of sources in Appendix A.) In recent years, drug and tobacco stocks in general suffered because of prevailing political attitudes. Also, certain stocks in particular (Microsoft in the late 1990s comes to mind) have seen their stock prices drop drastically because they were targets of government actions for reasons ranging from antitrust concerns to public safety issues.

Debt Is Too High or Unsustainable

Excessive debt is the kiss of death for a struggling company. During 2000–2002, many companies that experts thought were invincible went bankrupt. In 2001, a record 255 public companies filed for bankruptcy. The most obvious example is Enron. Many analysts and investment advisory publications actually touted Enron as a strong buy — even though the amount of problematic data could have made Godzilla gag. I still get a kick out of reading an old issue of a financial magazine that listed the defunct company the year before its demise as one of ten stocks "for the long haul!" Yikes! Writers like that end up getting hobbies like hang-gliding during hurricane season. Chapter 11 and Appendix B can help you read and understand a company's financial data clearly so that you can make an informed decision about buying or selling its stock.

Funny Accounting: No Laughing Here!

Throughout this book, I discuss the topic of accounting as an important way to see how well (or how poorly) a company is doing. Understanding a company's balance sheet and income statement, and making a simple comparison of these documents over a period of several years, can give you great insights into the company's prospects. You don't have to be an accountant to grasp key concepts. Enron is a perfect example of how you can avoid a stock investing disaster with some rudimentary knowledge of accounting.

Despite the fact that Enron hid many of its financial problems from public view, the information that was available made the message clear: "Danger Will Robinson! Houston, we have a problem!" If investors had done some simple homework, they would have plainly seen the following revealing points in 2000, over a year and a half before the collapse:

- ✔ **Enron's price to earnings (P/E) ratio hit 90 in 2000.** This stratospheric P/E kept most value investors (including myself) away. (See Chapter 10 for more information on P/E ratios.)

- ✔ **Its price to book (P/B) ratio hit 12.** For investors, this ratio meant that the market value of the company, compared to the company's book value (also called "accounting value"), was 12 to 1 — for every $12 of market value, investors were getting only $1 in book value. When you consider that a P/B ratio of 3 or 4 is considered nosebleed territory for value investors, you can see that Enron's P/B ratio was screaming, "Watch out below!"

- ✔ **The price to sales (P/S) ratio hit an incredible 22.** This ratio means that investors paid $22 in market value for every $1 of sales the company generated. When a P/S of 5 or 10 is considered too high, 22 is nosebleed territory!

I found this information in public filings that anyone could have seen. To understand these points more fully (along with other equally incisive and lucid accounting and financial points), and to know how to use the information to avoid similar mistakes in the future, see Chapters 10 and 11 and Appendix B.

Chapter 22

Ten Signals of a Stock Price Increase

*I*f you find a stock that has all ten signals listed in this chapter, back up the truck and load up. The odds are that you won't need all ten to indicate that it's a stock worth a closer look. Probably five or more signals are enough to merit further consideration. In any case, the more signals, the better your chances of choosing a winning stock.

Regardless of market conditions and investor sentiment (how investors "feel" about stocks and the economy), remember the three rules of stock investing success: profits, profits, profits, also known as earnings, earnings, earnings. This advice is as important as real estate's location, location, location. It's that important . . . uh . . . important, important.

Rise in Earnings

If a company earned $1 per share for the past three years and its earnings are now $1.20 per share (a 20 percent increase), consider this increase a positive harbinger. As the saying goes, "Earnings drive the market," so you need to pay attention to the company's profitability. The more a company makes, the greater the chance that its stock price will increase.

Some people wonder whether to invest in a company that was losing money and then finally turns a profit. Perhaps you're considering the stock of a company involved in new, untested technology. My advice is that you need to be careful in this situation. In such a case, predicting whether a second year of profits will show up is hard, but of course, that's what investors are hoping.

For the serious investor, a track record of positive earnings is important. Several years of earnings (especially growing earnings) are crucial in the decision-making process. As earnings rise, make sure that the growth is at a rate of 10 percent or higher.

Say that you're looking at the stock Buckets-o-Cash, Inc. (BOC). BOC had earnings of $1 per share in 2003, $1.10 in 2004, and $1.21 in 2005. First, you can see that the company is a profitable enterprise. Second (and more importantly), you can see that the earnings grew 10 percent each year. The fact that earnings grew consistently year after year is important because it indicates that the company is being managed well. Effective company management has a very positive effect on the stock price as the market notices the company's progress.

Growing earnings are important for another reason — inflation. If a company earns $1 per share in each year, that's, of course, better than earning less or losing money. But inflation erodes the purchasing power of money. If earnings stay constant, the company's ability to grow decreases, because the value of its money will decline as a result of inflation.

Increase in Assets as Debts Are Stable or Decreasing

Increasing assets while decreasing debts (or at least stabilizing them) is key to growing the book value of a company. *Book value* refers to the company's value as it appears on a balance sheet — equal to total assets minus liabilities. Book value usually differs significantly from market value (or market capitalization) because market value is based on supply and demand of the company's stock in the marketplace. For example, a company may have a book value of $10 million dollars (assets of $15 million less liabilities of $5 million) but a market value of $19 million (if, for example, it has 1 million shares that are currently trading at $19 per share). Usually, market value is higher (sometimes much higher) than book value.

Rising book value has a positive impact on market value, which, in turn, tends to drive the stock price up as well. Therefore, it pays to watch book value. Rising book value can be accomplished in one of two basic ways:

- ✔ Debt stays level as assets rise.
- ✔ Assets stay level as debts decline.

When looking at a company's assets and debts, the best scenario you can find is assets rising and debts declining.

At the most basic level, total assets should exceed total debt. Preferably, the company should have a ratio of at least 2-to-1 or better in terms of assets to debt. A ratio of 3-to-1 is better, and so on. The less debt, the better.

The best way to figure out a company's asset to debt ratio is to look at the company's most recent balance sheet and compare it to its balance sheet from prior periods (such as the year before or the same quarter last year). By comparing the figures over three or more years, you can see a trend developing. If the asset to debt ratio has been stable or improving over these three balance sheets, the company is showing growing financial strength, which will help the company's stock price increase in value.

Positive Publicity for Industry

When the media report that a company is doing well financially or that its products and services are being well received by both the media and the market, that news lets you know that this company's stock may be going places. This positive publicity ties in nicely with the other point made in this chapter about consumer acceptance for the company's products and services.

Positive press and consumer acceptance are important because they mean that the company is doing what's necessary to please its customers. The positive media coverage also may attract new customers to the company. Gaining customers means more sales and more earnings, which translates into a higher price for the stock. You can find corporate publicity at Web sites such as www.prnewswire.com and track the industries at www.hoovers.com.

Heavy Insider or Corporate Buying

Company insiders (such as the CEO and the treasurer) know better than anyone else about the health of a company. If insiders are buying stock by the boatload, then these purchases are certainly a positive sign for investors. Chapter 19 thoroughly covers insider trading, but I highlight the main points here. Insiders can do one of two things:

- ✔ **Buy stock for themselves:** If individuals such as the CEO or the treasurer are buying stocks for their personal portfolios, you can assume that they think the stock is a good investment.

- ✔ **Buy stock as a corporate decision:** When the corporation buys its own stock, it's usually considered a positive move. The corporation may see its own stock as a good investment. Additionally, corporate stock buying reduces the number of shares available in the market, potentially pushing the stock price higher.

All things being equal, either one will have a positive impact on the stock price. The odds are that you won't see a stampede of insiders buying the stock in a day or week, but you will see it over a period of months. This is generally true simply because each insider has different circumstances, and insider buying is usually done on an individual basis. An accumulation of purchases tells you that members of the management team believe so strongly that the company will do well that they're willing to put their own money at risk.

More Attention from Analysts

During 2000–2002, analysts were criticized for being zealously optimistic about stocks. I usually don't advise people to invest (or not invest) because of analysts' views, but they're important nonetheless. Many good analyst reviews, and the public's opinion of a single influential analyst, can make a stock's price move dramatically.

Analyze a stock according to its own merits first. Then watch the stock's price as more and more analysts start to direct the public's attention to it. In a sense, they're promoting your stock, an action that tends to boost the stock's price. Don't let the analyst's views sway you, though, because analysts may tout a stock for unsavory reasons. Perhaps the company is a client of the brokerage firm, or maybe the brokerage firm owns a lot of the company's shares and wants to unload them.

Rumors of Takeover Bids

I never want anyone to base an investment decision on a rumor of a takeover bid, but it doesn't hurt if you were considering the stock anyway — basing your decision on a variety of other solid factors, of course, such as strong fundamentals, earnings growth, popular products or services, and so on. A company that's rumored to be a takeover candidate (a company that may be potentially bought out by another company) may have an attractive aspect, such as a promising new patent or exclusive rights to certain properties, that could make it worthy for investors as well.

Rumors of a buyout are always welcome, but the bottom line is that it should alert you to a good value. Regardless of whether the buyout rumor proves true, you shouldn't even consider the stock if it isn't worth owning on its own merits. If it's a good stock, the rumor tends to increase its visibility so that the chances of a takeover do, in fact, increase. Rumor or not, the attention does tend to increase the stock's price.

Praise from Consumer Groups

A company is only as good as the profit it generates. The profit it generates is only as good as the revenues that the company generates. The revenues are based on whether customers are accepting (and shelling out money for) the company's products or services. Therefore, if what the company offers is popular with consumers, it bodes well for profits and consequently higher stock prices.

When you're ready to invest in stocks, look for high consumer satisfaction. Review consumer publications and Web sites and read the surveys and consumer feedback information. Good publicity and word-of-mouth consumer satisfaction are things that investors should be aware of. Stock-picking expert Peter Lynch (formerly of Fidelity Magellan fund fame) sees this popularity with consumers as very valuable stock-picking information. He likes to see what consumers buy because that's where the company's success starts.

Strong or Improving Bond Rating

In Chapter 9, I point out that a poor or deteriorating bond rating is a warning sign for the company. The creditworthiness of a company is a critical factor in determining the company's strength. Most people presume that the bond rating is primarily beneficial for bond investors, and they're correct. However, because the bond rating is assigned according to the company's ability to pay back the bond plus interest, it stands to reason that a strong bond rating (usually a rating of AAA or AA) indicates that the company is financially strong.

The work of independent bond rating firms, such as Standard & Poor's and Moody's, is invaluable for stock investors. For more about bond ratings, turn to Chapter 9.

Powerful Demographics

If you know that a company generates lots of profit from the teenage market and you find out that the teenage market is going to expand by 10 percent per year for the foreseeable future, what would you do? Exactly — you'd buy the stock of that company. If a company has strong fundamentals and appealing products or services and its market is expanding, that company has a winning combination.

Stay alert to growing trends in society. How are demographics changing? Which sectors of the population are growing? Shrinking? What shifts are expected in society in terms of age or ethnicity? Check out the data freely available at the Department of Commerce's Web site for the U.S. Census Bureau (www.census.doc.gov).

Take Sierra Pacific Resources (SRP). It services the fast-growing Las Vegas region of Nevada. The region experienced blistering growth during 2003–2005. SRP's stock price went from $3 in early 2004 and hit $14 by mid-2005. Population and economic expansion played a huge role in the company's growth and subsequent stock price rise.

A market that's growing in size isn't an indicator all by itself (in fact, no indicator gives you the green light all by itself anyway), but it should alert you to do some research. The fact that a strong company sees improving demographic shifts in its marketplace is a big plus.

Low P/E Relative to Industry or Market

The price to earnings (P/E) ratio is a critical number for investors. Value investors in particular scrutinize it. Because the stock price's future ability to rise is ultimately tied to the company's earnings (profits), you want to know that you're not paying too much for the stock. A low P/E ratio (low relative to some standard, such as the industry's average or the average P/E for the S&P 500) is generally considered safe, and the stock is a potential bargain.

If the industry's P/E ratio is 20 and you're looking at a stock that has a P/E of 15, all things being equal, that's great. The company has room for growth, and you have a good value.

Chapter 23

Ten Ways to Protect Yourself from Fraud

In This Chapter

▶ Looking to the SEC for help

▶ Adopting a skeptical attitude

▶ Steering clear of scams

Making money is tough enough without worrying about who is out to get your money. The usual suspects, such as the IRS and other government agencies, are trying to take your money legally. Fortunately, most of that money goes to beneficial pursuits (or so I hope). However, others are out to take your money by illegal methods. Fraud and theft schemes have always been there. Scammers are most prevalent during two economic conditions: when times are really, really good and when times are really, really bad. During the Great Depression, and a manic bull market alike, fraudsters were part of the human condition. Bottom line: Be alert and use the tips in this chapter to avoid being scammed.

Be Wary of Unsolicited Calls and E-mails

Phone calls or e-mails out of the blue to solicit money from you are always a bit questionable, but if they offer investments, you need to be particularly careful. But you knew that, right? You've read countless consumer reports warning you about investing through telemarketers and/or spammers. If the investment that's being pitched is so good, why is someone calling to sell you on it? Hasn't the financial press reported it? It probably has, but only as an advisory warning you to turn down any such offers. Find out more at Web sites such as www.fraudbureau.com and www.fraud.org.

Get to Know the SEC

Long before you invest your first dollar, whether in stocks or any other financial investment, get to know the Securities and Exchange Commission (SEC). It's there primarily to protect investors from fraud and other unlawful activity designed to fleece them. The federal government created the SEC during the early 1930s to crack down on abuses that continued to linger from the speculative and questionable trading practices that were in high gear during the stock market mania of the late 1920s.

The SEC has an excellent Web site at www.sec.gov. The site offers plenty of great articles and resources for both novice and experienced investors to help you watch out for fraud and better understand the financial markets and how they work. Look up the telephone numbers for regional offices and feel free to call with your questions about dubious investments and brokers or dealers. The SEC carries on a number of activities designed to help you invest with confidence. It maintains a database on file about complaints lodged against brokers and companies that have committed fraud or other abuses against the investing public.

Your tax dollars pay for this important agency. Find out about its free publications, services, and resources before you invest. If you've already been victimized by unscrupulous operators, call the SEC for assistance.

Don't Invest If You Don't Understand

Investments frequently can come in complicated forms that promise a great return but can be hard to understand. The premise of the investment — how it works and how it will create a great return on your money — may be hard to figure out. Scammers count on people being overwhelmed by the details to the point that they ignore the mechanics of the deal. Don't fall for such approaches. You should understand exactly what you're investing in, how it makes money, and what the risks are. If you still can't understand the investment (even if it's legitimate), then you're better off not plunging in with your hard-earned money.

If the investment still sounds intriguing, then at the very least get a second opinion by reviewing the details with advisors you trust.

Question the Promise of Extraordinary Returns

In good times and bad, people want to make as much money as possible with their investments. Hey, who doesn't? If your money is in a bank account earning a paltry 2 percent, what's wrong with putting some of it into some investment earning 17 percent compounded hourly? The extraordinary returns promised either end up being illusory or the result of great risk.

Misrepresenting or inflating promises of a great return on your money is common; sometimes even good brokers can unwittingly make them. Higher returns mean more exposure to loss.

If the investment is bona fide and is quoted as having a high rate of return (either in income or capital gains potential), then you can expect commensurate risk. The risk may not be immediately apparent, but it's there. As the Johnny-one-note that I am in this chapter, I recommend that you seek independent third parties for an informed second opinion. Appendix A has an extensive list of places and people to turn to.

A notable investment pro once remarked, "Sometimes, a return *on* your money is not as important as a return *of* your money." In other words, until you pick up more investing knowledge, keeping your original investment safe is better than risking it for questionable, pie-in-the-sky promises.

Verify the Investment

If anyone asks you to invest, first verify that the investment exists. Sounds weird, huh? Not really. Yes, many people have lost money in a bad or dubious investment, but you'd be surprised at how many people have been willing to fork over hard-earned money for phantom investments.

A man was prosecuted for fleecing millions from investors who were quick to jump into a dot-com IPO that he was peddling. After the SEC and other authorities investigated, they found that no such dot-com IPO existed at all. (Does that make it a dot-gone?) Sometimes, you can't trust a con man to be even partially truthful.

When someone offers you an investment and you're not certain what type of investment it is or where it's traded, ask questions of the person presenting the investment and of third parties who can offer verification. Here are some questions to ask:

- ✔ What exchange or market is this investment traded or sold on?
- ✔ What government agency oversees this investment, and how can I contact that agency?
- ✔ Have articles on this investment been published by major media sources, such as *The Wall Street Journal* and *Money* magazine?
- ✔ Can I find documents filed by this company at the SEC's document database called EDGAR (Electronic Document Gathering and Retrieval System found at `www.sec.gov`)?
- ✔ What literature do I have that I can present to my accountant and attorney?

Check Out the Broker

Sometimes the investment is legitimate, but the broker or dealer isn't. Scammers don't let the absence of a license stop them. When an unfamiliar financial products marketer contacts you, do some homework first. Contact one of the following to check the status of a broker or dealer:

- ✔ **Professional associations:** Do you want to know whether a marketer is a member in good standing? Associations help the public deal with unethical parties in the industry.
- ✔ **The National Association of Securities Dealers (NASD):** Visit one of its great Web sites at `www.nasdr.com`. This site informs the public about brokers and dealers who have been convicted or have complaints against them.
- ✔ **The SEC:** Are these marketers properly registered? The SEC can inform you about whether these marketers have been penalized or banned from further activity.

Beware of the Pump-and-Dump

The pump-and-dump is a classic scam that usually shows up in bull markets. The scam works best with small-cap or (even better) microcap stocks — in other words, small companies that have relatively few shares or small capitalization. Scams are at their most effective when they can play on the two most overworked emotions in the financial markets: greed and fear. In the pump-and-dump, greed is the operative emotion. In this example, the investor to be plucked is called Walter Pidjun (no relation to the actor Walter Pidgeon).

The insiders at the dubious company first try to promote the stock as a "hot investment." The company activates the "pump" when insiders and/or a stockbroker, in cahoots with the insiders, call up investors such as Mr. Pidjun to tout this fantastic opportunity. They promise an opportunity to get into a profitable stock that will skyrocket in value. As a result of the high-pressure sales tactics, investors start buying the stock. This demand pushes up the price easily because so few shares are available on this thinly-traded stock. Perhaps Mr. Pidjun didn't bite the first time the broker called, but the broker calls again.

"Hello again, Mr. Pidjun! This is Barry Kuda, account representative from the brokerage firm of Fleece, Peeples, & Scram. Do you remember that stock investment I brought to your attention last week? That's right . . . Titanic Bio-Tech, Inc. Have ya seen the way its price has zoomed since then? When I last spoke to you, it was at $3 a share. Now it's already at $47! Our respected research department tells me it should be at $93 by lunchtime and will probably triple again before the weekend. You don't want to miss this opportunity of a lifetime! Now how many shares would you like?"

Indeed, the price certainly went up dramatically as Mr. Kuda said it would. Mr. Pidjun puts the order in immediately while dollar signs dance in his head. The "pump" is working very well. After the fraudulent operators see that the stock has gone as high as possible, they immediately sell their stock at grossly inflated prices. The "dump" is complete, and they disappear into the woodwork. Mr. Pidjun and the other investors watch as their "hot" investment turns stone cold and the stock plummets to pennies on the dollar. Investors were so blinded by their greed that the pump-and-dump scam has successfully been done even in cases when no stock existed at all!

How can I do a warning about something legal in a chapter about fraud? Actually, isn't this entire chapter a warning? Yes, but sometimes you need a warning for things that aren't immediately apparent. As odd as this sounds, I want to warn you about something that technically isn't fraud. What is it? Well, a legal version of the pump-and-dump scheme does exist. It's not unusual for brokers and analysts to "pump" up a stock in the media. For example, a celebrated market strategist or high-profile CEO may talk up the wonderful potential of XYZ stock on a financial show. Then later you find out (through SEC filings, for instance) that while these people were recommending that people buy the stock, they had actually been furtively selling their holdings in the stock! You were hearing "buy, buy," yet they were really saying "bye-bye."

Watch Out for Short-and-Abort

Short-and-abort works on the same premise as pump-and-dump. The difference is that instead of playing on the greed emotion, the con works on the fear emotion. To understand this scam, you should keep in mind that one can profit even when a stock falls in price by "going short." Chapter 17 goes into detail about making money from going short on a stock, but here I want to briefly describe it.

Going short is a strategy that an investor can utilize in a margin account with just about any broker. An investor may consider going short on a stock if she expects the stock's price to fall. Say that you think the stock of the company Plummet Inc. (at $50 per share) will sink fast. When you tell the broker that you want to go short on 100 shares of Plummet Inc., the broker borrows 100 shares from the market, sells those shares, and credits $5,000 to your account (100 shares at $50 per share). Because this transaction is based on "borrowed stock," sooner or later you have to return the stock. Say that the stock price falls to $30; you could then instruct your broker to "close out the position." This order means that the broker debits your account for $3,000 (to buy 100 shares at $30) and returns the stock to the source. In this case, you make a $2,000 profit (the original $5,000 less the $3,000).

In the case of short-and-abort, the scammers want to make money from a stock's plummeting price. They may contact shareholders directly or plant phony stories or press releases in the media to cause concern and panic over a company's prospects. Naturally, shareholders in that particular company get anxious over their investment and decide to sell. The sudden, mass selling causes the stock's price to fall. The scammer then closes out the short position, takes the money, and runs.

Remember That Talk Is Cheap (Until You Talk to an Expert)

A fertile area for misleading investors is in the world of independent, third-party information sources. As the bull market reached its zenith in late 1999, some people were selling expensive stock-investing seminars and newsletters that promised get-rich-quick results. One promoter sold basic information (some of which was inaccurate) in a $5,000 seminar program. After many complaints, the authorities investigated and found out that the presenters made a lot of money from their seminars, but they actually lost money on their investment strategies! (It figures.)

Another information marketer published an expensive newsletter that promised lucrative stock picks. It was discovered that he wasn't recommending stocks found through diligent and honest research; he recommended the stocks because the companies paid him to tout their stocks.

Seminars and newsletters are excellent sources of information and expertise on a given topic, but you should stay away from marketers that use hard-sell approaches for outrageously priced seminars and other information products. If you're considering expensive seminars and information products, check with such sources as www.fraud.org and the Better Business Bureau at www.bbbonline.org for registered complaints.

Recovering (If You Do Get Scammed)

If, despite your best efforts to invest wisely, you have that sinking feeling that you've been conned, it's time to gain assistance from securities enforcement authorities. The SEC is a good place to start, but you can turn to other agencies, too.

If a scheme was promoted through the postal service, contact the postal service (www.usps.com). File a complaint with the postmaster in your town. Provide complete details in writing, including your account of what happened and copies of literature you received from the offending organization.

Also contact the offices of appropriate state government attorneys general. Find out more from the National Association of Attorneys General (www.naag.org). See Appendix A for more resources.

Chapter 24

Ten Challenges and Opportunities for Stock Investors

*O*ver the years, I have found that the easiest way to make money with stocks (or the easiest way to avoid losing money with stocks) was to simply be aware of the economic environment in which they operate. Stocks can be the best (or worst) investment given the economic/political environment. There are many economic challenges facing the stock market and they include what is happening with government policy, societal trends, and national/international geopolitical conditions. You need to be aware of "The big picture" by regularly checking in with great Web sites such as Financial Sense (www.financialsense.com), Free Market News Network (www.freemarketnews.com), and the Mises Institute (www.mises.org). See Appendix A for more resources.

In this chapter, I discuss the most important issues or megatrends that can affect you and your loved ones as well as your stock investments.

Debt, Debt, and More Debt

In early 2005, the United States' Gross Domestic Product (GDP) hit the $12 trillion mark. Great! However, the total level of debt in the country hit $38 trillion. Ugh . . . NOT great. What has kept the economy afloat and "growing" during the past eight to ten years has been massive and pervasive debt that must be dealt with. Debt in just about every category is at record levels. This includes mortgage, consumer, margin, corporate, and government debt. The problem is that this debt must be either paid off or wiped out through bankruptcy.

Either one will have its negative consequences for the economy. Either one can do great harm to stocks in general and/or your portfolio in particular.

Make sure that you are dealing with your debt level now. Reduce it as much as possible and make sure that you are analyzing your stocks in the same light. Companies that carry too much debt will be at great risk. If the company sinks, your stock will follow. If the company goes into bankruptcy, your stock's value will be vaporized.

If you want to see something fascinating (and scary at the same time), check out the total debt figures by viewing the Grandfather Economic Report by Michael Hodges at `http://mwhodges.home.att.net` (if the Web site is no longer there feel free to e-mail me at paul@mladjenovic.com and I'll get the info for you). It is sobering stuff!

Derivatives

Deriv . . . what? You might say "what the hell are they?" unless, of course, you're my church's pastor. Derivatives are the largest financial market in the world. As of July 2005, the total dollar value exceeds $280 trillion. It easily dwarfs the world economy. Easily! Now, you don't have to understand them but you should be aware of what could go wrong if a derivatives problem occurs. The once-mighty Enron imploded very quickly primarily due to tragic errors in their derivatives portfolio. Derivatives "accidents" have dotted the financial landscape over the past 10 to 15 years and they had (and will have) the potential to do major damage to the stock market.

There's no use fretting about derivatives. While you're at it, you might as well worry about meteors, presidential campaigns, and the chance you might get O. J. Simpson as your neighbor. Just take common sense approaches to protect your portfolio as you grow your wealth. Look into diversifying, trailing stops, and myriad strategies throughout this book and in the resources cited.

Real Estate

In much the same way that everyone was enamored and overzealous with stocks a few years ago, the same is true with real estate circa 2004. The real estate mania has turned into a dangerous bubble and it is an ominous development for the economy and yes . . . stocks. The expansion of the money supply, excessive credit and debt growth, and the lowering of lending standards have acted like rocket fuel for the real estate market causing prices to rise beyond reasonable market value. Millions of homeowners, investors, and speculators will be adversely affected. And listen, I'm not just talking about property owners. The tentacles of the housing bubble reach far beyond bricks and mortar. Mortgages in the hundreds of billions have been packaged and resold as securities and purchased by many mutual funds, insurance companies, Fortune 500 companies, and pension plans. Because a huge chunk of these are "sub-prime" (risky) debt, that means huge problems as interest rates rise, the economy sags, and so on.

The message to you is clear: Make sure you have your mortgage under control and your debt at manageable levels. Make sure that you avoid stocks of companies that are overly exposed to what will most likely be a bubble that could dwarf the stock bubble of 1998–2002.

Inflation

The last time inflation was a major problem was the late 1970s and . . . you guessed it . . . the market was having a rough time. Interest rates soared to over 18 percent and it was economic headaches for everyone. Although inflation was generally tame during the '80s and '90s, it is showing renewed life during this decade due to a massive expansion of the money supply that started in earnest in 1995. I think that it is a minor scandal that the official inflation rate (Consumer Price Index or CPI) excludes food and energy costs. This significantly understates what our daily costs of living are. Without food and energy, the inflation rate recently hovered in the 2 ƒ 1/2 to 3 percent range. Just think: As long as you don't eat, turn on your lights, or drive, you're doing great! If these costs were realistically included, the inflation rate would easily be two to three times higher.

For stock investors, this means that having your money grow is more important than ever. Understanding the pernicious effects of inflation should be factored into your stock picks. Some stocks will suffer (mortgage companies with fixed-debt portfolios) while others (precious metals mining companies) will prosper.

Pension Crisis

You've seen all the headlines: "Pension plans are a growing crisis." "San Diego has pension crisis." "People are living longer lives." "People are not saving enough for retirement." Many state/local governments and large companies will experience shortfalls in their financial ability to meet retirement plan obligations. Millions of people will, at the very least, not get as much as they expect when they retire. In addition, the Pension Benefit Guaranty Corporation (see www.pbgc.gov) does not have enough funds to cover the shortfall of company pension plans. According to a survey cited by Forbes magazine, 313 (62 percent!) of the 500 companies listed in the S&P 500 do not have enough funds to cover their future expected financial obligations (as of early 2005). America is not alone; Europe, Japan, and even China are in the same (or worse!) predicament.

The message is clear: People need to save and invest more to fill in the financial gaps that seem to be inevitable. Stocks are a wealth-building tool that is well suited for long-term needs such as your retirement concerns. Start now because the future has a way of sneaking up on you faster than you think.

Government's Unfunded Liabilities

Social Security and Medicare are certain to be gigantic challenges during the next few decades. As of June 2005, the total liabilities for these mammoth programs exceed $44 trillion. That's not a typo; it's a combined liability that is nearly four times our nation's gross domestic product (GDP). Current beneficiaries will likely not be affected, but anyone under 65 will certainly be. Let's face it: We're living longer than ever before and we will need to be more proactive about our personal responsibility in our senior years. To find out more, review your rights and responsibilities with the Social Security Administration (www.ssa.gov) and Medicare (www.medicare.gov). Also check out some excellent private sites such as www.socialsecurity.org, www.Medicare.org, and www.MedicareNewsWatch.com.

Recession/Depression

History tells us that stock investing during a recession or depression is best avoided. Declines in economic growth always follow artificial economic booms. In this decade, the likelihood of a recession or depression is remarkably high due to the fact that economic problems and imbalances (such as debt, housing bubble, and so on) need to be addressed, and that means a significant downturn. Become more aware about economics and how it operates. Find out more at reader-friendly sites such as Dismal Scientist (www.economy.com), American Institute for Economic Research (www.aier.org), and Foundation for Economic Education (www.fee.org).

In rough economic times, the best stocks are defensive (food, beverage, utilities, and so on) because people will buy these things no matter how good or bad the economy is. Cyclical stocks will get beaten down so it might be a good idea to shop around for real values after the economy turns around. In the meanwhile, play it safe and protect your money with solid, financially sound companies and deploy protective strategies with your money.

Commodities

A shrewd man once said, "History may not repeat but it can often rhyme" (Okay, it was me!). In many respects, this decade resembles the 1970s. Stocks were having a dreadful time as inflation, the energy crisis, and international tensions escalated. However, it was a great time to invest in energy, precious metals, and commodities. Gold and silver hit all-time highs by the end of the decade. Stock investors that scooped up shares of companies in these specific industries racked up tremendous gains. The lesson for us to understand is that conditions in this decade offer opportunities in natural resources that mirror the late 1970s. In addition, China and India are growing and they will need more commodities (grains, base metals, energy, water, and so on) for their expanding economies and populations.

As demand continues to outpace supply, the stocks of companies that provide products and services in natural resources will shine.

Energy

The world's appetite for energy (oil, gas, and so on) has caused prices to hit record highs, and the coming years promise more demand. The energy markets have seen a sea of change that makes current conditions far more different and more serious than we've seen in recent decades. We have entered the age of "Peak Oil" (see more about this at www.peakoil.net), which means that cheap and readily available energy is a thing of the past. In August 2005, oil hit $67 per barrel as gasoline topped $3 per gallon in many spots across the country. All of a sudden, $100 oil and $7 gas doesn't seem so farfetched. Supply and demand is nowhere more evident than the world's energy market.

For stock investors, this at least means the chance to grow your money both directly (energy companies, obviously) and indirectly (alternate energy companies). If we want our wealth to grow, then we need to understand the impact that energy will have on our portfolios. To get some excellent information on the energy sector, try a resource such as Doug Casey's Energy Speculator (www.caseyresearch.com). For more information, check out Chapter 13.

Dangers from Left Field

Gee, after being beaten up by the previous nine points, what else is needed? This reminds me of the episode of "Get Smart" where the arch villain says "You've been whipped, beaten, and tortured, but the picnic is over!" (I still use that great line at parties.) In any case, I hope that I have impressed upon you that it is a brave, new world fraught with dangers for the clueless, but filled with wealth-building opportunities for the "clued in." The fact is that no one knows what will hit our economy and society from out of the blue. Events such as 9/11, the tsunami in Asia, and Hurricane Katrina certainly tell us the world has unseen perils for us and our prosperity. The point is that terrorism and other factors will have an impact. Fortunately, you can make changes . . . even slight changes . . . that can protect or grow your wealth.

Whether you're talking about healthcare stocks that boom in response to new health threats or concerns (mad cow disease, and so on) or stocks of companies that prosper due to homeland security issues, your stock investing program can survive and thrive. Stay informed and understand that successful stock investing doesn't happen in a vacuum.

Part VI
Appendixes

The 5th Wave   By Rich Tennant

"I take it your stocks are still trading high on the 'yawn index'."

In this part . . .

Check out the appendixes for resources that aid you in making informed investment decisions. Whether the topic is stock investing terminology, economics, or avoiding capital gains taxes, I include a treasure trove of resources for you. Whether you go to a bookstore, the library, or the Internet, Appendix A gives you some great places to turn to for help. In Appendix B, I explain financial ratios. These important numbers help you better determine whether to invest in a particular company's stock.

Appendix A

Resources for Stock Investors

· ·

*G*etting and staying informed is an ongoing priority for stock investors. The lists in this appendix represent some the best information resources available.

Financial Planning Sources

To find a financial planner to help you with your general financial needs, contact the following organizations:

Certified Financial Planner Board of Standards
1670 Broadway, Suite 600
Denver, CO 80202-4809
888-237-6275
www.CFP-Board.org
Get a free copy of the CFP Board's pamphlet *10 Questions to Ask When Choosing a Financial Planner*. Be sure to ask for a financial plannerthat specializes in investing.

Financial Planning Association (FPA)
1615 L Street, N.W. Suite 650
Washington, DC 20036-5606
800-322-4237
www.fpanet.org

National Association of Personal Financial Advisors
3250 North Arlington Heights Road
Suite 109
Arlington Heights, IL 60004
800-366-2732
www.napfa.org

The Language of Investing

Dictionary of Financial Terms
By Virginia Morris and Kenneth Morris
Published by Lightbulb Press, Inc.
A nicely laid out A-to-Z publication for investors mystified by financial terms. It explains the important investing terms you come across every day.

Investor Words
www.investorwords.com
One of the most comprehensive sites on the Internet for beginning and intermediate investors for learning words and phrases unique to the financial world.

Investopedia
www.investopedia.com
Another excellent site with plenty of information on investing for beginners and intermediate investors.

Textual Investment Resources

Stock investing success is not an event; it's a process. The periodicals and magazines listed (along with their Web sites) have offered many years of guidance and information for investors, and they're still top-notch. The books and pamphlets provide much wisdom that is either timeless or timely (covering problems and concerns every investor should be aware of now).

Periodicals and magazines

Barron's
www.barrons.com

Forbes magazine
www.forbes.com

Investor's Business Daily
www.investors.com

Kiplinger's Personal Finance magazine
www.kiplinger.com

Money magazine
www.money.com

SmartMoney
www.smartmoney.com

The Wall Street Journal
www.wsj.com

Books and pamphlets

Austrian Economics for Investors
By Mark Skousen
Published by Pickering & Chatto Ltd.

Common Stocks and Uncommon Profits
By Philip A. Fisher
Published by Wiley Publishing, Inc.

Elliott Wave Principle: Key to Market Behavior
By Robert Prechter and A. J. Frost
Published by New Classics Library

Forbes Guide to the Markets
By Marc M. Groz
Published by John Wiley & Sons, Inc.

How to Buy Stocks
By Louis Engel and Henry Hecht
Published by Little, Brown and Company

How to Pick Stocks Like Warren Buffett: Profiting from the Bargain Hunting Strategies of the World's Greatest Value Investor
By Timothy Vick
Published by McGraw-Hill Professional Publishing

The Intelligent Investor: A Book of Practical Counsel
By Benjamin Graham (preface by Warren Buffett)
Published by HarperCollins

"Invest Wisely: Advice From Your Securities Regulators" (pamphlet)
www.sec.gov/consumer/inws.htm
This publication provides basic information to help investors select a brokerage firm and sales representative, make an initial investment decision, monitor an investment, and address an investment problem.

Secrets of the Great Investors (audiotape series)
Published by Knowledge Products
800-876-4332
www.knowledgeproducts.net

Standard & Poor's Stock Guide (available in the library reference section)
Ask your reference librarian about this excellent reference source, which gives one-page summaries on the major companies and has detailed financial reports on all companies listed on the New York Stock Exchange, American Stock Exchange, and major companies in Nasdaq.

Unofficial Guide to Picking Stocks
By Paul Mladjenovic
Published by Wiley
www.wiley.com
My shameless plug for another great book. Seriously, the book has several hundred resources and tips that add tremendously to your stock investing knowledge.

The Wall Street Journal Guide to Understanding Money and Investing
By Kenneth Morris, Virginia Morris, and Alan Siegel
Published by Fireside Press

Special books of interest to stock investors

These titles provide more in-depth information for Chapters 13 and 23.

The Coming Collapse of the Dollar and How to Profit from It: Make a Fortune by Investing in Gold and Other Hard Assets
By James Turk and John Rubino
Published by Double Day

The Coming Crash in the Housing Market: 10 Things You Can Do Now to Protect Your Most Valuable Investment
By John R. Talbott
Published by McGraw-Hill

Financial Reckoning Day: Surviving the Soft Depression of the 21st Century
By William Bonner and Addison Wiggin
Published by John Wiley & Sons, Inc.

*Hot Commodities: How Anyone Can Invest Profitably
in the World's Best Market*
By Jim Rogers
Published by Random House

*Twilight in the Desert: The Coming Saudi Oil Shock
and the World Economy*
By Matthew R. Simmons
Published by John Wiley & Sons, Inc.

Investing Web sites

How can any serious investor ignore the Internet? You can't and you shouldn't.
The following are among the best information sources available.

General investing Web sites

Bloomberg
www.bloomberg.com

Free Market News Network
www.freemarketnews.com

MarketWatch
www.marketwatch.com

Money Central
www.moneycentral.msn.com

Stock investing Web sites

Allstocks.com
www.allstocks.com

Contrarian Investing.com
www.contrarianinvesting.com

Daily Stocks
www.dailystocks.com

Investools
www.investools.com

Market Guide
www.investor.reuters.com

Quote.com
www.quote.com

RagingBull
www.ragingbull.lycos.com

Standard and Poor's
www.standardandpoors.com

Super Money Links
www.supermoneylinks.com

Yahoo! Finance
www.finance.yahoo.com

Investor Associations and Organizations

American Association of Individual Investors (AAII)
625 North Michigan Ave.
Chicago, IL 60611-3110
800-428-2244, 312-280-0170
ww.aaii.org

National Association of Investors Corp. (NAIC)
877-275-6242
www.betterinvesting.org

Stock Exchanges

American Stock Exchange
www.amex.com

Nasdaq
www.nasdaq.com

New York Stock Exchange
www.nyse.com

OTC Bulletin Board
www.otcbb.com

Finding Brokers

The following sections offer both sources to help you evaluate brokers and an extensive list of brokers (telephone numbers and Web sites) so that you can do your own shopping.

Choosing brokers

Gomez & Associates
www.watchfire.com
This firm acts like the "J.D. Power & Associates" of the stock brokerage industry.

Smart Money Magazine
www.smartmoney.com
They do a comprehensive annual review and comparison of stock brokers.

Stock Brokers
www.stockbrokers.com

Brokers

A. B. Watley
866-492-8539
www.abwatley.com

Accutrade
800-882-4887
www.accutrade.com

A. G. Edwards & Co.
877-835-7877
www.agedwards.com

Ameritrade
800-669-3900
www.ameritrade.com

Brown & Company
800-822-2021
www.brownco.com

Charles Schwab & Co.
800-540-9874
www.schwab.com

E*TRADE
800-etrade-1
www.etrade.com

Fidelity Brokerage
800-fidelity
www.fidelity.com

Harris Direct
800-825-5723
www.harrisdirect.com

Merrill Lynch
800-merrill
www.ml.com

Muriel Siebert & Co.
800-872-0444
www.siebertnet.com

R. F. Lafferty & Co.
800-513-6930
www.laffertyny.com

Scottrade
800-619-SAVE
www.scottrade.com

Smith Barney Citigroup
800-221-3636
www.smithbarney.com

TD Waterhouse Securities, Inc.
800-934-4448
www.waterhouse.com

Vanguard Brokerage Services
877-662-7447
www.vanguard.com

Wall Street Access
800-774-0163
www.wsaccess.com

Investment Sources

The following are fee-based subscription services. Many of them also offer excellent free e-mail newsletters tracking the stock market and related news.

Daily Reckoning (Agora Publishing)
www.dailyreckoning.com

The Elliott Wave Theorist
770-536-0309
www.elliottwave.com

Hulbert Financial Digest
www.hulbertdigest.com
Part of MarketWatch.com

Louis Rukeyser's Wall Street
800-892-9702
www.rukeyser.com

Martin Weiss's Safe Money Report
800-844-1773
www.safemoneyreport.com

Motley Fool
www.fool.com

Richard Russell's Dow Theory Letters
www.dowtheoryletters.com

The Value Line Investment Survey
800-654-0508
www.valueline.com

Dividend Reinvestment Plans

Buy and Hold, Inc.
www.buyandhold.com

DRIP Central
www.dripcentral.com

First Share
www.firstshare.com

Share Builder
www.sharebuilder.com

Sources for Analysis

The following sources give you the chance to look a "little deeper" at some critical aspects regarding stock analysis. Whether its earnings estimates and insider selling or a more insightful look at a particular industry, these sources are among my favorites.

Earnings and earnings estimates

Earnings Whispers
www.earningswhispers.com

Thomson Financial's First Call
www.firstcall.com

Zacks Summary of Brokerage Research
www.zacks.com

Industry analysis

Hoover's
www.hoovers.com

MarketWatch
www.marketwatch.com

Standard & Poor's
www.standardandpoors.com

Factors that affect market value

Understanding basic economics is so vital to making your investment decisions that I had to include this section. These great sources have helped me understand "the big picture" and what ultimately affects the stock market.

Economics and politics

American Institute of Economic Research (AIER)
Box 100
Great Barrington, MA 01230
www.aier.org
Note: AIER also has a great little booklet on budgeting for consumers.

Center for Freedom and Prosperity
www.freedomandprosperity.org

Economy.com, Inc.
600 Willowbrook Lane
West Chester, PA 19382
866-275-3266
www.economy.com
www.dismal.com
www.freelunch.com

Federal Reserve Board
www.federalreserve.gov

Financial Sense
Box 1269
Poway, CA 92074
858-486-3939
www.financialsense.com

Foundation of Economic Education
30 South Broadway
Irvington, NY 10533
800-960-4FEE
www.fee.org

Le MetroPole Café
www.lemetropolecafe.com

Ludwig von Mises Institute
518 West Magnolia Ave.
Auburn, AL 36832
334-321-2100
www.mises.org

Securities and Exchange Commission (SEC)

www.sec.gov

The SEC has tremendous resources for investors. In addition to information on investing, the SEC also monitors the financial markets for fraud and other abusive activities. For stock investors, it also has EDGAR (Electronic Data Gathering, Analysis, and Retrieval system), which is a comprehensive, searchable database of public documents that are filed by public companies.

Federal laws

Go to any of these sites to find out about new and proposed laws. The on-site search engine will help you find laws either by their assigned number or a keyword search.

Library of Congress

Thomas legislative search engine

http://thomas.loc.gov

U.S. House of Representatives

www.house.gov

U.S. Senate

www.senate.gov

Technical analysis

Big Charts (Provided by www.Marketwatch.com)

www.bigcharts.com

Elliott Wave Theorist

www.elliottwave.com

Stockcharts.com, Inc.

www.stockcharts.com

Insider trading

FreeEDGAR

www.freeedgar.com

Securities and Exchange Commission (SEC)

www.sec.gov

Street Insider
www.streetinsider.com

10-K Wizard
www.10kwizard.com

Tax Benefits and Obligations

Americans for Tax Reform
www.atr.org

Fair Mark
www.fairmark.com

Fidelity Investments
www.401k.com

J. K. Lasser's series of books on taxes
By J. K. Lasser
John Wiley & Sons, Inc.
www.wiley.com

National Taxpayers Union
www.ntu.org

Roth IRA
www.rothira.com

Taxes 2006 For Dummies
By Eric Tyson, Margaret A. Munro, and David J. Silverman
John Wiley & Sons, Inc.
www.wiley.com

Fraud

Consumer Information Center
www.pueblo.gsa.gov
Investing publications for consumers from the Consumer Information Center
catalog are available for downloading at this Web site at no charge.

National Association of Securities Dealers
1735 K Street, N.W.
Washington, DC 20006
800-289-9999
202-728-8000
www.nasdr.com
This Web site gives you information and assistance on reporting fraud or
other abuse by brokers.

The National Fraud Center
www.fraud.org

North American Securities Administrators Association
888-846-2722
www.nasaa.org

Securities and Exchange Commission (SEC)
www.sec.gov
The government agency that regulates the securities industry.

Securities Industry Association
1401 I Street, N.W.
Washington, DC 20005
202-296-9410
www.siainvestor.com

Appendix B

Financial Ratios

As dull or cumbersome as the topic sounds, financial ratios are indeed the "meat" of analyzing stocks. Sadly, most investors don't exercise their due diligence when it comes to doing some relatively easy things to make sure that the company they're investing in is a good place for their hard-earned investment dollars. This appendix lists the most common ratios that investors should be aware of and use. A solid company doesn't have to pass all these ratio tests with flying colors, but at a minimum, it should comfortably pass the ones regarding profitability and solvency:

✔ **Profitability:** Is the company making money? Is it making more or less than it did in the prior period? Are sales growing? Are profits growing?

You can answer these questions by looking at the following ratios:

- Return on Equity
- Common Size Ratio (Income Statement)
- Return on Assets

✔ **Solvency:** Is the company keeping debts and other liabilities under control? Are the company's assets growing? Is the company's net equity (or net worth or stockholders' equity) growing?

You can answer these questions by looking at the following ratios:

- Debt-to-Net-Equity
- Working Capital
- Quick Ratio

While you examine ratios, keep these points in mind:

✔ Not every company and/or industry is the same. A ratio that seems problematic in one industry may be just fine in another. Investigate.

✔ A single ratio isn't enough on which to base your investment decision. Look at several ratios covering the major aspects of a company's finances.

✔ Look at two or more years of a company's numbers to judge whether the most recent ratio is better, worse, or unchanged from the previous year's ratio. Ratios can give you early warning signs regarding the company's prospects.

Liquidity Ratios

Liquidity means the ability to quickly turn assets into cash. Liquid assets are simply assets that are easier to convert to cash. Real estate, for example, is certainly an asset, but it's not liquid because converting it to cash could take weeks, months, or even years. Current assets such as checking accounts, savings accounts, marketable securities, accounts receivable, and inventory are much easier to sell or convert to cash in a very short period of time.

Paying bills or immediate debt takes liquidity. Liquidity ratios help you understand a company's ability to pay its current liabilities. The most common liquidity ratios are the current ratio and the quick ratio; the numbers to calculate them are located on the balance sheet.

Current ratio

The current ratio is the most commonly used liquidity ratio. It answers the question "Does the company have enough financial cushion to meet its current bills?" It's calculated as follows:

Current ratio = total current assets ÷ total current liabilities

If Holee Guacamolee Corp. (HGC) has $60,000 in current assets and $20,000 in current liabilities, the current ratio is 3 because the company has $3 of current assets for each dollar of current liabilities. As a general rule, a current ratio of 2 or more is desirable. A current ratio of less than 1 is a red flag that the company may have a cash crunch that could cause financial problems. Although many companies strive to get the current ratio to equal 1, I like to see a higher ratio (in the range of 1–3) to keep a cash cushion should the economy slow down.

Quick ratio

The quick ratio is frequently referred to as the "acid test" ratio. It's a little more stringent than the current ratio in that you calculate it without inventory. I'll use the current ratio example discussed in the preceding section. What if half of the assets are inventory ($30,000 in this case)? Now what? First, here's the formula for the quick ratio:

Quick ratio = (Current assets less inventory) ÷ current liabilities

In the example, the quick ratio for HGC is 1.5 ($30,000 divided by $20,000). In other words, the company has $1.50 of "quick" liquid assets for each dollar of current liabilities. This amount is okay. *Quick liquid assets* include any money in the bank, marketable securities, and accounts receivable. If quick liquid assets at the very least equal or exceed total current liabilities, that amount is considered adequate.

The acid test that this ratio reflects is embodied in the question "Can the company pay its bills when times are tough?" In other words, if the company can't sell its goods (inventory), can it still meet its short-term liabilities? Of course, you must watch the accounts receivable as well. If the economy is entering rough times, you want to make sure that the company's customers are paying invoices on a timely basis.

Operating Ratios

Operating ratios essentially measure the company's efficiency. "How is the company managing its resources?" is a question commonly answered with operating ratios. If, for example, a company sells products, does it have too much inventory? If it does, that could impair the company's operations. The following sections present common operating ratios.

Return on equity (ROE)

Equity is the amount left from total assets after you account for total liabilities. (This can also be considered a profitability ratio.) The net equity (also known as shareholders' equity, stockholders' equity, or net worth) is the bottom line in the company's balance sheet, both geographically as well as figuratively. It's calculated as

Return on equity (ROE) = net income ÷ net equity

The net income (from the company's income statement) is simply the total income less total expenses. Net income that isn't spent or used up increases the company's net equity. Looking at net income is a great way to see whether the company's management is doing a good job growing the business. You can check this out by looking at the net equity from both the most recent balance sheet and the one from a year earlier. Ask yourself whether the current net worth is higher or lower than the year before. If it's higher, by what percentage is it higher? Use the ROE in conjunction with the ROA ratio (see the following section) to get a fuller picture of a company's activity.

Return on assets (ROA)

The ROA may seem similar to the ROE, but it actually gives a perspective that completes the picture when coupled with the ROE. The formula for figuring out ROA is

Return on assets = net income ÷ total assets

The ROA reflects the relationship between a company's profit and the assets used to generate it. If the company HGC makes a profit of $10,000 and has total assets of $100,000, the ROA is 10 percent. This percentage should be as high as possible, but it will generally be less than the ROE.

Say that the company has an ROE of 25 percent but an ROA of only 5 percent. Is that good? It sounds okay, but a problem exists. If the ROA is much lower than the ROE, it indicates that the higher ROE may have been generated by something other than total assets — debt! The use of debt can be a leverage to maximize the ROE, but if the ROA doesn't show a similar percentage of efficiency, then the company may have incurred too much debt. In that case, investors should be aware that it could cause problems (see the section, "Solvency Ratios," later in this appendix).

Sales to receivables ratio (SR)

The sales to receivables ratio (SR) gives investors an indication of a company's ability to manage what customers owe it. This ratio uses data from both the income statement (sales) and from the balance sheet (accounts receivable, or AR). The formula is expressed as

Sales to receivables ratio = sales ÷ receivables

Say that you have the following data for HGC:

Sales in 2005 are $75,000. On 12/31/05, receivables stood at $25,000.

Sales in 2006 are $80,000. On 12/31/06, receivables stood at $50,000.

Based on this data, you can figure out that sales went up 6.6 percent, but receivables went up 100 percent! In 2005, the SR was 3 ($75,000 divided by $25,000). However, the SR in 2006 sank to 1.6 ($80,000 divided by $50,000), or nearly cut in half. Yes, sales did increase, but the company's ability to collect money due from customers fell dramatically. This information is important to notice for one main reason: What good is selling more when you can't get the money? From a cash flow point of view, the company's financial situation deteriorated.

Solvency Ratios

Solvency just means that the company isn't overwhelmed by its liabilities. Insolvency means "Oops! Too late." You get the point. Solvency ratios have never been more important than they are now. Solvency ratios look at the relationship between what the company owns and what it owes. Here are two of the primary solvency ratios.

Debt to net equity ratio

The debt to net equity ratio is an indicator of the company's solvency. It answers the question "How dependent is the company on debt?" In other words, it tells you how much the company owes and how much it owns. You calculate it as follows:

Debt to net equity ratio = total liabilities ÷ net equity

If the company HGC has $100,000 in debt and $50,000 in net worth, the debt to net equity ratio is 2. The company has two dollars of debt to every dollar of net worth. In this case, what the company owes is twice the amount of what it owns. Whenever a company's debt to net equity ratio exceeds 1 (as in the example), that isn't good. In fact, the higher the number, the more negative the situation. If the number is too high and the company isn't generating enough income to cover the debt, the company runs the risk of bankruptcy.

Working capital

Technically, working capital isn't a ratio, but it does belong to the list of things that serious investors look at. *Working capital* means what the company has in current assets and its relationship to current liabilities. It's a simple equation:

Working capital = total current assets − total current liabilities

The point is obvious: Does the company have enough to cover the current bills? Actually, you can formulate a useful ratio. If current assets are $25,000 and current liabilities are $25,000, then that's a 1-to-1 ratio, which is cutting it close. Current assets should be at least 50 percent higher than current liabilities (say, $1.50 to $1.00) to have enough cushion to pay bills and have some money for other purposes. Preferably, the ratio should be 2 to 1 or higher.

Common Size Ratios

Common size ratios offer simple comparisons. You have common size ratios for both the balance sheet (where you compare total assets) and the income statement (where you compare total sales):

✔ **To get a common size ratio from a balance sheet,** the total assets figure is assigned the percentage of 100 percent. Every other item on the balance sheet is represented as a percentage of total assets. For example, if Holee Guacamolee Corp. (HGC) has total assets of $10,000 and debt of $3,000, you know that total assets equal 100 percent, while debt equals 30 percent (debt divided by total assets or $3,000 ÷ $10,000, which equals 30 percent).

✔ **To get a common size ratio from an income statement (or profit and loss statement),** you compare total sales. For example, if a company has $50,000 in total sales and a net profit of $8,000, then you know that the profit equals 16 percent of total sales.

Keep in mind the following points with common size ratios:

✔ **Net profit:** What percentage of sales is it? What was it last year? How about the year before? What percentage of increases (or decreases) is the company experiencing?

✔ **Expenses:** Are total expenses in line with the previous year? Are any expenses going out of line?

✔ **Net equity:** Is this item higher or lower than the year before?

✔ **Debt:** Is this item higher or lower than the year before?

Common size ratios are used to compare the company's financial data not only with prior balance sheets and income statements but also with other companies in the same industry. You want to make sure that the company is not only doing better historically but also as a competitor in the industry.

Valuation Ratios

Understanding the value of a stock is very important for stock investors. The quickest and most efficient way to judge the value of a company is to look at valuation ratios. The type of value that you deal with throughout the book is the *market value* (essentially the price of the company's stock). You hope to buy it at one price and sell it later at a higher price — that's the name of the game. But what's the best way to determine whether what you're paying for now is a bargain or is fair market value? How do you know whether your stock investment is undervalued or overvalued? The valuation ratios in this appendix can help you answer these questions. In fact, they're the same ratios that value investors have used with great success for many years.

Price-to-earnings ratio (P/E)

The price-to-earnings ratio can also double as a profitability ratio because it's a common barometer of value that many investors and analysts look at. I cover this topic in Chapter 10, but because it's such a critical ratio, I also include it here. The formula is

P/E ratio = price (per share) ÷ earnings (per share)

For example, if a company's stock price per share is $10 and the earnings per share are $1, the P/E is 10 (10 divided by 1).

The P/E ratio answers the question "Am I paying too much for the company's earnings?" Value investors find this number to be very, very important. Here are some points to remember:

✔ Generally, the lower the P/E ratio, the better (from a financial strength point of view). Frequently, a low P/E ratio indicates that the stock is undervalued (or the company is failing).

✔ A company with a P/E ratio significantly higher than its industry average is a red flag that its stock price is too high (or that it is growing faster than its competitors).

✔ Don't invest in a company with no P/E ratio (it has a stock price, but the company experienced losses). Such a stock may be good for a speculator's portfolio but not for your retirement account.

✔ Any stock with a P/E higher than 40 should be considered a speculation and not an investment. Frequently, a high P/E ratio indicates that the stock is overvalued.

When you buy a company, you're really buying its power to make money. In essence, you're buying its earnings. Paying for a stock that's priced at 10 to 20 times earnings is a conservative strategy that has served investors well for nearly a century. Make sure that the company is priced fairly and use the P/E ratio in conjunction with other measures of value (such as the ratios in this appendix).

Price to sales ratio (PSR)

The price to sales ratio (PSR) is another method for valuing the company. It helps to answer the question "Am I paying too much for the company's stock based on the company's sales?" This is a useful valuation ratio that I recommend using as a companion tool with the company's P/E ratio. You calculate it as follows:

PSR = stock price (per share) ÷ total sales (per share)

This ratio can be quoted on a per-share basis or on an aggregate basis. For example, if a company's market value (or market capitalization) is $1 billion and annual sales are also $1 billion, the PSR is 1. If the market value in this example is $2 billion, then the PSR is 2. For investors trying to make sure that they're not paying too much for the stock, the general rule is that the lower the PSR, the better. Stocks with a PSR of 2 or less are considered undervalued.

Be very hesitant about buying a stock with a PSR greater than 5. If you buy a stock with a PSR of 38, that means you're paying $38 for each dollar of sales — not exactly a bargain.

Price to book ratio (PBR)

The price to book ratio (PBR) is yet another valuation method. This ratio compares the market value to the company's accounting (or book) value. Recall that the book value refers to the company's net equity (assets minus liabilities). The company's market value is usually dictated by external factors such as supply and demand in the stock market. The book value is indicative of the company's internal operations. Value investors see the PBR as another perspective to valuing the company to determine whether you're paying too much for the stock. The formula is

Price to book ratio (PBR) = market value ÷ book value

An alternate method is to calculate the ratio on a per-share basis, which yields the same ratio. If the company's stock price is $20 and the book value (per share) is $15, then the PBR is 1.33. In other words, the company's market value is 33 percent higher than its book value. Investors seeking an undervalued stock like to see the market value as close as possible to (or even better, below) the book value.

Keep in mind that the PBR may vary depending on the industry and other factors. Also, judging a company solely on book value may be misleading because many companies have assets that aren't adequately reflected in the book value. Software companies are a good example. Intellectual properties, such as copyrights and trademarks, are very valuable yet aren't fully covered in book value. Just bear in mind that, generally, the lower the market value is in relation to the book value, the better for you (especially if the company has strong earnings and the outlook for the industry is positive).

Index

• *E* •